ACCESS TO MEDICINES AS A HUMAN RIGHT

IMPLICATIONS FOR PHARMACEUTICAL INDUSTRY
RESPONSIBILITY

Edited by Lisa Forman and Jillian Clare Kohler

Access to Medicines as a Human Right

Implications for Pharmaceutical Industry Responsibility

UNIVERSITY OF TORONTO PRESS
Toronto Buffalo London

ISBN 978-1-4426-4397-0

Printed on acid-free, 100% post-consumer recycled paper
with vegetable-based inks.

Library and Archives Canada Cataloguing in Publication

Access to medicines as a human right: implications for pharmaceutical
industry responsibility / edited by Lisa Forman and Jillian Clare Kohler.

Includes bibliographical references.
ISBN 978-1-4426-4397-0

1. Pharmaceutical industry – Moral and ethical aspects. 2. Pharmaceutical
ethics. 3. Human rights – Health aspects. 4. Social responsibility of business. 5. Social responsibility of business – Case studies. I. Forman, Lisa,
1970– II. Kohler, Jillian Clare

HD9665.5.A24 2012   174.2'951   C2012-902241-1

This book has been published with the help of a grant from the Canadian
Federation for the Humanities and Social Sciences, through the Aid to
Scholarly Publications Program, using funds provided by the Social Sciences
and Humanities Research Council of Canada.

University of Toronto Press acknowledges the financial assistance to its publishing program of the Canada Council for the Arts and the Ontario Arts Council.

 Canada Council **Conseil des Arts**
for the Arts **du Canada**   **ONTARIO ARTS COUNCIL**
CONSEIL DES ARTS DE L'ONTARIO

University of Toronto Press acknowledges the financial support of the
Government of Canada through the Canada Book Fund for its publishing
activities.

Contents

Acknowledgments

We have many people to thank for their vital roles in producing this volume. First and foremost, we are grateful to the Canadian Institute for Health Research, the Lupina Foundation, and Comparative Program on Health and Society for institutional and financial support to an earlier conference at the Munk School of Global Affairs, which provided the impetus for this volume. We thank in particular Peter Warrian and Margret Hovanec for their wholehearted support, generosity, and openness. We also wish to thank our extraordinary research team: Matthew Lee, Viktoria Prokorova, Sneha Rathod, Roshina Babaei Rad, and Kelly Tai. We are grateful to the anonymous reviewers whose constructive suggestions strengthened this manuscript, and to Daniel Quinlan at the University of Toronto Press for his guidance throughout this process.

We are grateful too for the support we receive from our families, which in all ways makes the production of works such as this possible. This work is dedicated to them, particularly Lorraine and Sidney Forman. Lastly, we dedicate this volume to all the people in the world who still lack access to the medicines they need.

Lisa Forman and Jillian Clare Kohler, November 2011

ACCESS TO MEDICINES AS A HUMAN RIGHT

IMPLICATIONS FOR PHARMACEUTICAL INDUSTRY
RESPONSIBILITY

1 Introduction: Access to Medicines as a Human Right – What Does It Mean for Pharmaceutical Industry Responsibilities?

LISA FORMAN AND JILLIAN CLARE KOHLER

Introduction

Pharmaceuticals are one of the cornerstones of human development, as their rational consumption can reduce morbidity and mortality rates and enhance quality of life. Yet dramatic gaps in regular access to medicines persist between and within countries, despite a growing international recognition of the individual and public health importance of ensuring access to medicines, and a plethora of international programs and financial aid focused on improving drug access. Almost two billion people, one-third of the global population, lack regular access to essential medicines, and in poorest Africa and Asia, this lack of regular access rises to half of the population.[1] This gap in access to medicines is not only a moral but also a human rights dilemma: within international human rights law, access to essential medicines has been authoritatively interpreted to constitute a minimum core entitlement under the human right to the highest attainable standard of health ('the right to health'), placing correlative duties on a range of actors to enable and ensure access.[2] This book focuses on the right to health, with authors investigating whether pharmaceutical companies can be understood to hold consequent ethical and/or legal duties towards populations in developing countries needing to access affordable medicines, and if so, what the appropriate content and scope of such duties should be.

The central inquiry of this book responds to the growing legal and political recognition of the right to health[3] and the prioritized duties that this right places on states to provide access to affordable medicines. Increasingly, these duties are understood to place limitations on the exercise of pharmaceutical patents and to require governments and even companies to realize affordable access to medicines in developing countries.[4] These duties are in apparent tension with corporate imperatives to maximize profits, including through the global enforcement of trade-related intellectual property rights.

The key role of drugs in health care and the ostensibly divergent imperatives of a for-profit industry raise pressing and controversial questions as well as implicating broader scholarly and political debates: about the appropriate relationship between the market, health care and human rights, about the appropriate allocation of responsibilities in resolving the dilemma of inaccessible and unaffordable drugs in developing countries, and about the legal, social, or political mechanisms necessary to appropriately mediate these relationships.[5] This book's investigation is located, therefore, within converging legal, political, and social trends that seek to resolve these questions, including through conceptions of corporate social responsibility and explorations of whether and how international law can and should apply to non-state actors such as multinational corporations.

We want to be clear at the outset that we are not suggesting that global drug access can be improved solely through the actions of pharmaceutical companies. Responsibilities to resolve the barriers to drug access lie with a range of actors, including governments, donor governments, and agencies and international organizations. Nor are we suggesting that pharmaceutical companies are the primary duty bearers responsible for assuring human rights entitlements to medicines are realized: states continue to hold primary responsibility under international human rights law for the realization of such rights, including the right to health. Nonetheless, while we recognize the important roles played by this broad range of actors, and the primary responsibilities of states, this volume focuses on the contributory role and responsibilities of pharmaceutical corporations, in line with the growing recognition of this sector's role in influencing access to affordable medicine in low- and middle-income countries.[6] Accordingly, the collection brings together a multidisciplinary team of experts to explore the implications for pharmaceutical corporations of viewing access to medicines as a human right, and the tensions that companies may experience in balancing their social and business responsibilities.

While this volume may raise more questions than answers, its intent is to invite further discussion and debate about the role of the private sector in relation to drug supply for those populations that fall outside the boundaries of profitable markets. Indeed, the book is aimed at the vast field of scholars, legal practitioners, civil society, and domestic and international policymakers who grapple with corporate conduct in relation to medicines access in developing countries. In this introduction, we first expand on the international human rights law framework relevant to this issue and then outline how our contributors have responded to the central questions driving this collection regarding the nature, scope, and content of pharmaceutical company duties to address drug access in the developing world.

Corporate Responsibility in International Law in Context

The discussions in this book are presented against the backdrop of broader debates about whether corporations hold responsibilities under international law, including in relation to the realization of human rights.[7] Such debates have intensified as transnational companies have grown in size and economic power, prompting mounting concerns about product safety, corporate labour practices, environmental damage, and collusion with oppressive governments in the global South.[8] These apprehensions have grown particularly acute in the face of the sizeable corporate contribution to the global recession that began in 2008 and has deepened since.[9]

Long before international law became concerned with corporations, the concept of 'corporate social responsibility' had been coined to encompass the notion of corporate duties outside the business context.[10] Certainly as Lee and Kohler point out in their chapter in this collection, the term refers to a broad, complex, and evolving concept, which is ambiguous and subjective. Nonetheless, the expansive development of the concept of corporate social responsibility suggests a shift away from the neoclassical economic view that business responsibilities are exclusively to shareholders,[11] towards responsibility to a considerably wider range of social stakeholders, including 'workers, creditors, suppliers, consumers and even the wider community.'[12] What these duties encompass and how they should be enforced remains the key question in this area.

Over time, these concerns have led not simply to increasing calls for state regulation of corporations, but to the elaboration of human rights responsibilities applying directly to corporations – a trend in apparent contradiction to the traditional Westphalian international legal system premised on the primacy of the nation state.[13] The inadequacy of the

state-centric system of international law to govern increasingly powerful non-state actors and institutions is particularly apparent in relation
to health, given the health impacts of economic globalization and the
emergence and re-emergence of deadly infectious disease pandemics.[14]
In response to the negative confluence of these transnational structural
and epidemiological determinants of health, scholars have developed
an alternative paradigm of global health governance.[15] Instead of relying on state-centric international law, this new vision of global health
governance incorporates 'the means or mechanisms used by various
public and private actors, acting at sub-national, national and international levels, that seek to control, regulate or ameliorate [the] global
system of disease [produced at the nexus of economic globalization
and health].'[16]

One outcome of this impetus towards diverse collective responses to
remediate structural drivers of health inequities has been a prolifera-
tion of 'soft' (non-binding) and voluntary codes of corporate conduct,
in areas such as labour and employment,[17] culminating in the universally relevant United Nations Global Compact. In the Global Compact,
companies undertake to enact ten universal principles within their
'spheres of influence' (a core term not defined within the Compact),
including undertaking to respect human rights and not to be complicit
in human rights abuses. The Global Compact and other multilateral
agreements addressing corporations suggest the emergence of a new
international normative paradigm applicable to corporations, rooted
not simply in law but in increasingly mainstream expectations that
business can and should contribute to public welfare (and sustainable
development).[18]

Despite these emerging norms and social expectations, it remains
controversial whether corporations hold 'hard' (binding) human
rights duties in international law, and whether 'soft' corporate duties
can ever be enforced directly, other than through state regulation.[19]
Certainly international treaties contain suggestions that human rights
duties do not rest on governments alone and that all social actors –
including individuals and organs of society – hold human rights duties to the community.[20] These duties are explicitly elaborated in the
non-binding 1999 United Nations *Declaration on the Rights and
Responsibilities of Individuals, Groups and Organs of Society*, which recognizes that while human rights are largely individual rights invok-
ing corresponding state duties, non-state actors have important roles
to play in promoting human rights generally, and particularly in

promoting everyone's right to a social and international order in which human rights can be fully realized.[21] These duties are extended towards health by the United Nations Committee on Economic, Social, and Cultural Rights in its *General Comment 14 on the Right to Health*, where the committee recognizes that while only states are parties to the *Covenant on Economic, Social and Cultural Rights* and thus accountable for compliance with it, all members of society, including the private business sector, have responsibilities for the realization of the right to health.[22]

Yet the form and content of these duties remain uncertain, particularly given the failure of efforts at the United Nations to articulate binding international human rights responsibilities for corporations. In 2003, the United Nations Sub-Commission on Human Rights introduced draft norms on the human rights responsibilities of transnational corporations, which suggested that corporations have human rights responsibilities within their 'sphere of influence,' the term used in the Global Compact, but similarly undefined in these norms.[23] To facilitate the passage of the norms, the United Nations Commission on Human Rights appointed John Ruggie as the secretary-general's special representative on business and human rights, with the mandate of clarifying law relating to human rights and corporations and defining key concepts. Ruggie's first report in his tenure as special representative effectively defeated the adoption of the norms. Ruggie suggested that the norms reflected a tremendous doctrinal overreach and that no binding international law presently placed direct human rights duties on companies (aside from the customary international law rule that corporations not commit gross human rights violations).[24] Ruggie's later reports nonetheless concede that corporations do hold a limited variety of direct human rights duties – including to respect human rights and not infringe on the rights of others.[25] For companies to comply with these duties, Ruggie suggests that they must engage in an 'ongoing process of human rights due diligence, whereby companies become aware of, prevent, and mitigate adverse human rights impacts.'[26]

As these conflicts within international law suggest, there is little clarity within international law about the binding legality of corporate duties. Yet even if Ruggie's approach reflects a particularly cautious assessment of the binding legality of international law on corporations, it suggests nonetheless that international law requires corporations to abstain from obstructing human rights. This duty alone may hold particularly momentous implications for the pharmaceutical industry, given the potentially restrictive impacts of intellectual property rights on drug affordability and accessibility in low- and middle-income countries. These and other duties are explored from numerous legal, ethical, and social perspectives by the authors in this collection, including in particular within Khosla and Hunt's 'Human Rights Guidelines for Pharmaceutical Companies.'

Human Rights, Pharmaceutical Companies, and Access to Medicines in Developing Countries

The question of corporate duties has particular resonance in relation to pharmaceutical companies, in light of growing controversy and consequent hostility in the relationship between the pharmaceutical industry and the public. Santorro and Gorrie suggest that these controversies have seen the unravelling of a tacit 'grand bargain' between the pharmaceutical industry and society that allowed the modern global pharmaceutical industry to emerge in the second half of the twentieth century, whereby industry's immense profits were balanced by the social enjoyment of a wide variety of life-saving and life-enhancing drugs.[27]

Concerns about an imbalance between pharmaceutical industry profits and social benefit have intensified since 1995, when the World Trade Organization's *Agreement on Trade-Related Aspects of Intellectual Property Rights (TRIPS)* was introduced,[28] internationalizing powerful legal protection for pharmaceutical patents and enabling companies to charge monopoly pricing for twenty years in all countries globally, irrespective of the disease burden or level of development of such countries.[29] Questions about the impact of this agreement on access to medicines came to a sharp focus in light of the explosive growth of the global AIDS pandemic in Sub-Saharan Africa, and the inability of millions of people infected with HIV and AIDS to access expensive antiretroviral medicines protected under *TRIPS* rules.[30] At approximately fifteen thousand U.S. dollars a year per person, drug prices presented a primary stumbling block to broader access in developing countries. At the same time, focus has intensified on the deficiencies of the medical innovation system for producing medicines to meet the pharmaceutical needs of developing countries. This gap is exemplified in the fact that in a twenty-five-year period, only 0.1 per cent of new chemical entities produced were for tuberculosis and 'tropical diseases' (diseases primarily experienced in low- and middle-income countries).[31]

The conflict between drug pricing and public access has raised pressing questions about the relevance of international human rights law to medicines, trade-related intellectual property rights, and indeed pharmaceutical companies themselves.[32] As Alkoby points out in his chapter, corporate efforts to protect *TRIPS* rights at the expense of access to AIDS medicines for poor populations, as evidenced in the infamous corporate litigation in South Africa in 2001, coalesced focus not simply on the impact of *TRIPS* on access to medicines, but also on the ethical and indeed human rights legitimacy of such actions.[33] This issue became the focal point of what Obijiofor Aginam characterizes as a 'life versus profit' debate, in which *TRIPS* 'firmly pitted corporate profit against vulnerable populations living with HIV/AIDS globally, human rights to life against intellectual property rights, and civil society groups against transnational pharmaceutical corporations.'[34]

These debates motivated the international human rights community to develop interpretations of the international human rights framework relevant to medicines, including in particular the right to health. At least since 2000, UN bodies tasked with interpreting international treaties have understood this right to include certain essential elements, irrespective of a country's developmental levels, including the state duty to ensure that essential drugs be available, accessible, acceptable, and of good quality, and a minimum core duty to provide essential medicines.[35] Multiple declarations from international human rights bodies have reiterated that the right to health includes as a fundamental element the duty to provide access to medication,[36] and that states hold a range of duties to respect, protect, and fulfil access to affordable medicines.[37]

While the focus of these duties has been primarily on states – the primary duty-bearers under international law – there has also been a move to elaborate and codify corporate human rights duties with regard to medicines. As Paul Hunt and Rajat Khosla explore in detail in chapter 2 and in the collection's annex, in 2008 Hunt – who was then the UN special rapporteur on the right to health – released guidelines detailing human rights responsibilities for pharmaceutical companies in relation to access to medicines. As the discussion above indicates, the application of human rights to non-state actors like the pharmaceutical industry is not a settled question within international law. Nonetheless in creating these guidelines, Khosla and Hunt make an important normative advance by interpreting human rights norms relevant to specific pharmaceutical industry practices: the guidelines are drafted with considerable specificity and detail, they adopt the language of rights and correlative obligations, and they insist on accountability. Thus, in their use of the language and frameworks of human rights, the guidelines go considerably further than simply offering ethical guidance to pharmaceutical companies, by providing companies with a concrete framework to guide human rights–compliant action in relation to developing countries.

These quasi-legal developments are matched by the emergence of new global policy approaches to this issue. Despite the gross lacunae in drug access and innovation for developing countries, this topic received little or weak attention in international efforts to address global health challenges until the early 2000s. It was only in response to tremendous social pressures at that time that global policy actors moved to address deficiencies in drug innovation and access in low- and middle-income countries.[38] One of the most important of these initiatives was the 2006 establishment by the World Health Organization of an Intergovernmental Working Group on Public Health, Innovation and Intellectual Property, with the mandate of preparing a global strategy and plan of action to promote new thinking on access to medicines and assure essential health research and development relevant to the disease burdens of low- and middle-income countries.[39] Two aspects of the strategy are worth highlighting in the context of this book's inquiry. First, the plan of action explicitly identifies pharmaceutical companies as stakeholders necessary to contribute to achieving key elements of the strategy. Second, the strategy recognizes as a founding principle that the enjoyment of the right to health is a fundamental right of every human person.[40] While the strategy is markedly weak in identifying the implications of the human right to health for medicines for specific actors, it can be viewed nonetheless as signifying the emergence of a new global ethical paradigm on collective responsibilities to resolve access and innovation deficiencies in the developing world, including within the pharmaceutical industry.

Structure of the Book

The book is composed of three sections exploring rights, norms, and ethics regarding pharmaceuticals; tensions between the social and business responsibilities of companies; and case studies of different approaches to resolving ethical or legal questions about corporate conduct.

In Part One, Paul Hunt and Rajat Khosla explore the legal and ethical duties of the pharmaceutical industry, drawing from international human rights law on health. In his capacity as United Nations special rapporteur on the right to health, Hunt, along with Khosla, drafted *Human Rights Guidelines for Pharmaceutical Companies*, an innovative effort to provide practical and constructive assistance to pharmaceutical companies to better understand and discharge their responsibilities in relation to medicines, according to the standards drawn from international law. In their chapter, Khosla and Hunt explore the context and content of these guidelines, emphasizing the importance of cooperation with the pharmaceutical industry to improve drug access. Khosla and Hunt's chapter can be read in conjunction with the guidelines themselves, annexed in full at the conclusion of the collection.

Asher Alkoby focuses on international law and the actors that shape normative change in access to essential medicines. Alkoby indicates that non-state norm entrepreneurs have often been key in advancing broader normative changes that become reflected in international law. Even so, he suggests that laws are dynamic and that their clarification, interpretation, and implementation are constantly renegotiated and reflected upon in light of changing circumstances. Alkoby suggests that a key to enhancing corporate compliance with the right to health is to open up relevant legislative processes to all relevant actors.

Patricia Illingworth explores the question of corporate duties from an ethical perspective, particularly the argument that pharmaceutical companies have a duty to provide essential medicines to those who need them but cannot afford them. She argues that, given the medical mission that pharmaceutical companies have, they, like physicians and some other professionals, should be understood as moral hybrids and not simply as profit-making organizations. Drawing on the reasoning that has been used to justify physician fiduciary duties, she argues from analogy that the arguments that apply to physicians also apply to pharmaceutical companies. In addition, she shows that counter-arguments that appeal to shareholder claims do not override the life-and-death claims of the sick and dying.

In Part Two, authors explore tensions between social and business duties for corporations, and innovative methods for monitoring and guiding compliance with corporate social responsibilities.

Matthew Lee and Jillian Kohler explore the trend of benchmarking the pharmaceutical industry on their corporate social responsibility performance in access to medicines. They suggest that benchmarking creates a competitive inter-business environment and acts as an incentive for improving corporate social responsibility. Lee and Kohler's chapter conducts a qualitative analysis of pharmaceutical industry feedback in response to criticism from benchmarking reports. Their conclusions suggest that benchmarking assures increasing transparency in the pharmaceutical industry, which may translate into actual access to medicine practices.

Joel Lexchin focuses on how corporate activity in developing nations is motivated by business interests rather than efforts to provide social assistance. He points out that marketing in developing countries has different ethical implications, given weak regulatory systems. As a result, a large number of products that are sold in developing countries are irrationally used, dangerous, or just useless, many of which are not sold in developed nations. As an example, Lexchin indicates how direct advertising to health-care workers is prevalent in developing countries, and how many of them are misleading. Self-regulation by industry for marketing standards has little effect when industry violates the code. While organizations like the WHO provide codes for drug promotion and rational use of medicine, governments must adopt and enforce them.

In Part Three, human rights and ethical considerations are explored more concretely in application to specific legal mechanisms and country experiences. Richard Elliott focuses on the practical implications of the right to health for corporate duties with regards to medicines. In doing so, he focuses on the role of compulsory licensing to allow states to promote the greater affordability of medicines, by overcoming medicine monopolies and creating competition. He pays particular attention to Canada's Access to Medicines Regime and highlights the sluggish process of the legislation and its inefficiencies. He concludes that the basic mechanism for licensing the production and export of generic versions of patented drugs, as set out in the WTO Decision, is flawed, and Canada can and should legislate a simpler, more user-friendly process for both developing country purchasers and generic suppliers.

Judith King and Stephanie Nixon explore the case study of how corporate responsibility has been addressed in South Africa. They focus in particular on a policy process called the *King II Report* on corporate governance in South Africa, which postulates a means for businesses to balance economics and social goals, specifically in relation to antiretroviral access. The King Report focused on companies participating in the Johannesburg Stock Exchange but has been adopted for corporate governance in Africa and many European countries. It is based on the concept of *ubuntu*, an African communitarian philosophy that serves as the foundational principle for the report, stressing collectiveness, interdependence, consensus, and humility. This concept provides a uniquely African solution to corporate governance that highlights the interdependence of corporations and communities. The *King II Report* calls for triple bottom-line reporting, which means that in addition to reporting economic data, companies must also provide social and environmental data yearly.

Conclusion

As many of our contributors note, broader questions about the existence, nature, and extent of corporate duties are subject to debate and intense contestation. These debates highlight the importance of continued academic, political, and social explorations of these pressing and essentially unresolved political and legal questions. The chapters in this volume are intended to disaggregate some of these issues in this area, explore alternative legal and ethical approaches to understanding the notion of corporate duties regarding pharmaceutical access in the developing world, and identify potential solutions capable of being applied in global and domestic forums. The dilemma of inaccessible medicines in low- and middle-income countries will not be resolved by these strategies alone. However, the book is motivated by the hope that further academic and policy elaboration of corporate duties in the developing world may elucidate concrete actions and strategies capable of contributing to better public health outcomes globally. We hope that the articles in this volume provide illuminating context for readers and that they raise provocative questions to guide future research in this realm.

NOTES

1 World Health Organization, *WHO Medicines Strategy: Countries at the Core 2004–2007* (Geneva: WHO, 2004), 3.
2 United Nations Committee on Economic, Social, and Cultural Rights, General Comment No. 14 (2000), *The Right to the Highest Attainable Standard of Health, Article 12 of the International Covenant on Economic, Social and Cultural Rights*, U.N. Doc. E/C.12/2000/4, paras 43, 44.
3 See, for example, E.D. Kinney and B.A. Clark, 'Provisions for Health and Healthcare in the Constitutions of the Countries of the World,' *Cornell International Law Journal* 37 (2004): 287.

4 See United Nations Committee on Economic, Social and Cultural Rights, General Comment No. 17 (2005), *The Right of Everyone to Benefit from the Protection of the Moral and Material Interests Resulting from Any Scientific, Literary or Artistic Production of Which He or She Is the Author* (Article 15, Paragraph 1[c], of the Covenant 12 Jan. 2006, UN Doc. E/C.12/GC/17 (2005); and United Nations Commission on Human Rights, *The Impact of the Agreement on Trade-Related Aspects of Intellectual Property Rights on Human Rights: Report of the High Commissioner*, UN Doc. E/CN.4/Sub.2/2001/13 (2001).

5 See, for instance, Daniel Callahan and Angela A. Wassuna, *Medicine and the Market: Equity v. Choice* (Baltimore, MD: Johns Hopkins University Press, 2008); Ralph Hamann, Stu Woolman, and Courtenay Sprague, *The Business of Sustainable Development in Africa: Human Rights, Partnerships, Alternative Business Models* (Pretoria, South Africa: UNISA Press, 2008); Adriana Petryna, Andrew Lakoff, and Arthur Kleinman, eds., *Global Pharmaceuticals: Ethics, Markets, Practices* (Durham NC: Duke University Press, 2006); and Michael A. Santoro and Thomas M. Gorrie, *Ethics and the Pharmaceutical Industry: Business, Government, Professional and Advocacy Perspectives* (West Nyack, NY: Cambridge University Press, 2005).

6 See, for example, World Health Organization, *Public Health Innovation and Intellectual Property Rights: Report of the Commission on Intellectual Property Rights, Innovation, and Public Health* (Geneva: WHO, 2006).

7 A growing scholarly literature explores these topics. See, for example, Andrew Clapham, *The Human Rights Obligations of Non-State Actors* (Oxford: Oxford University Press, 2006); Paula Darvas, 'Grounding the "Social Responsibility" of Companies in the Language of Human Rights: A Survey of the Issues,' *Australian Journal of Corporate Law* 20 (2007): 129–56; Janet Dine, *Companies, International Trade and Human Rights* (Cambridge, UK: Cambridge University Press, 2005); David Kinley and Junko Tadaki, 'From Talk to Walk: The Emergence of Human Rights Responsibilities for Corporations at International Law,' *Virginia Journal of International Law* 44, no. 4 (2004): 931–1023; Justine Nolan and Luke Taylor, 'Corporate Responsibility for Economic, Social and Cultural Rights: Rights in Search of a Remedy?' *Journal of Business Ethics* 87, no. 2 (2009): 433–51; and Steven R. Ratner, 'Corporations and Human Rights: A Theory of Legal Responsibility,' *Yale Law Journal* 111 (2001): 443–545.

8 Sarah Joseph, 'Pharmaceutical Corporations and Access to Drugs: The "Fourth Wave of Corporate Human Rights Scrutiny,"' *Human Rights Quarterly* 25 (2003): 425–52.

9 See, for example, Joseph Stiglitz, 'A Crisis of Confidence,' *Guardian*, 22 Oct. 2008.

10 From the earliest reference to corporate social responsibility (Howard R. Bowen, *Social Responsibilities of the Businessman* [New York: Harper & Brothers, 1953]), a large literature has emerged. Important publications from the last decade include M. Blowfield and J.G. Frynas, 'Setting New Agendas: Critical Perspectives on Corporate Social Responsibility in the Developing World,' *International Affairs* 8, no. 3 (2005): 499–513; A. Crane, A. McWilliams, and D. Matten, *The Oxford Handbook of Corporate Social Responsibility* (Oxford: Oxford University Press, 2008); Andy Crane and Dirk Matten, *Business Ethics: Managing Corporate Citizenship and Sustainability in the Age of Globalization*, 2nd ed. (Oxford: Oxford University Press, 2007); I. Maignan and O.C. Ferrell, 'Corporate Social Responsibility and Marketing: An Integrative Framework,' *Journal of the Academy of Marketing Science* 32, no. 1 (2004): 3 19; D. Matten and J. Moon, '"Implicit" and "Explicit" CSR: A Conceptual Framework for a Comparative Understanding of Corporate Social Responsibility," *Academy of Management Review* 33, no. 2 (2008): 404–24; A. McWilliams, D.S. Siegel, and P.M. Wright, 'Corporate Social Responsibility: Strategic Implications,' *Journal of Management* 43, no. 1 (2005): 1–18.

11 A view encapsulated most famously by Milton Friedman, 'The Social Responsibility of Business Is to Increase Its Profits,' *New York Times Magazine*, 13 Sept. 1970.

12 Paula Darvas, 'Grounding the "Social Responsibility" of Companies in the Language of Human Rights: A Survey of the Issues,' *Australian Journal of Corporate Law* 20 (2007): 139.

13 Obijiofor Aginam, 'Between Life and Profit: Global Governance and the Trilogy of Human Rights, Public Health and Pharmaceutical Patents,' *North Carolina Journal of International Law and Commercial Regulation* 31 (2006): 903.

14 See, for example, World Health Organization Commission on the Social Determinants of Health, *Closing the Gap in a Generation: Health Equity through Action on the Social Determinants of Health* (Geneva: WHO, 2008).

15 See, for example, Aginam, 'Between Life and Profit'; Andrew F. Cooper, John J. Kirton and Ted Schrecker, eds., *Governing Global Health: Challenge, Response, Innovation* (Aldershot, UK: Ashgate, 2007); and Andrew F. Cooper, John J. Kirton, and Ted Schrecker, eds., *Innovation in Global Health Governance: Critical Cases* (Aldershot: Ashgate, 2009); David P. Fidler, 'Constitutional Outlines of Public Health's "New World Order,"' *Temple Law Review* 77 (2004): 247.

16 Adrian Kay and Owain David Williams, 'Introduction: The International Political Economy of Global Health Governance,' in *Global Health*

Governance: Crisis, Institutions and Political Economy, ed. Adrian Kay and Owain David Williams (Basingstoke, Hampshire: Palgrave Macmillan, 2009), 1–2.

17 See, for example, the International Labour Organization's *Tripartite Declaration of Principles concerning Multinational Enterprises and Social Policy* (OB Vol. LXI, 1978, Series A, No. 1), UN Doc. 28197701 (adopted by the Governing Body of the International Labour Office at its 204th Session, Geneva, Nov. 1977); and the Organization for Economic Cooperation and Development, *Guidelines for Multinational Enterprises*, Daffe/IME/WPG (2000)15/Final, 31 Oct. 2001.

18 Ralph Hamann, 'Introducing Corporate Citizenship,' in *The Business of Sustainable Development in Africa: Human Rights, Partnerships, Alternative Business Models*, ed. Ralph Hamann, Stu Woolman, and Courtenay Sprague (Pretoria, South Africa: UNISA Press, 2008), 2.

19 See, for example, Kinley and Tadaki, 'From Talk to Walk'; and Ratner, 'Corporations and Human Rights.'

20 See, for example, *International Covenant on Civil and Political Rights*, G.A. Res. 2200A (XXI), 21 UNGAOR Supp. (No. 16), UN Doc. A/6316 (1966), preamble; United Nations, *International Covenant on Economic, Social, and Cultural Rights*, 16 Dec. 1966, 993 U.N.T.S. 3, preamble; and United Nations, *Universal Declaration of Human Rights*, GA Res. 217 (III), UNGAOR, 3d Sess. Supp. No. 13, UN Doc. A/810 (1948) 71, article 29.

21 United Nations General Assembly, *Declaration on the Right and Responsibility of Individuals, Groups and Organs of Society to Promote and Protect Universally Recognized Human Rights and Fundamental Freedoms*, UN Doc. A/Res/53/144, 8 Mar. 1999, articles 18.1, 18.2, and 18.3.

22 United Nations Committee on Economic, Social and Cultural Rights, General Comment No. 14 (2000), *The Right to the Highest Attainable Standard of Health (Article 12 of the International Covenant on Economic, Social and Cultural Rights)*, UN Doc. E/C.12/2000/4, 11 Aug. 2000, para. 42.

23 United Nations Commission on Human Rights, *Norms on the Responsibilities of Transnational Corporations and Other Business Enterprises with Regard to Human Rights*, UN Doc. E/CN.4/Sub.2/2003/12/Rev.2, 26 Aug. 2003.

24 John Ruggie, *Interim Report of the Special Representative of the Secretary General on the Issue of Human Rights and Transnational Corporations and Other Business Enterprises*, UN Doc. E/CN.4/2006/97 (2006), para. 59.

25 John Ruggie, *Business and Human Rights: Towards Operationalizing the 'Protect, Respect and Remedy' Framework: Report of the Special Representative of the Secretary-General on the Issue of Human Rights and Transnational Corporations and Other Business Enterprises*, UN Doc. A/HRC/11/13, 22 Apr. 2009, para. 46.

26 Ibid., para. 49.
27 Santoro and Gorrie, *Ethics and the Pharmaceutical Industry*, 1.
28 *Agreement on Trade-Related Aspects of Intellectual Property Rights (TRIPS)*,
    Annexure 1C to the Marrakesh Agreement Establishing the World Trade
    Organization, signed in Marrakesh, Morocco, 15 Apr. 1994.
29 These measures include parallel imports (whereby countries import
    cheaper patented medicines) and compulsory licensing (whereby coun-
    tries manufacture or import generics under strict conditions). See *TRIPS*,
    articles 6 and 31.
30 See, for example, Carlos Correa, 'Public Health and Intellectual Property
    Rights,' *Global Public Policy* 2, no. 3 (2002): 261; Holger Hestermeyer,
    Human Rights and the WTO: The Case of Patents and Access to Medicines
    (Oxford: Oxford University Press, 2007); Zita Lazzarini, 'Making Access to
    Pharmaceuticals a Reality: Legal Options under TRIPS and the Case of
    Brazil,' *Yale Human Rights Journal* 6 (2003): 103; Richard D. Smith, Carlos
    Correa, and Cecilia Oh, 'Trade, TRIPS and Pharmaceuticals,' *Lancet* 373
    (2009): 687; and Ellen F.M. 'T Hoen, (2002). 'TRIPS, Pharmaceutical Patents
    and Access to Essential Medicines: A Long Way from Seattle to Doha,'
    Chicago Journal of International Law 3, no. 2 (2002): 27.
31 P. Trouiller, P. Olliaro, E. Torreele, J. Orbinski, R. Laing, and N. Ford.,
    'Drug Development for Neglected Diseases: A Deficient Market and a
    Public Health Policy Failure,' *Lancet* 359 (2002), 2188. While corporate
    innovation for neglected disease has increased since the early part of this
    century, this increase is not attributed to commercial incentives but to
    efforts to minimize reputational damage resulting from their failure to
    address developing country needs. See M. Moran, 'A Breakthrough in
    R&D for Neglected Diseases: New Ways to Get the Drugs We Need,' *PLoS
    Medicine* 2, no. 9 (2005): e302.
32 See, for example, Frederick M. Abbott, 'The "Rule of Reason" and the
    Right to Health: Integrating Human Rights and Competition Principles in
    the Context of TRIPS,' in *Human Rights and International Trade*, ed. Thomas
    Cottier, Joost Pauwelyn, and Elisabeth Burgi (Oxford: Oxford University
    Press, 2005) 279; Philippe Cullet, 'Patents and Medicines: The Relationship
    between TRIPS and the Human Right to Health,' *International Affairs* 79,
    no. 1 (2003): 139–60; Lisset Ferreira, 'Access to Affordable HIV/AIDS
    Drugs: The Human Rights Obligations of Multinational Pharmaceutical
    Corporations,' *Fordham Law Review* 71 (2002): 1133; Joseph, 'Pharma-
    ceutical Corporations and Access to Drugs,' 425; Sisule F. Musungu, 'The
    Right to Health, Intellectual Property and Competition Principles,' in
    Cottier, Pauwelyn, and Burgi, *Human Rights and International Trade*, 301;
    and Alicia Ely Yamin, 'Not Just a Tragedy: Access to Medications as a

Right under International Law,' *Boston University International Law Journal* *21 (2003):* 325.

33 See also Lisa Forman, '"Rights" and Wrongs: What Utility for the Right to Health in Reforming Trade Rules on Medicines?' *Health and Human Rights* 10, no. 2 (2008): 37.

34 Aginam, 'Between Life and Profit,' 903.

35 United Nations Committee on Economic, Social and Cultural Rights, General Comment No. 14, para. 12.

36 United Nations Commission on Human Rights, *Access to Medication in the Context of Pandemics such as HIV/AIDS*, UN Doc. E/CN.4/RES/2001/33, 20 Apr. 2001, at para. 1, as well as resolutions 2002/32, 2003/29, and 2004/26.

37 United Nations Commission on Human Rights, *Impact of the Agreement on Trade-Related Aspects of Intellectual Property Rights on Human Rights*; United Nations Commission on Human Rights, *Intellectual Property Rights and Human Rights: Report of the Secretary-General*, UN Doc. E/CN.4/ Sub.2/2001/12 (2001); United Nations Commission on Human Rights, Resolutions 2001/33 (23 Apr. 2001), 2002/32 (6 Mar. 2002), 2003/29 (22 Apr. 2003), and 2004/26 (16 Apr. 2004); United Nations Committee on Economic, Social and Cultural Rights, *Human Rights and Intellectual Property*, UN Doc. No. E/C.12/2001/15 (2001); United Nations Office of the High Commissioner for Human Rights and UNAIDS, HIV/AIDS and Human Rights International Guidelines, Revised Guideline 6: *Access to Prevention, Treatment, Care and Support, Third International Consultation on HIV/AIDS and Human Rights*, UNAIDS/02.49E, HR/PUB/2002/1 (Geneva: UN, 2002).

38 See, for example, British Commission on Intellectual Property Rights, *Integrating Intellectual Property Rights and Development Policy: Report of the Commission on Intellectual Property Rights* (London: UK Department of International Development, 2002); United Nations Commission on Human Rights, *Intellectual Property Rights*; United Nations Commission on Human Rights, *Impact of the Agreement*.

39 World Health Assembly, *Global Strategy and Plan of Action on Public Health, Innovation and Intellectual Property*, 61st World Health Assembly, WHA61.21, 24 May 2008.

40 Ibid., para. 16.

REFERENCES

Aginam, Obijiofor. 'Between Life and Profit: Global Governance and the Trilogy of Human Rights, Public Health and Pharmaceutical Patents.' *North*

Carolina Journal of International Law and Commercial Regulation 31, no. 4 (2006): 901–22.

Agreement on Trade-Related Aspects of Intellectual Property Rights (TRIPS). Annexure 1C to the Marrakesh Agreement Establishing the World Trade Organization, signed in Marrakesh, Morocco, 15 Apr. 1994.

Blowfield, M., and J.G. Frynas. 'Setting New Agendas: Critical Perspectives on Corporate Social Responsibility in the Developing World.' *International Affairs* 81, no. 3 (2005): 499–513.

Bowen, Howard R. *Social Responsibilities of the Businessman*. New York: Harper & Brothers, 1953.

British Commission on Intellectual Property Rights. *Integrating Intellectual Property Rights and Development Policy: Report of the Commission on Intellectual Property Rights*. London: UK Department of International Development, 2002.

Callahan, Daniel, and Angela A. Wassuna. *Medicine and the Market: Equity v. Choice*. Baltimore, MD: Johns Hopkins University Press, 2008.

Clapham, Andrew. *The Human Rights Obligations of Non-State Actors*. Oxford: Oxford University Press, 2006.

Cooper, Andrew F., John J. Kirton, and Ted Schrecker, eds. *Governing Global Health: Challenge, Response, Innovation*. Aldershot, UK: Ashgate, 2007.

– *Innovation in Global Health Governance: Critical Cases*. Aldershot, UK: Ashgate, 2009.

Correa, Carlos. 'Public Health and Intellectual Property Rights.' *Global Public Policy* 2, no. 3 (2002): 261–78.

Cottier, Thomas, Joost Pauwelyn, and Elisabeth Burgi, eds. *Human Rights and International Trade*. Oxford: Oxford University Press, 2005.

Crane, A., A. McWilliams, and D. Matten. *The Oxford Handbook of Corporate Social Responsibility*. Oxford: Oxford University Press, 2008.

Crane, Andy, and Dirk Matten. *Business Ethics: Managing Corporate Citizenship and Sustainability in the Age of Globalization*. 2nd ed. Oxford: Oxford University Press, 2007.

Cullet, Philippe. 'Patents and Medicines: The Relationship between TRIPS and the Human Right to Health.' *International Affairs* 79, no. 1 (2003): 139–60.

Darvas, Paula. 'Grounding the "Social Responsibility" of Companies in the Language of Human Rights: A Survey of the Issues.' *Australian Journal of Corporate Law* 20, no. 2 (2007): 129–56.

Dine, Janet. *Companies, International Trade and Human Rights*. Cambridge, UK: Cambridge University Press, 2005.

Ferreira, Lisset. 'Access to Affordable HIV/AIDS Drugs: The Human Rights Obligations of Multinational Pharmaceutical Corporations.' *Fordham Law Review* 71 (2002): 1133–79.

Fidler, David P. 'Constitutional Outlines of Public Health's "New World Order."' *Temple Law Review* 77, no. 2 (2004): 247–90.

Forman, Lisa. '"Rights" and Wrongs: What Utility for the Right to Health in Reforming Trade Rules on Medicines?' *Health and Human Rights* 10, no. 2 (2008): 37–52.

Friedman, Milton. 'The Social Responsibility of Business Is to Increase Its Profits.' *New York Times Magazine*, 13 Sept. 1970.

Hamann, Ralph, Stu Woolman, and Courtenay Sprague. *The Business of Sustainable Development in Africa: Human Rights, Partnerships, Alternative Business Models* Pretoria, South Africa: UNISA Press, 2008.

Hestermeyer, Holger. *Human Rights and the WTO: The Case of Patents and Access to Medicines*. Oxford: Oxford University Press, 2007.

International Covenant on Civil and Political Rights. G.A. Res. 2200A (XXI), 21 UNGAOR Supp. No. 16, UN Doc. A/6316 (1966).

International Labour Organization. *Tripartite Declaration of Principles concerning Multinational Enterprises and Social Policy* (OB Vol. LXI, 1978, Series A, No. 1), UN Doc. 28197701 (adopted by the Governing Body of the International Labour Office at its 204th Session, Geneva, Nov. 1977).

Joseph, Sarah. 'Pharmaceutical Corporations and Access to Drugs: The "Fourth Wave" of Corporate Human Rights Scrutiny.' *Human Rights Quarterly* 25 (2003): 425–52.

Kay, Adrian, and Owain David Williams. 'Introduction: The International Political Economy of Global Health Governance.' In *Global Health Governance: Crisis, Institutions and Political Economy*, edited by Adrian Kay and Owain David Williams, 1–23. Basingstoke, Hampshire: Palgrave Macmillan, 2009.

Kinley, David, and Junko Tadaki. 'From Talk to Walk: The Emergence of Human Rights Responsibilities for Corporations at International Law.' *Virginia Journal of International Law* 44, no. 4 (2004): 931–1023.

Kinney, E.D., and B.A. Clark. 'Provisions for Health and Healthcare in the Constitutions of the Countries of the World.' *Cornell International Law Journal* 37 (2004): 285–355.

Lazzarini, Zita. 'Making Access to Pharmaceuticals a Reality: Legal Options under TRIPS and the Case of Brazil.' *Yale Human Rights Journal* 6 (2003): 103–38.

Maignan, I., and O.C. Ferrell. 'Corporate Social Responsibility and Marketing: An Integrative Framework.' *Journal of the Academy of Marketing Science* 32, no. 1 (2004): 3–19.

Matten, D., and J. Moon. '"Implicit" and "Explicit" CSR: A Conceptual Framework for a Comparative Understanding of Corporate Social Responsibility.' *Academy of Management Review* 33, no. 2 (2008): 404–24.

McWilliams, A., D.S. Siegel, and P.M. Wright. 'Corporate Social Responsibility: Strategic Implications.' *Journal of Management* 43, no. 1 (2006): 1–18.

Moran, M. 'A Breakthrough in R&D for Neglected Diseases: New Ways to Get the Drugs We Need.' *PLoS Medicine* 2, no. 9 (2005): e302.

Nolan, Justine, and Luke Taylor. 'Corporate Responsibility for Economic, Social and Cultural Rights: Rights in Search of a Remedy?' *Journal of Business Ethics* 87, no. 2 (2009): 433–51.

Organization for Economic Cooperation and Development (OECD). *Guidelines for Multinational Enterprises.* Daffe/IME/WPG (2000) 15/Final, 31 Oct. 2001.

Petryna, Adriana, Andrew Lakoff, and Arthur Kleinman, eds. *Global Pharmaceuticals: Ethics, Markets, Practices.* Durham, NC: Duke University Press, 2006.

Ratner, Steven R. 'Corporations and Human Rights: A Theory of Legal Responsibility.' *Yale Law Journal* 111 (2001): 443–545.

Ruggie, John. *Business and Human Rights: Towards Operationalizing the "Protect, Respect and Remedy" Framework; Report of the Special Representative of the Secretary-General on the Issue of Human Rights and Transnational Corporations and Other Business Enterprises.* UN Doc. A/HRC/11/13 (2009).

– *Interim Report of the Special Representative of the Secretary General on the Issue of Human Rights and Transnational Corporations and Other Business Enterprises.* UN Doc. E/CN.4/2006/97 (2006).

Santoro, Michael A., and Thomas M. Gorrie. *Ethics and the Pharmaceutical Industry: Business, Government, Professional and Advocacy Perspectives.* West Nyack, NY: Cambridge University Press, 2005.

Smith, Richard D., Carlos Correa, and Cecilia Oh. 'Trade, TRIPS and Pharmaceuticals.' *Lancet* 373 (2009): 684–91.

Stiglitz, Joseph. 'A Crisis of Confidence.' *Guardian,* 22 Oct. 2008.

'T Hoen, Ellen F.M. 'TRIPS, Pharmaceutical Patents and Access to Essential Medicines: A Long Way from Seattle to Doha.' *Chicago Journal of International Law* 3, no. 2 (2002): 27–46.

Trouiller, P., P. Olliaro, E. Torreele, J. Orbinski, R. Laing, and N. Ford. 'Drug Development for Neglected Diseases: A Deficient Market and a Public Health Policy Failure.' *Lancet* 359 (2002): 2188–94.

United Nations. *International Covenant on Economic, Social, and Cultural Rights.* 16 Dec. 1966, 993 U.N.T.S. 3.

– *Universal Declaration of Human Rights.* GA Res. 217 (III), UNGAOR, 3d Sess., Supp. No. 13, UN Doc. A/810 (1948).

United Nations Commission on Human Rights. *Access to Medication in the Context of Pandemics such as HIV/AIDS.* UN Doc. E/CN.4/RES/2001/33 (2001), and resolutions 2002/32, 2003/29, and 2004/26.

- *The Impact of the Agreement on Trade-Related Aspects of Intellectual Property Rights on Human Rights: Report of the High Commissioner.* UN Doc. E/CN.4/Sub.2/2001/13 (2001).
- *Intellectual Property Rights and Human Rights: Report of the Secretary-General.* UN Doc. E/CN.4/Sub.2/2001/12 (2001).
- *Norms on the Responsibilities of Transnational Corporations and Other Business Enterprises with Regard to Human Rights.* UN Doc. E/CN.4/Sub.2/2003/12/Rev.2 (2003).

United Nations Committee on Economic, Social and Cultural Rights. General Comment No. 14 (2000). *The Right to the Highest Attainable Standard of Health (Article 12 of the International Covenant on Economic, Social and Cultural Rights).* UN Doc. E/C.12/2000/4 (2000).
- General Comment No. 17 (2006). *The Right of Everyone to Benefit from the Protection of the Moral and Material Interests Resulting from Any Scientific, Literary or Artistic Production of Which He or She Is the Author.* Article 15, Paragraph 1(c), of the Covenant 12 January 2006. UN Doc. E/C.12/GC/17 (2005).
- *Human Rights and Intellectual Property.* UN Doc. E/C.12/2001/15 (2001).

United Nations General Assembly. *Declaration on the Right and Responsibility of Individuals, Groups and Organs of Society to Promote and Protect Universally Recognized Human Rights and Fundamental Freedoms.* UN Doc. A/Res/53/144 (1999).

United Nations Office of the High Commissioner for Human Rights and UNAIDS. HIV/AIDS and Human Rights International Guidelines, Revised Guideline 6. *Access to Prevention, Treatment, Care and Support, Third International Consultation on HIV/AIDS and Human Rights.* UNAIDS/02.49E, HR/PUB/2002/1 (Geneva: UN, 2002).

World Health Assembly. *Global Strategy and Plan of Action on Public Health, Innovation and Intellectual Property.* 61st World Health Assembly, WHA61.21, 24 May 2008.

World Health Organization. *Public Health Innovation and Intellectual Property Rights: Report of the Commission on Intellectual Property Rights, Innovation, and Public Health* (Geneva: WHO, 2006).
- *WHO Medicines Strategy: Countries at the Core 2004–2007* (Geneva: WHO, 2004).

World Health Organization Commission on the Social Determinants of Health. *Closing the Gap in a Generation: Health Equity through Action on the Social Determinants of Health* (Geneva: WHO, 2008).

Yamin, Alicia Ely. 'Not Just a Tragedy: Access to Medications as a Right under International Law.' *Boston University International Law Journal* 21 (2003): 325–71.

PART ONE

Rights, Norms, and Ethics

2 Human Rights Responsibilities of Pharmaceutical Companies in Relation to Access to Medicines

RAJAT KHOSLA AND PAUL HUNT

Introduction

A consensus is emerging that business enterprises, like all actors in society, have some legal and ethical human rights responsibilities. According to its Preamble, the *Universal Declaration of Human Rights* gives rise to some human rights responsibilities for 'every organ of society,' which must include business enterprises.[1] The United Nations Global Compact, with more than 4,700 participating companies, affirms that businesses should support and respect the protection of international human rights.[2] The Organization for Economic Cooperation and Development's *Guidelines for Multinational Enterprises* require businesses to 'respect the human rights of those affected by their activities consistent with the host Government's obligations and commitments.'[3] While holding that the draft *Norms on the Responsibilities of Transnational Corporations and Other Business Enterprises with Regard to Human Rights of the UN Sub-Commission on the Promotion and Protection of Human Rights* had no legal standing, the UN Commission on Human Rights found that the *Norms* contained 'useful elements and ideas.'[4] Some national courts have recognized the impact of pharmaceutical company pricing policies on the human rights of patients. Significantly, some companies have prepared their own guidelines and other statements explicitly affirming their human rights responsibilities.[5]

As observed by the UN special representative of the secretary-general on the issue of human rights and transnational corporations and other business enterprises, 'It is essential to achieve greater conceptual clarity with regard to the respective responsibilities of States and corporations ... In doing so we should bear in mind that companies are constrained not only by legal standards but also by social norms and moral considerations.'[6]

Today, two key issues are to clarify the scope and content of the human rights responsibilities of the private sector, and to identify which are legal and which are ethical responsibilities. The *Human Rights Guidelines for Pharmaceutical Companies in Relation to Access to Medicines* that are considered in this chapter focus on the first of these issues in the specific context of pharmaceutical companies: the right to health and access to medicines. As for the second, it is inconceivable that some human rights do not place legal responsibilities on business enterprises.[7]

This chapter introduces *Human Rights Guidelines for Pharmaceutical Companies in Relation to Access to Medicines*, which were published by the UN in August 2008. After research and consultations over several years, the *Guidelines* were written by the authors of the present chapter while one served as the UN special rapporteur on the right to the highest attainable standard of health (2002–8), and the other was senior researcher supporting the UN mandate-holder.[8] Drawing upon this experience, the chapter includes some brief remarks about the global medicine context, the origins of the *Guidelines*, the process by which they were drafted, and the right-to-health analytical framework that helped to shape them. Then, by way of illustration, the chapter briefly introduces a few of the forty-seven *Guidelines*.

Global Medicine Context

Almost two billion people lack access to essential medicines.[9] This deprivation causes immense and avoidable suffering: ill health, pain, fear, and loss of dignity and life.[10] Improving access to existing medicines could save ten million lives each year, four million of them in Africa and Southeast Asia.[11] Besides deprivation, gross inequity in access to medicines remains the overriding feature of the world pharmaceutical situation.[12] Average per capita spending on medicines in high-income countries is 100 times higher than in low-income countries. High-income countries spend about US$400, as compared to low-income countries, which spend only US$4. The World Health Organization estimates that 15 per cent of the world's population consumes over 90 per cent of the world's production of pharmaceuticals.[13]

National and international policies, rules, and institutions give rise to these massive deprivations and inequalities. National supply systems for medicines seldom reach those living in poverty, but if they do, the medicines are often unaffordable. Historically, research and development has not addressed the priority health needs of those living in poverty. Alternative arrangements are feasible, and reforms are urgently required. Indeed, they are demanded by legal and ethical duties, including those arising from international human rights law.

Millennium Development Goals (MDGs), such as reducing child mortality, improving maternal health, and combating HIV/AIDS, malaria, and other diseases, depend upon improving access to medicines. Moreover, one of the MDG targets is to provide, 'in cooperation with pharmaceutical companies, access to affordable essential drugs in developing countries.'[14] Crucially, implementation of the right to the highest attainable standard of health can help to achieve the health-related goals.[15]

Medical care in the event of sickness, as well as the prevention, treatment, and control of diseases, are central features of the right to the highest attainable standard of health.[16] These features depend upon access to medicines. Thus, access to medicines forms an indispensable part of the right to the highest attainable standard of health. Numerous court cases, as well as resolutions of the UN Commission on Human Rights, confirm that access to essential medicines is a fundamental element of the right to health.[17] Some of the cases also confirm that access to essential medicines is closely connected to other human rights, such as the right to life.

States have the primary responsibility to implement the right to the highest attainable standard of health and enhance access to medicines for all. This extremely important state responsibility is discussed elsewhere.[18] Here, however, we make a few introductory remarks about the human rights responsibilities of pharmaceutical companies in relation to access to medicines. Of course, pharmaceutical companies have human rights responsibilities extending beyond access to medicines and encompassing other elements of the right to health. Moreover, their human rights responsibilities extend beyond the right to health. Nonetheless, our focus in this chapter remains pharmaceutical companies and access to medicines.

A Shared Responsibility

While states have the primary responsibility to enhance access to medicines, this is a shared responsibility. If there is to be an increase in access to medicines, numerous national and international actors have an indispensable role to play. As already signalled, the Millennium Development Goals recognize that pharmaceutical companies are among those who share this responsibility.

In 2005, a British government policy paper on access to medicines elaborated on this point: 'Responsibility for increasing access to essential medicines rests with the whole international community. Progress depends on everyone working in partnership to build health systems in developing countries, increase financing, make medicines more affordable, and increase the amount of new medicines developed for diseases affecting developing countries.'[19] Significantly, the paper continued, 'In this context there is a particular role for pharmaceutical companies. As the producers of existing, and developers of new, medicines they can – and do – make a difference within their sphere of influence.' The paper then sets out a promising 'framework for good practice in the pharmaceutical industry.'[20]

The pharmaceutical sector has a profound impact – positive and negative – on the implementation of the right to the highest attainable standard of health. States and others have criticized the pharmaceutical sector for high prices, erratic drug donations, imbalanced research and development, lobbying for 'TRIPS-plus' standards, inappropriate drug promotion, problematic clinical trials, and other practices that are seen to obstruct a state's ability to discharge its right-to-health responsibilities.[21] However, states and others have also commended significant progress in recent years, such as the more widespread use of differential pricing, predictable and sustainable drug donations, and a renewed commitment to research and development into neglected diseases.[22]

There is considerable congruity among corporate responsibility, good practices, and the right to health. However, while a number of pharmaceutical companies report on their corporate citizenship or corporate responsibility activities, few make specific references in their corporate mission statements to human rights in general, or the right to health in particular. Even fewer appear to have carefully examined their policies through the lens of the right to the highest attainable standard of health. This is a missed opportunity because all pharmaceutical companies, whether large or small, research-based or generic, and whether or not their reach is global, would find it beneficial to adopt a rights-based approach to their businesses, as outlined in the joint publication of the UN Global Compact, Business Leaders Initiative on Human Rights (BLIHR), and UN Office of the High Commissioner for Human Rights.[23]

The *Guidelines'* Origins: The Drafting Process

In 2000, the UN Committee on Economic, Social and Cultural Rights (CESCR) confirmed that the private business sector has responsibilities for realizing the right to the highest attainable standard of health.[24] While this general statement of principle is important, it provides no practical guidance to pharmaceutical companies and others.

In recent years, the general understanding of economic, social, and cultural rights has deepened.[25] If this momentum is to be maintained, it is important to move from general discussions about economic, social, and cultural rights to consideration of specific rights, in relation to specific sectors, actors, and issues. This point has now been reached in relation to pharmaceutical companies and the right to health. As recently observed by the UN special representative of the secretary-general on the issue of human rights and transnational corporations and other business enterprises, 'Broad aspirational language may be used to describe respect for human rights, but more detailed guidance in specific functional areas is necessary to give those commitments meaning.'[26] Today, general statements about pharmaceutical companies and economic, social, and cultural rights provide the indispensable foundation for a more detailed examination of specific right-to-health issues arising in the pharmaceutical sector. In short, it is time to explore further the right-to-health responsibilities of pharmaceutical companies that were acknowledged in general terms by CESCR in 2000.

In September 2007, immediately following a consultation at the University of Toronto, the UN special rapporteur on the right to the highest attainable standard of health published draft *Human Rights Guidelines for Pharmaceutical Companies in relation to Access to Medicines*. Placed on the websites of the UN Office of the High Commissioner for Human Rights, the University of Essex, and elsewhere, the draft was available for public comment for eight months until mid-May 2008.

The draft *Guidelines* drew upon the growing jurisprudence on the right to the highest attainable standard of health, and aimed to help pharmaceutical companies enhance their contribution to these vital human rights issues. Additionally, the draft aimed to assist those who wish to monitor the human rights performance of the pharmaceutical sector in relation to access to medicines. The text considered specific issues, such as differential pricing, donations, research and development for neglected diseases, public–private partnerships, drug promotion, clinical trials, and corruption.[27]

Under his mandate, the special rapporteur is requested, among other things, to develop a regular dialogue and discuss possible areas of co-operation with all relevant actors; to report on good practices most beneficial to the enjoyment of the right to the highest attainable standard of health, as well as obstacles encountered domestically and internationally; and to support states' efforts by making recommendations. Given this mandate, the special rapporteur formed the view that it was important to examine, and clarify, the human rights responsibilities of states and pharmaceutical companies in relation to access to medicines.

Accordingly, the special rapporteur engaged in many substantive discussions on access to medicines with numerous parties, including states, the WHO, pharmaceutical companies, investor groups, civil society organizations (including the International Federation of Pharmaceutical Manufacturers and Associations), and academics. These discussions were informed by the publications of numerous actors such as pharmaceutical companies, the UN Global Compact, the UN Office of the High Commissioner for Human Rights, the WHO, BLIHR, civil society organizations, and others.[28] More recently, the project benefited from the reports of the UN special representative of the secretary-general on the issue of human rights and transnational corporations and other business enterprises.

The special rapporteur on the right to the highest attainable standard of health received a large number of comments on the draft *Guidelines*. Additionally, after September 2007, he discussed the draft with numerous stakeholders, including the International Federation of Pharmaceutical Manufacturers and Associations, as well as investors in the pharmaceutical sector. Pharmaceutical companies were approached to meet and discuss the draft but, unfortunately, all declined, with the exception of NovoNordisk. A few companies sent helpful written comments on the draft. Forty stakeholders sent written comments, all of which were placed on the web, with a small handful of exceptions where confidentiality was requested. The comments were varied: while many were supportive, some were critical. In summary, extensive written and oral comments on the draft were received from a very wide range of stakeholders encompassing states, institutional investors, pharmaceutical companies, specialized agencies, national human rights institutions, non-governmental organizations, academics, and others.

In light of this feedback, the draft was extensively revised. The final version of the *Guidelines* was published in the special rapporteur's report to the General Assembly of August 2008 and should be read with

Chapter IV of the same report.[29] Following the preamble, the *Guidelines* are grouped by themes, such as transparency; management, monitoring and accountability; pricing; and ethical marketing.

In the Background: The Right-to-Health Analytical Framework

The right to the highest attainable standard of health is complex and extensive. In recent years it has been analysed by courts, CESCR as well as other international human rights treaty-bodies, the WHO, civil society organizations, academics, and others, with a view to making it easier for states, and others, to apply in practice.

The key elements of this right-to-health analysis may be briefly summarized as follows:[30]

1. *National and international human rights laws, norms, and standards*: The laws, norms, and standards relevant to the particular issue (such as access to medicines), program, or policy must be identified.[31]
2. *Resource constraints and progressive realization*: International human rights law recognizes that the realization of the right to health is subject to resource availability. Thus, what is required of a developed state today is of a higher standard than what is required of a developing state. However, a state is obliged – whatever its resource constraints and level of economic development – to realize progressively the right to the highest attainable standard of health.[32]
3. *Obligations of immediate effect*: Despite resource constraints and progressive realization, the right to health also gives rise to some obligations of immediate effect, such as the duty to avoid discrimination.[33] These are obligations without which the right would be deprived of its raison d'être and as such they are not subject to progressive realization, even in the presence of resource constraints.[34]
4. *Freedoms and entitlements*: The right to health includes freedoms (such as freedom from discrimination) and entitlements (such as the provision of a system of health protection that includes minimum essential levels of water and sanitation). For the most part, freedoms do not have budgetary implications, while entitlements do.[35]

5. *Available, accessible, acceptable, and good quality*: All health services, goods, and facilities should comply with each of these four requirements; in other words, a particular health service must be available, accessible (for example, affordable and physically accessible), culturally acceptable, and of good quality.[36] There is a similarity between this element of the right-to-health analysis and the public health requirements set out in the Declaration of Alma-Ata (1978): geographical accessibility, financial accessibility, cultural accessibility, and functional accessibility.[37]

6. *Respect, protect, and fulfil*: States have duties to respect, protect, and fulfil the right to the highest attainable standard of health, as explained and used by CESCR and the UN Committee on the Elimination of Discrimination against Women.[38]

7. *Non-discrimination, equality, and vulnerability*: Because they are crucially important, the analytical framework demands that special attention be given to non-discrimination, equality, and vulnerability in relation to all elements of the right to the highest attainable standard of health.[39]

8. *Active and informed participation*: The right to health requires that there be an opportunity for individuals and groups to participate actively, and in an informed manner, in health policymaking processes that affect them.[40]

9. *International assistance and cooperation*: In line with obligations envisaged in the UN *Charter* and some human rights treaties,[41] developing countries have a responsibility to seek international assistance and cooperation, while developed states have some responsibilities towards the realization of the right to health in developing countries.[42]

10. *Monitoring and accountability*: Transparent, effective, and accessible monitoring and accountability mechanisms, including redress, are among the most crucial characteristics of the right to the highest attainable standard of health.[43]

This analysis has been developed while keeping in mind the responsibilities of states, yet many of its elements are also instructive in relation to the responsibilities of non-state actors, including pharmaceutical companies. As we will see, for example, the requirement that health services shall be accessible places duties upon both states and non-state actors, as does the requirement that there should be effective monitoring and accountability mechanisms.

Human Rights Guidelines for Pharmaceutical Companies in Relation to Access to Medicines

After the preamble, the forty-seven *Guidelines* are grouped into overlapping thematic categories, keeping in mind the analytical framework outlined above. In the *Guidelines*, each thematic category is followed by a brief Commentary. While the full text is available in annex 1, this section provides a brief introduction to a few of the *Guidelines*.

Some General Guidelines

Formal, express recognition of the importance of human rights, and the right to the highest attainable standard of health, helps to establish a firm foundation for the company's policies and activities on access to medicines. Thus, *Guideline 1* requires that a company's corporate mission statement should expressly recognize the importance of human rights generally, and the right to the highest attainable standard of health in particular, in relation to the strategies, policies, programs, projects, and activities of the company.

Formal recognition, however, is not enough: operationalization is the challenge. Accordingly, *Guideline 2* requires that a company should integrate human rights, including the right to the highest attainable standard of health, into its strategies, policies, programs, projects, and activities. Many of the *Guidelines* suggest ways in which human rights considerations can be operationalized, or integrated into, the company's activities. *Guidelines 9–14*, for example, address the critical human rights issue of monitoring and accountability, while *Guidelines 39–41* apply the general principle of transparency to the specific issue of ethical promotion and marketing.

Disadvantaged Individuals, Communities, and Populations

Equality and non-discrimination are among the most fundamental features of international human rights, including the right to the highest attainable standards of health. They are akin to the crucial health concept of equity. Equality, non-discrimination and equity have a social justice component. Accordingly, the right to the highest attainable standard of health has a particular preoccupation with disadvantaged individuals, communities, and populations, including children, the elderly, and those living in poverty. Like equity, the right to health also requires that particular attention be given to gender. *Guideline 5* reflects these concerns and requires a company to give particular attention to the needs of disadvantaged individuals, communities, and populations, including 'the poorest in all markets.'

Neglected Diseases

The right to health encompasses an obligation to engage in research and development that addresses the health needs of the entire population, including disadvantaged groups. All pharmaceutical companies have a large number of compelling and competing research and development needs. Space does not permit this chapter to explore how prioritization of research and development can take place in a manner that is respectful of the right to health.[44] However, an essential point is that prioritization must take into account the health needs of those living in poverty, as well as other disadvantaged groups. This rarely happens. Historically, research and development has not addressed the priority health needs of low-income and middle-income countries. More specifically, health research and development has given insufficient attention to neglected diseases (such as lymphatic filariasis, sleeping sickness, and river blindness) that mainly afflict the poorest people in the poorest countries, although there is evidence that some pharmaceutical companies are taking measures to reverse this trend.[45]

The right to the highest attainable standard of health not only requires that existing medicines are accessible without discrimination, but also that much-needed new medicines are developed and thereby become available to those who need them. From the perspective of the right to the highest attainable standard of health, neglected diseases demand special attention, because they tend to afflict the most disadvantaged and vulnerable. For this reason, the *Guidelines* require that a company should make a public commitment to contribute to research and development for neglected diseases (*Guideline 23*) and consult with relevant organizations to enhance its contribution to research and development for neglected diseases (*Guideline 24*). Of course, it might not be appropriate for all companies to themselves embark on research and development into neglected diseases. Thus, *Guideline 23* provides that the company 'should either provide in-house research and development for neglected diseases; or support external research and development for neglected diseases; or both.' And it concludes, 'In any event, it should disclose how much it invests in research and development for neglected diseases.' Lastly, *Guideline 25* requires companies to 'engage constructively with key international and other initiatives that are searching for new, sustainable and effective approaches to accelerate and enhance research and development for neglected diseases.'

Patents and Licensing

The right to the highest attainable standard of health requires that medicines are available and accessible.[46] Intellectual property rights affect the availability and accessibility of medicines; they attempt to strike a balance among the interests of various stakeholders, for example by establishing 'flexibilities' within the *TRIPS* regime.[47] In 2001, the Doha *Declaration on the TRIPS Agreement and Public Health* recognized that the *TRIPS Agreement* 'can and should be interpreted and implemented in a manner supportive of WTO Members' right to protect public health and, in particular, to promote access to medicine for all.'[48] The *Declaration* confirmed the right of countries to use safeguards, such as compulsory licences, to protect public health and promote access to medicines for all. The *Decision by the TRIPS Council of the WTO on Implementation of Paragraph 6 of the Doha Declaration* (August 2003) confirms that countries producing generic copies of patented drugs under compulsory licence may export drugs to countries with little or no manufacturing capacity, and it sets out the requirements for doing so.[49]

The right to the highest attainable standard of health tends to reinforce these *TRIPS* 'flexibilities.' *Guidelines 26–32* aim to ensure that the features of intellectual property rights (such as the *TRIPS* 'flexibilities') that reinforce the right to health of individuals and communities are recognized, respected, and applied.

Pricing, Discounting, and Donations

The right to the highest attainable standard of health also requires that medicines must be affordable for all. Equity demands that poorer households not be disproportionately burdened with health expenses as compared to richer households.[50] Thus *Guideline 33* requires, 'When formulating and implementing its access to medicines policy, the company should consider all the arrangements at its disposal with a view to ensuring that its medicines are affordable to as many people as possible,' and it sets out some of the available 'arrangements,' such as differential pricing among countries, differential pricing within countries, commercial voluntary licences, and so on. In international human rights law, the right to health is subject to resource availability. In other words, more is expected of a high-income, than of a low-income, country. *Guideline 34* on pricing reflects this concept and applies it to the human rights responsibilities of pharmaceutical companies by requiring a company to take into consideration a country's stage of economic development when setting its prices. The *Guideline* also requires a company to take into account 'the differential purchasing power of populations within a country,' and it concludes that the same medicine 'may be priced and packaged differently for the private and public sectors within the same country.'

Guidelines 36–8 on discounting and donations recognize that carefully targeted donations, while unsustainable in the long term, have a role to play in ensuring access, especially to those living in poverty and other disadvantaged individuals and communities in low-income countries.

Corruption

The pharmaceutical system is susceptible to fraud and corruption in manufacturing, registration, selection, procurement, distribution, prescribing, and dispensing.[51] Corruption is a major obstacle to the enjoyment of the right to the highest attainable standard of health, including access to medicines. Those living in poverty are disproportionately affected by corruption in the health sector, because they are less able to pay for private alternatives where corruption has depleted public health services. Features of the right to health, such as participation, transparency, access to information, monitoring, and accountability, help to establish an environment in which corruption cannot survive. A right-to-health policy is also an anti-corruption policy. These considerations animate several of the *Guidelines*, including 15 and 16. *Guideline 15* requires a company to 'publicly adopt effective anti-corruption policies and measures, and comply with relevant national law implementing the UN Convention against Corruption,' while *Guideline 16* calls upon companies 'in collaboration with States' to 'take all reasonable measures to address counterfeiting.'

Monitoring and Accountability

International human rights empower individuals and communities by granting them entitlements and placing legal obligations on others.

Critically, rights and obligations demand accountability: unless supported by a system of accountability, they can become no more than window dressing. Accordingly, a human rights – or right to health – approach emphasizes obligations and requires that all duty-holders be held to account for their conduct.[52]

All too often, *accountability* is used to mean blame and punishment.[53] But this narrow understanding of the term is much too limited. A right-to-health accountability mechanism establishes which health policies and institutions are working and which are not, and why, with the objective of improving the realization of the right to health. Such an accountability device has to be effective, transparent, and accessible.[54]

The absence of external, independent accountability mechanisms in relation to corporate social responsibility is striking. Some companies' reporting initiatives are impressive, such as the Novartis publication *Improving Access to Leprosy Treatment* and GlaxoSmithKline's *Facing the Challenge: Two Years On*.[55] Public, candid self-reporting is very welcome. But self-reporting of this sort is no substitute for the type of accountability anticipated by human rights, including the right to the highest attainable standard of health.

Usually, a mix of mechanisms (both internal and external) is required to assure effective accountability. Because of their critical importance, monitoring and accountability are addressed at several places in the *Guidelines*. *Guidelines 9–13* address internal corporate monitoring and accountability, while *Guideline 14* addresses external and independent monitoring and accountability. For example, a human rights accountability mechanism would evaluate whether or not a company, in collaboration with other actors, including the state, has taken all reasonable steps to enhance access for not only the urban elite, but also the rural poor.

Conclusion

States have primary responsibility for ensuring the right to the highest attainable standard of health, including access to medicines. However, this is a shared responsibility. If access to medicines is to be enhanced, numerous national and international actors have an indispensable role to play. There is more literature on states' human rights duties in relation to access to medicines than on the human rights responsibility of pharmaceutical companies in access to medicines. In our view, it is unhelpful and unfair to urge pharmaceutical companies to comply with their right-to-health responsibilities without explaining what those responsibilities are. For this reason, we embarked on a project to clarify the human rights responsibilities of pharmaceutical companies in relation to access to medicines. After some years, this project generated the *Guidelines* that were published by the UN in August 2008 and which we have introduced in this chapter. We were, and remain, firmly of the view that a document consisting of only five or six general principles would fail to provide adequate practical, operational guidance to the interested parties. Like the UN special representative of the secretary-general on the issue of human rights and transnational corporations and other business enterprises, we are convinced that 'detailed guidance in specific functional areas' is what is needed – and this is what the *Guidelines*, firmly based on fundamental human rights principles, endeavour to provide. We encourage companies that wish to enhance their contribution to the realization of human rights, and other actors who wish to monitor and hold companies accountable, to use the *Guidelines* in their indispensable work.

NOTES

1 Mary Robinson, 'The Business Case for Human Rights,' United Nations High Commissioner for Human Rights, http://www.unhchr.ch/huricane/huricane.nsf/0/E47D352DEDC39697802566DE0043B28E?opendocument; S.V. de Mello, 'Human Rights: What Role for Business?' *New Academy Review* 2, no. 1 (2003): 19–25.
2 For more information on the Global Compact, see http://www.unglobalcompact.org/.
3 Organisation for Economic Co-operation and Development, *OECD Guidelines for Multinational Enterprises* (Paris: OECD, 2000).
4 United Nations Sub-Commission on Promotion and Protection of Human Rights, *Norms on the Responsibilities of Transnational Corporations and Other Business Enterprises with regard to Human Rights*, UN Doc. E/CN.4/Sub.2/2003/12/Rev.2 (2003). Also see the *Guiding Principles on Business and Human Rights: Implementing the United Nations 'Protect, Respect and Remedy' Framework*, prepared by the Special Representative of the Secretary-General on the Issue of Human Rights and Transnational Corporations, and endorsed by the UN Human Rights Council in 2011: A/HRC/RES/17/4, 16 June 2011, and A/HRC/17/31, 21 March 2011. These *Guiding Principles* were completed and adopted after the completion of this chapter.

5 Novartis Foundation for Sustainable Development, *Novartis Corporate Citizenship Guideline 4 (Human Rights)*, http://www.corporatecitizenship. novartis.com/downloads/people-communities/cc_guideline_4.pdf.

6 United Nations Commission on Human Rights, *Report of the Special Representative of the Secretary-General on the Issue of Human Rights and Transnational Corporations*, UN Doc. E/CN.4/2006/97 (2006), para. 70.

7 For a view consistent with the reports of the UN special representative of the secretary-general on the issue of human rights and transnational corporations, see, for example, ibid., para. 61, last sentence; and generally, United Nations Human Rights Council, *Report of the Special Representative of the Secretary-General on the Issue of Human Rights and Transnational Corporations and Other Business Enterprises*, UN Doc. A/HRC/8/5 (2008). Also see Andrew Clapham, *Human Rights Obligations of Non-State Actors* (London: Oxford University Press, 2006).

8 United Nations General Assembly, *Report of the Special Rapporteur on the Right of Everyone to the Enjoyment of the Highest Attainable Standard of Physical and Mental Health*, UN Doc. A/63/263 (2008).

9 World Health Organization, *Medicines Strategy: Countries at the Core, 2004–2007* (Geneva: WHO, 2004).

10 Some of this chapter draws upon the Montreal Statement on the Human Right to Essential Medicines (2005). See Stephen Marks, ed., *Health and Human Rights: Basic International Documents* (Cambridge, MA: Harvard University Press, 2006). It also draws from Paul Hunt and Rajat Khosla, 'The Human Right to Medicines,' *Sur: International Journal on Human Rights* 8 (2008): 99–114; and United Nations General Assembly, *Report of the Special Rapporteur on the Right of Everyone to the Enjoyment of the Highest Attainable Standard of Physical and Mental Health*, UN Doc. A/61/338 (2006); and United Nations General Assembly, *Report of the Special Rapporteur on the Right of Everyone to the Enjoyment of the Highest Attainable Standard of Physical and Mental Health*, UN Doc. A/63/263 (2008).

11 United Kingdom, Department of International Development, *Increasing Access to Essential Medicines in the Developing World: UK Government Policy and Plans* (London: DFID, 2004).

12 World Health Organization, *Medicines Strategy 2004–2007* (Geneva: WHO, 2004), n10.

13 Ibid.

14 Millennium Development Goals (MDGs), 2000, Target 17 of Goal 8, accessed 8 February 2008, http://www.undp.org/mdg/.

15 As shorthand, we use the terms 'the right to the highest attainable standard of health' and 'the right to health' instead of the full formulation,

'the right of everyone to the enjoyment of the highest attainable standard of physical and mental health.' For a discussion about the contribution of the right to health to the achievement of the health-related MDGs, see United Nations General Assembly, *Report of the Special Rapporteur on the Right of Everyone to the Enjoyment of the Highest Attainable Standard of Physical and Mental Health*, UN Doc. A/59/422 (2004).

16 *International Covenant on Economic, Social and Cultural Rights (ICESCR)*, 1976, articles 12 (2) (c) and (d), http://www2.ohcr.org/English/law/cesr.htm.

17 For an excellent summary of relevant national jurisprudence, see Hans Hogerzeil Melanie Samson, Jaume Vidal Casanovas, and Ladan Rahmani-Ocora, 'Is Access to Essential Medicines as Part of the Fulfilment of the Right to Health Enforceable through the Courts?' *Lancet* 368 (2006): 305. See also United Nations Commission on Human Rights, *Human Rights Resolutions: Access to Medication in Context of Pandemics such as HIV/AIDS, Tuberculosis and Malaria*, UN Doc. E/CN.4/Res/2003/29 (2003); UN Doc. E/CN.4/Res/2004/26 (2004); UN Doc. E/CN.4/Res/2005/23 (2005).

18 United Nations General Assembly, *Report of the Special Rapporteur* (2006). See also Hans Hogerzeil, 'Essential Medicines and Human Rights: What They Can Learn from Each Other,' *Bulletin of the World Health Organisation* 84, no. 5 (2006): 371–5.

19 United Kingdom, Department for International Development, *Increasing People's Access to Essential Medicines in Developing Countries: A Framework for Good Practice in the Pharmaceutical Industry* (London: DFID, 2005).

20 Ibid., 8–16.

21 Some of this information has been provided to the UN special rapporteur on the right to the highest attainable standard of health while on mission, and confirmed in, for example, Philippe Cullet, 'Patents and Medicines: The Relationship between TRIPS and the Human Right to Health,' *International Affairs* 79, no. 1 (2003): 139–60; and United Nations Millennium Project, *Report of Task Force 5 Working Group on Access to Essential Medicines* (New York: UNMP, 2005).

22 On the latter, see Mary Moran, Anne-Laure Ropars, Javier Guzman, Jose Diaz, and Christopher Garrison, *The New Landscape of Neglected Disease Drug Development* (London: Welcome Trust, 2005).

23 BLIHR, Global Compact, and OHCHR, *A Guide for Integrating Human Rights into Business Management*, http://www.integrating-humanrights.org.

24 UN Committee on the Economic, Social and Cultural Rights (CESCR), General Comment No. 14, *The Right to the Highest Attainable Standard of Health*, UN Doc. E/C.12/2000/4 (2000), para 42.

25 At the international level, for example, recent General Comments promulgated by the UN CESCR have helped to clarify the nature and scope of economic, social, and cultural rights. Also, recent international, regional, and national case law has shed light on the contours and content of economic, social, and cultural rights; see, for example, V. Gauri and D.M. Brinks, eds., *Courting Social Justice: Judicial Enforcement of Social and Economic Rights in the Developing World* (Cambridge, UK: Cambridge University Press, 2008).

26 United Nations Human Rights Council, *Report of the Special Representative* (2008), para 64.

27 The relevant literature is extensive and includes Consumers International, *Branding the Cure* (London: Consumers International, 2006); Klaus Leisinger, 'On Corporate Responsibility and Human Rights,' 2006, http://www.novartisfoundation.org/mandant/apps/publication/index.asp?MenuID=270&ID=612&Menu=3&Item=46; and United Kingdom, *Increasing Access* (2005).

28 For instance, BLIHR, Global Compact, and OHCHR, *Guide*; Commission on Intellectual Property, Innovation and Public Health, *Public Health, Innovation and Intellectual Property Rights* (Geneva: CIPIH, 2006); Novartis, *Novartis Corporate Citizenship*; United Nations Millennium Project, *Report*.

29 United Nations General Assembly, *Report of the Special Rapporteur* (2008). The Guidelines are also available in Rajat Khosla and Paul Hunt, *Human Rights Guidelines for Pharmaceutical Companies in Relation to Access to Medicines: The Sexual and Reproductive Health Context* (Colchester, Essex: Human Rights Centre, 2009).

30 The various reports of the special rapporteur on the right to the highest attainable standard of health set out, and apply, this right-to-health analysis in considerable detail, e.g., in relation to mental disability, United Nations Commission on Human Rights, *Report of the Special Rapporteur on the Right of Everyone to the Enjoyment of the Highest Attainable Standard of Physical and Mental Health*, UN Doc. E/CN.4/2005/51 (2005).

31 United Nations Commission on Human Rights, *Report of the Special Rapporteur on the Right of Everyone to the Enjoyment of Physical and Mental Health*, UN Doc. E/CN.4/2003/58 (2003).

32 *ICESCR*, article 2(1).

33 UN CESCR, General Comment 14, para. 43.

34 Ibid., General Comment 3, para. 10.

35 Ibid., General Comment 14, para. 8.

36 Ibid., para. 12.

37 World Health Organization, *A Joint Report by the Director-General of the WHO and the Executive Director of UNICEF Presented at the International Conference on Primary Health Care Alma-Ata* (Geneva: WHO, 1978).

38 See UN Committee on the Economic, Social and Cultural Rights (CESCR), General Comment 14, para. 33; United Nations Committee on the Elimination of Discrimination against Women, General Recommendation 24, 1999, para. 13.

39 UN CESCR, General Comment 14, paras 18–19.

40 Ibid., para. 54. See Helen Potts, *Participation and the Right to the Highest Attainable Standard of Health* (Colchester, Essex: Human Rights Centre, 2009).

41 For example, *ICESCR*, article 2(1).

42 UN Human Rights Council, *Report of the Special Rapporteur* (2008).

43 Helen Potts, *Accountability and the Right to the Highest Attainable Standard of Health* (Colchester, Essex: Human Rights Centre, 2008).

44 For a preliminary attempt to consider prioritization in the health sector generally, in the context of the right to the highest attainable standard of health, see United Nations General Assembly, *Report of the Special Rapporteur on the Right of Everyone to the Enjoyment of the Highest Attainable Standard of Physical and Mental Health*, UN Doc. A/62/214 (2007).

45 Moran et al., *New Landscape*.

46 UN CESCR, General Comment 14, para. 12.

47 For an introduction to these issues, see *United Nations Commission on Human Rights, Report of the Special Rapporteur on the Right of Everyone to the Enjoyment of the Highest Attainable Standard of Physical and Mental Health on mission to WTO*, UN Doc. E/CN.4/2004/49.Add.1 (2004).

48 World Trade Organization, *Declaration on TRIPS Agreement and Public Health*, Doha, WT/Min (01)/Dec/W/2 (2001).

49 World Trade Organization, *Implementation of Paragraph 6 of the Doha Declaration on the TRIPS Agreement and Public Health*, Decision of General Council, WT/L/540 (2003).

50 UN CESCR, General Comment 14, para 12 (b).

51 Jillian Clare Cohen, 'Pharmaceuticals and Corruption: A Risk Assessment', in *Global Corruption Report*, 77–85 (London: Transparency International, 2006).

52 Potts, *Accountability*.

53 Lynn P. Freedman, 'Human Rights, Constructive Accountability and Maternal Mortality in the Dominican Republic: A Commentary,' *International Journal of Gynaecology and Obstetrics* 82 (2003), 111–14.

54 The accountability device should clarify who has the responsibility to do what – and whether each has done it. If no one has done it, the device should explore why not, with a view to ensuring that it is properly done next time.

55 Novartis, *Improving Access to Leprosy Treatment* (Basel: Novartis Foundation, 2005); GlaxoSmithKline, *Facing the Challenge: Two Years On* (London: GlaxoSmithKline, 2004).

REFERENCES

BLIHR, Global Compact, and OHCHR. *A Guide for Integrating Human Rights into Business Management.* http://www.integrating-humanrights.org/.

Clapham, Andrew. *Human Rights Obligations of Non-State Actors.* London: Oxford University Press, 2006.

Cohen, Jillian Clare. 'Pharmaceuticals and Corruption: A Risk Assessment.' In *Global Corruption Report,* 77–85. London: Transparency International, 2006.

Commission on Intellectual Property, Innovation and Public Health. *Public Health, Innovation and Intellectual Property Rights.* Geneva: CIPIH, 2006.

Consumers International. *Branding the Cure.* London: Consumers International, 2006.

Cullet, Philippe. 'Patents and Medicines: The Relationship between TRIPS and the Human Right to Health.' *International Affairs* 79, no. 1 (2003): 139–60.

De Mello, S.V. 'Human Rights: What Role for Business?' *New Academy Review* 2, no. 1 (2003): 19–22.

Freedman, Lynn P. 'Human Rights, Constructive Accountability and Maternal Mortality in the Dominican Republic: A Commentary.' *International Journal of Gynaecology and Obstetrics* 82 (2003): 89–103.

Gauri, V., and D.M. Brinks, eds. *Courting Social Justice: Judicial Enforcement of Social and Economic Rights in the Developing World.* Cambridge, UK: Cambridge University Press, 2008.

GlaxoSmithKline. *Facing the Challenge: Two Years On.* London: GlaxoSmith-Kline, 2004.

Hogerzeil, Hans. 'Essential Medicines and Human Rights: What They Can Learn from Each Other.' *Bulletin of the World Health Organisation* 84, no. 5 (2006): 371–5.

Hogerzeil, Hans, Melanie Samson, Jaume Vidal Casanovas, and Ladan Rahmani-Ocora. 'Is Access to Essential Medicines as Part of the Fulfilment of the Right to Health Enforceable through the Courts?' *Lancet* 368 (2006): 305–11.

Hunt, Paul, and Rajat Khosla. 'The Human Right to Medicines.' *Sur: International Journal on Human Rights* 8 (2008): 99–114.

International Covenant on Economic, Social and Cultural Rights (ICESCR). 1976. http://www2.ohchr.org/english/law/cescr.htm.

Khosla, Rajat, and Paul Hunt. *Human Rights Guidelines for Pharmaceutical Companies in Relation to Access to Medicines: The Sexual and Reproductive Health Context.* Colchester, Essex: Human Rights Centre, 2009.

Leisinger, Klaus. *On Corporate Responsibility for Human Rights.* 2006. http://www.novartisfoundation.org/mandant/apps/publication/index.asp?MenuID=270&ID=612&Menu=3&Item=46.1.

Marks, Stephen, ed. *Health and Human Rights: Basic International Documents.* Cambridge, MA: Harvard University Press, 2006.

Moran, Mary, Anne-Laure Ropars, Javier Guzman, Jose Diaz, and Christopher Garrison. *The New Landscape of Neglected Disease Drug Development* (London: Welcome Trust, 2005).

Novartis. *Improving Access to Leprosy Treatment* (Basel: Novartis Foundation, 2005).

Novartis Foundation for Sustainable Development. *Novartis Corporate Citizenship Guideline 4 (Human Rights).* http://www.novartisfoundation. com. Accessed 12 Feb. 2008.

Organisation for Economic Co-operation and Development. *OECD Guidelines for Multinational Enterprises.* Paris: OECD, 2000.

Potts, Helen. *Accountability and the Right to the Highest Attainable Standard of Health.* Colchester, Essex: Human Rights Centre, 2008.

– *Participation and the Right to the Highest Attainable Standard of Health.* Colchester, Essex: Human Rights Centre, 2009.

Robinson, Mary. 'The Business Case for Human Rights.' United Nations High Commissioner for Human Rights. http://www.unhchr.ch/huricane/ huricane.nsf/0/E47D352DEDC39697802566DE0043B28E?opendocument.

United Kingdom. Department for International Development. *Increasing Access to Essential Medicines in the Developing World: UK Government Policy and Plans.* London: DFID, 2004.

– *Increasing People's Access to Essential Medicines in Developing Countries: A Framework for Good Practice in the Pharmaceutical Industry.* London: DFID, 2005.

United Nations Commission on Human Rights. *Human Rights Resolutions: Access to Medication in Context of Pandemics such as HIV/AIDS, Tuberculosis and Malaria.* UN Doc. E/CN.4/Res/2003/29 (2003); UN Doc. E/CN.4/ Res/2004/26 (2004); and UN Doc. E/CN.4/Res/2005/23 (2005).

– *Report of the Special Rapporteur on the Right of Everyone to the Enjoyment of Physical and Mental Health.* UN Doc. E/CN.4/2003/58 (2003).

– *Report of the Special Rapporteur on the Right of Everyone to the Enjoyment of the Highest Attainable Standard of Physical and Mental Health on Mission to WTO.* UN Doc. E/CN.4/2004/49.Add.1 (2004).

– *Report of the Special Rapporteur on the Right of Everyone to the Enjoyment of the Highest Attainable Standard of Physical and Mental Health.* UN Doc. E/ CN.4/2005/51 (2005).

– *Report of the Special Representative of the Secretary-General on the Issue of Human Rights and Transnational Corporations.* UN Doc. E/CN.4/2006/97 (2006).

United Nations Committee on the Economic, Social and Cultural Rights. General Comment No. 14. *The Right to the Highest Attainable Standard of Health.* UN Doc. E/C.12/2000/4 (2000).

United Nations Committee on the Elimination of Discrimination against Women, General Recommendation 24, *Women and Health,* UN Doc. A/54/38 (1999).

United Nations General Assembly. *Report of the Special Rapporteur on the Right of Everyone to the Enjoyment of the Highest Attainable Standard of Physical and Mental Health.* UN Doc. A/59/422 (2004).

– *Report of the Special Rapporteur on the Right of Everyone to the Enjoyment of the Highest Attainable Standard of Physical and Mental Health.* UN Doc. A/61/338 (2006).

– *Report of the Special Rapporteur on the Right of Everyone to the Enjoyment of the Highest Attainable Standard of Physical and Mental Health.* UN Doc. A/62/214 (2007).

– *Report of the Special Rapporteur on the Right of Everyone to the Enjoyment of the Highest Attainable Standard of Physical and Mental Health.* UN Doc. A/63/263 (2008).

United Nations Human Rights Council. *Report of the Special Rapporteur on the Right of Everyone to the Enjoyment of Physical and Mental Health.* UN Doc. A/HRC/7/11/Add.2 (2008).

– *Report of the Special Representative of the Secretary-General on the Issue of Human Rights and Transnational Corporations.* UN Doc. A/HRC/8/5 (2008).

United Nations Millennium Project. *Report of Task Force 5 Working Group on Access to Essential Medicines.* New York: UNMP, 2005.

United Nations Sub-Commission on Promotion and Protection of Human Rights. *Norms on the Responsibilities of Transnational Corporations and Other Business Enterprises with regard to Human Rights.* UN Doc. E/CN.4/Sub.2/2003/12/Rev.2 (2003).

World Trade Organization. *Declaration on TRIPS Agreement and Public Health.* Doha, WT/Min (01)/Dec/W/2, 2001.

– *Implementation of Paragraph 6 of the Doha Declaration on the TRIPS Agreement and Public Health.* Decision of General Council, WT/L/540, 30 Aug. 2003.

World Health Organization. *A Joint Report by the Director-General of the WHO and the Executive Director of UNICEF Presented at the International Conference on Primary Health Care Alma-Ata.* Geneva: WHO, 1978.

– *Medicines Strategy: Countries at the Core, 2004–2007.* Geneva: WHO, 2004.

3 Improving Access to Essential Medicines: International Law and Normative Change

ASHER ALKOBY

Introduction

This chapter seeks to gain insights into the struggle to improve access to essential medicines from the empirical and conceptual contributions to the study of normative change in international law and international relations scholarships. Each of the essays collected in this volume addresses the question of normative change, by exploring the potential of corporate responsibility for improving access to medicines. Much of the current scholarly work on the responsibilities of corporations for human rights attempts to measure corporate activities against an international normative framework for the protection of human rights. This discussion often oscillates between the descriptive (pointing to existing norms, conventions, or principles and measuring corporate compliance with them) and the prescriptive (such as an argument for the right to health as a global moral imperative). However, to speak of compliance of states with an obligation to protect the right to health, or the responsibility of corporations to respect such a right, is to imply that such a norm exists in international law and that it is currently binding on states – an argument that is not uncontroversial. This norm is one of a number of politically charged social, economic, and cultural rights that have been historically resisted because of their subjectivity, and because of the difficulty in assigning responsibility for these norms to governments who may not have the capacity to comply with them.

More importantly, the discussion of 'responsibility' must also take into account the dynamic nature of international lawmaking today, particularly in the areas of trade and human rights. Any attempt to understand (or predict) normative change in the right to health, and the intellectual property rights that sometimes stand in conflict to it, cannot assume that these norms have meanings that are stable over time. It would be helpful to take a broader perspective and consider, for example, how norms protecting intellectual property rights came about, the processes through which they are being revised, elaborated, and interpreted, and how these norms, in turn, change the meaning and content of the human right to health. The ongoing elaboration and interpretation of norms is typically done within specific international institutions and therefore applies only among the states that contracted by treaty to respect them. When a conflict arises with a norm that was created in a separate normative framework, the question becomes whether the resolution of an issue in a given legal regime should depend on, or be depended upon, the resolution of the issue in another regime, and if so, what the nature of such interdependence of regimes might be.

When considering the way in which the debate over increased access to essential medicines has unfolded so far, it becomes evident that the forces behind the significant normative shifts have not been only states but networks of non-state actors as well. This chapter aims to locate this involvement in the broader context of international normative change and suggest what the way forward should be. The second section begins by examining studies that aim to predict conditions under which international normative change is likely to take place, and focuses on two of the propositions that this body of work has generated. The first proposition is that value-laden, contested, international norms often emerge as a result of concerted efforts of norm entrepreneurs who advance their agenda and mobilize support around it. Their power often lies in their moral authority rather than military or economic might, yet they engage other international actors in an attempt to either convince or coerce them to accept the new normative standard. The third section shows that this hypothesis is largely confirmed by the case under study. Faced with a sustained campaign led by like-minded activists, states and corporate actors have slowly begun to accept the right to health as an emerging normative standard and the responsibility for implementing it is increasingly recognized.

Some studies of international normative change further suggest that processes of lawmaking within international institutions may be designed to facilitate discursive interaction among all stakeholders, out of which reasoned consensus may be reached. Examples of successful implementation of discursive lawmaking arrangements, notably in the area of environmental governance, suggest that inclusive lawmaking will produce norms that are legitimate in the eyes of their addressees, and these norms will be better complied with for that reason. The implication is that opening up institutions of global governance to the input of all who may be affected by their decisions will enhance their legitimacy. More to the point, the responsibility of corporations for the human right to health would be greatly enhanced if both human rights groups and corporate actors will be able to partake in the processes through which the right to health is given meaning to, interpreted, elaborated, and revised. In the last section I suggest that while this hypothesis may have been confirmed in other areas of global governance, it may not apply with equal force to the case under study. When the preconditions for discursive engagement are unlikely to be met within a lawmaking institution, opening up this institution to civil society input should proceed with caution because it is not likely to produce the desired effect.

International Lawmaking and the Study of Normative Change

The traditional view of international lawmaking considers law as a collection of formalized and institutional features. Many scholars studying international norms continue to work within this conceptual framework: they treat the act of contractual obligation as the defining moment when a law comes into being, and they measure the behaviour of states with reference to that point in time.[1] What these analyses often fail to acknowledge is that, given the nature and reach of international law in the past few decades, these traditional categories must be reexamined. Very often, the formal act of accepting a legal obligation is only a point in a broad process of lawmaking, and it only signals the beginning of such a process.[2]

International lawmaking is thus often more about process than about form.[3] An increasing number of voices, especially in the community of international lawyers, advocate a more expansive view of law and aim to situate it in a broader social context.[4] Like all law, international law is 'jurisgenerative': a law-creating process in which interpretive communities create and give meaning to law through their narratives and precepts.[5] The meaning, as well as the level of acceptance of a legal rule by its addressees, may change over time. Since law is an inevitably incomplete construction, lawmaking and application of the law cannot be viewed as radically separate from each other: they are part of the same continuum.[6] In many areas of international governance, the pattern of lawmaking reflects this view of law as an activity rather than an act. States first negotiate a set of general principles or statements of intent (sometimes in the form of a 'declaration'), followed by more concrete principles, procedural provisions, and information-sharing mechanisms (usually in the form of a 'convention'), and only later do they develop a more substantive set of binding commitments ('treaties' or 'protocols'). Even after binding commitments are made, their clarification, interpretation, and implementation are constantly renegotiated and reflected upon in light of changing circumstances or new information.[7]

Since lawmaking and application of the law are part of the same continuum, the question of international normative change does not begin at a moment when law is formally created, but in the process through which norms are made, elaborated, and revised. Studies of international normative change tend to focus on the main loci of this ongoing lawmaking activity: international institutions. The dominant institutionalist perspective explains the emergence of international norms in a rational choice framework and posits that states will usually cooperate with each other, and develop normative frameworks that support such cooperation, only when it is in their best interest to do so.[8] Self-interestedness, however, is manipulable: institutions may be designed to create incentives and punishments that could have impact on the behaviour of states. Institutionalists point to two kinds of 'games' between states in explaining the evolution of international norms. The first is coordination games, in which all actors benefit from a rule or a standard and therefore they all have an incentive to enact such a rule and then comply with it (such as the rules of international aviation). The second type of game is a cooperation game, where actors have a strong incentive not to comply and to free-ride (such as rules governing international trade or environmental protection). Much of this literature aims to identify why cooperation failed in certain situations as well as predict which institutional arrangements will be more suitable for stable cooperation.[9] This approach, however, faces some difficulties in explaining (or predicting) normative change. It fails to explain what brings actors to adopt certain preferences in the first place, and it cannot explain how preferences may change. Actors leave the 'game' with the same set of preferences with which they entered into it.

Further, institutionalism does not fully account for the involvement of non-state entities in international lawmaking, in and outside of international institutions.[10] Within institutions, these analysts agree that states are likely to make use of non-state entities when they see fit, mostly to minimize research and implementation expenditures. The involvement of these actors has to be devised, therefore, to fit the broader undertakings of states within the institution. Indeed, for institutionalists, states continue to be the only relevant players on the international playing field. In many areas of international lawmaking, however – including the case under study, as the following section will show – non-state actors are assuming key roles in the making and application of international norms.

A growing body work in the past two decades, often labelled 'constructivism,' has attempted to challenge institutionalism and has shown that institutions have the power to do more than constrain behaviour through using costs and benefits: they may also shape the identities of actors operating within them and their interests as a result.[11] Some empirical work has demonstrated that international actors do not always act out of material self-interest. Sometimes they create norms, and they comply with such norms, even when doing so appears to be against their interest. What often guides the behaviour of states is socially shared understandings that point to what is normatively appropriate.[12]

Constructivist studies also suggest that states are not the only international actors involved in the process of normative change. Many of these studies centre on the role played by civil society actors in the evolution and diffusion of international norms, through the use of both coercive and persuasive methods.[13] Research into norms of international relations suggests that two elements contribute to the successful diffusion of new international norms: the involvement of non-state networks of 'norm entrepreneurs' in the introduction of the norm (by bringing attention to the need for the norm and mobilizing support for it) and the availability of organizational platforms from which entrepreneurs can operate.[14] After norm entrepreneurs manage to persuade a critical number of states to act as 'norm leaders,' it is possible to say that the norm has reached a tipping point (and possibly an agreement is signed), after which a 'norm cascade' begins: an active international socialization intended to induce those who violate what now is an established norm to comply with it.[15]

Once again, however, this 'tipping point' is typically not the end of the lawmaking enterprise. It may mark a significant normative shift, but the process through which the norm is further interpreted (for example, by decisions of dispute settlement tribunals), operationalized, and revised, very often requires continuous dialogue. In some areas of lawmaking, notably environmental regimes, studies point to the ways in which this ongoing dialogue takes shape. They have found evidence for international deliberation involving civil society groups in international lawmaking processes. Here too, non-state actors were found to be instrumental to the ways in which international norms are further developed. Networks of both activist and corporate associations typically provide information and expertise, participate to some extent in negotiations within institutional settings, introduce new issues and values to the debate, and contribute to the reproduction of the political consensus.[16]

Drawing on analyses of institutional deliberation, I have argued elsewhere that this dialogic process of international lawmaking resembles the idea of discourse ethics developed by Jürgen Habermas.[17] The notion of discourse builds on the need to allow participants in political deliberation to account for their beliefs and actions in terms that would be intelligible to others, who may accept them or contest them.[18] Principles, norms, or any institutional arrangement can be said to be valid only if they meet the approval of those affected by them.[19] Discourse theory rejects the vision of democracy as an agglomeration of private preferences and instead introduces the notion of 'institutionalized discourses' as the processes through which political consensus is formed. Legitimacy, under this view, requires that decisions rest on 'good arguments' made by participants in the debate. It derives from a mutual respect for the rules of argumentation: that participants must be free and equal actors who challenge the validity of each other's claims, that they seek a reasoned consensus about their situation and justifications for the norms chosen, and that they are open to being persuaded by the better argument.[20] Participants advance reasons for why certain behaviour ought to be avoided and another should be adopted. Once a consensus is reached, these reasons internally motivate the participants to behave appropriately.

When mapped onto the international relations realm, this conceptual schema suggests that the public sphere is where informally organized global networks create and legitimate norms through discourse. In the political sphere, networks act strategically in order to gain recognition, achieve benefits, and influence the political discourse. This offensive, political mode of action is not focused upon material gains only; it also involves 'the politics of influence,' targeting political actors and making them more receptive to the needs and self-understandings of actors in civil society. International relations scholars have found evidence for such discursive construction of norms at the interstate level and have demonstrated how patterns of persuasive argumentation are found in the adoption of international norms through an interaction among international actors.[21]

It should be stressed that the inclusiveness requirement under this framework applies to all potentially affected participants rather than entities representing public interest only. Some argue that the inclusion of corporate entities in international lawmaking is not a desirable development, since these actors are motivated by economic self-interest and their participation in treaty-making would impede progress in issues such as human rights or environmental protection. Nongovernmental organizations (NGOs), on the other hand, are free from profit-making constraints and promote the public interest by representing the beneficiaries of the prescribed international norms.[22] This argument assumes, however, that NGOs represent the global public in some aggregative sense – an assumption that is very difficult to defend. Under the deliberative approach to lawmaking, on the other hand, the reason to allow both NGO and business entities to participate in the creation and application of international norms is not because they represent the public, but because they bring a diversity of perspectives into the institutional dialogue, out of which informed and reasoned consensus may be reached.[23]

The assumption underlying a deliberative approach to lawmaking is that the best decisions are made by including a multitude of perspectives in the process, because actors are engaged in a genuine dialogue where relations of power recede in the background. Power relations, however, are hardly ever absent from human interaction – particularly when powerful corporate actors are involved – and this concern is often raised by critics of discursive approaches to global governance. The idea of discourse, they contend, is good in theory, but it rarely takes place in practice.[24] Yet the requirements for genuine discourse are not absolute. The idea of discourse 'is a regulative idea, a counterfactual stance from which to assess and criticize non-deliberative processes and power politics.'[25] In this sense, the procedural fairness as required by a discourse approach should be viewed as an aspiration rather than as a goal that could be entirely achieved. The insight that this approach provides, however, remains forceful nonetheless: the closer the lawmaking process comes to reaching this regulative ideal, the more legitimate the norms that it produces will be.

Furthermore, discourse may do more than convince participants of the rightness of the arguments raised. It also has the power to discipline actors through language and rhetoric. Therefore, even corporate actors who may enter the debate without the requisite openness to be persuaded by others may find themselves entrapped by the precepts, norms, and ideas that are used by all participants in the debate. This appears to have happened in the climate change regime, for example, where corporate associations who initially opposed climate-change mitigation policies of any kind (as well as denied the science of climate change) were arguably socialized into the regime through active participation in the negotiations leading up to the signing of a treaty. A significant shift is witnessed in the positions of many of the multinational oil companies who took an active role in the institutional debate.[26] This finding is crucial for the debate over corporate responsibility for the human right to health, because if this assumption holds, it suggests that the key to enhancing the compliance of corporate actors with the right to health is to allow them to take an active role in the lawmaking processes where the norm is developed and revised.

This insight may be crucial for the study of global health governance, where the tremendous effect of non-state actors on lawmaking processes is widely recognized, but their role in reshaping the landscape of global public health is articulated mostly in terms of indirect influence on states and institutions (as the first hypothesis suggests), or as a direct influence on governance through the provision of resources and expertise. In this latter role, NGOs work to strengthen international institutions such as the World Health Organization (WHO) vis-à-vis sovereign states by partnering with these institutions and bringing to the table their scientific expertise.[27] When such partnerships are not conceivable, activist networks step in to fill voids in areas of governance neglected by states.[28] Their potential role as participants in the continuous lawmaking processes taking place within different institutional settings affecting the governance of global health, however, remains largely unexplored.[29]

To conclude this part, studies of normative change leave us with two hypotheses on the emergence and evolution of international norms. First, it is very often non-state norm entrepreneurs who bring about normative change by advancing their agenda and mobilizing support around it. Second, international norms continue to evolve, often within institutional settings, and the level of participation of all stakeholders in the process through which these norms are given meaning has direct bearing on the legitimacy of the norms and their effectiveness as a result. The deliberative approach predicts that when norms are the product of consensus among the participants – reached through an inclusive discourse – they will be viewed as legitimate in the eyes of their addressees. Indeed, the concept of legitimacy is central to a deliberative approach to lawmaking.[30] Legitimacy under this view is 'rooted in a "thick" acceptance of the need for emerging norms, an acceptance promoted by reference to past practice, contemporary aspirations and the deployment of reason by analogy.'[31] It is achieved when law is created, interpreted, and applied through an active participation of all those affected by the resultant norms. The discussion below examines the two hypotheses against the access campaign to suggest that while the human right to health in the context of access to medicines may have reached the 'tipping point' of normative change as a result of activist norm entrepreneurship, the continued development of the relevant norms may be impeded by institutional imperatives preventing the emergence of a genuinely discursive framework.

Access to Medicines: Non-State Norm Entrepreneurs as Key Players

The state of public health care in developing countries, particularly with relation to HIV/AIDS infections, is one of the most pressing international problems of our time. Poverty and inadequate resources significantly restrict access to essential medicines in most of sub-Saharan Africa, the Caribbean, and parts of Asia and Central America. But at the more immediate level, the high prices of antiretroviral (ARV) drugs has been the main obstacle to improving access of people with HIV/AIDS to life-saving treatment.[32] Efforts by developing countries' governments to reduce the prices of ARV drugs by allowing for generic substitution or parallel importation of expensive patented drugs have encountered the fierce resistance of patent-holding multinational corporations as well as their host countries. This resistance enjoys the backing of a powerful international institution – the WTO and its *Agreement on Trade-Related Aspects of Intellectual Property* (*TRIPS*). This agreement extends intellectual property protection to pharmaceutical patents, which were unprotected in most developing countries until the agreement came along. Patents are protected for twenty years. They are valid whether the products are imported or locally produced, and they apply to all patent holders, foreign and domestic.[33]

Shortly after its conclusion in the Uruguay Round in 1994, it was clear that *TRIPS* will become the main battleground between those struggling to improve access to essential medicines and others who seek to protect patent rights. While interaction in the WTO is exclusively between states, the main drivers of the normative shifts in the access campaign have been global networks of non-state actors: business networks on the one hand (through patent-holding governments) and activist networks (often coalescing with developing countries' governments) on the other.

Business networks were the main driving force behind the *TRIPS* agreement.[34] Leading these efforts were twelve CEOs of U.S.-based multinational corporations who formed the Intellectual Property Committee (IPC) as early as 1986, just before the Uruguay Round was launched. Four of these corporations were pharmaceutical companies. In an increasingly globalized economy, these companies were concerned about the extent to which foreign governments would protect U.S. patents and therefore began seeking the support of the U.S. government in pressuring foreign governments to adopt and enforce strict patent-protection laws.[35] This campaign involved mobilizing a private sector coalition, pressing international institutions, pleading their case to government and business representatives in countries with lax intellectual property protection, and even participating in the U.S. delegation at the Uruguay Round.[36] The IPC's success was remarkable: after forging industry consensus with its European and Japanese counterparts, it achieved more than it expected – an intellectual property code that was a wholesale reflection of the private sector's interests. In fact, a draft paper prepared by the IPC's consultant in 1985 essentially outlines what later became *TRIPS*.[37]

Among the reasons for the business associations' success, Susan Sell claims, are the great economic power that they wield (their ability to offer expertise, the lobbying activities, and the institutional access that the latter brings), as well as the discursive effects of their efforts.[38] Despite the fact that extending monopoly privileges to patent holders means, ironically, *less* free trade and *less* competition, the business network succeeded in introducing a stringent intellectual property code to an institution founded on trade liberalization. It did so by framing the issue of intellectual property protection as a solution for the U.S. trade deficit and convincing U.S. policymakers that patent protection would be beneficial for the U.S. economy. The IPC also managed to persuade the negotiating states that this approach will benefit not only the IPC (and the United States) but the entire world trading system.

It would not be an overstatement to conclude that *TRIPS* was hijacked by the private sector. As the UN Development Programme report from 1999 points out, this agreement was adopted 'before most governments and people understood the social and economic implications of patents on life. They were also negotiated with far too little participation from developing countries now feeling the impact of their conditions.'[39] Networks of activists campaigning for improved access to medicines became involved in the process much too late.[40] Spearheaded by Médecins sans frontières (MSF) and the South African Treatment Action Campaign (TAC), these activists began supporting governments that are fighting to increase access to health drugs by using various strategies to curtail the potentially devastating impact of a strict enforcement of *TRIPS*. Opposition to *TRIPS* first became visible in the activities leading up to the street protests during the WTO Seattle Ministerial Conference in 1999. Networks of activists picked up the support of the UN Development Programme and the WHO, calling governments to ensure access to essential drugs and to re-examine the institutional arrangements impeding access to essential medicines.[41] But the first major victory of the campaign was in the high-profile episode of the lawsuit filed by forty-one multinational pharmaceutical firms against the South African government alleging that South African law violated *TRIPS* by allowing parallel imports and generic substitution of medicines.[42] In addition to their direct involvement in the South African litigation as *amicus curiae*, activist networks led by TAC and MSF launched a worldwide campaign against Big Pharma and the U.S. government. On the first day of the hearing in court, TAC called for an international day of action, holding demonstrations in thirty cities around the world. MSF initiated petitions against the case and persuaded several European governments to support the cause by passing resolutions calling for the case to be dropped. This broad campaign, involving contentious political manoeuvres and acts of shaming against drug companies and their host states, was a clear turning point in the struggle. The campaign conveyed the message that protecting the drug revenues of pharmaceutical companies means that people with HIV/AIDS in developing countries would die. It soon became clear to the drug companies that pursuing the claim in court would only worsen the public relations disaster they were now faced with, and thus decided to drop the case.[43]

In November 2001, the campaign yielded another significant normative outcome. The WTO members agreed to a ministerial declaration at
Doha, which stated, 'The TRIPS agreement does not and should not
prevent Members from taking measures to protect public health.' They
agreed that *TRIPS* 'should be interpreted and implemented in a manner supportive of WTO Members' right to protect public health.'[44]
Shortly before this declaration, and in light of the new political climate,
the United States decided to withdraw its WTO case against Brazil for
violating patents rights under *TRIPS* by enabling compulsory licensing
of essential drugs.[45]

While the *Doha Declaration* is not considered a formal amendment of
TRIPS, it could have some influence on the interpretation and application of the treaty. It allows countries to use parallel importation to promote public health, as well as use compulsory licensing to manufacture
or import generic medicines.[46] But while it reinforces the need for flexibility in countries' duties to protect intellectual property rights, it does
not do much more than 'leave open all the possibilities that existed under the *TRIPS* agreement, without providing clear guidance as to which
one of the options would be best to achieve the desired results.'[47] It has
therefore been argued that the declaration, as well as the subsequent
TRIPS Council decision of 2003 that aimed to further elaborate on the
exceptions to intellectual property protection, may be seen as no more
than a public relations exercise by the WTO.[48]

The key forces in this battle so far have been non-state actors. Business
networks are responsible for initiating and carving out what became an
international code for the protection of intellectual property rights, and
they have done so through an intensive, focused campaign, convincing
governments to adopt standards that reflected the interests of the private sector. The formal adoption of *TRIPS*, however, merely signalled
the beginning of the lawmaking enterprise. Once *TRIPS* was adopted,
business networks worked to bring violating countries to comply with
TRIPS by pressing the U.S. government to impose unilateral sanctions
against those states and bring complaints against violations in both domestic and international adjudicative bodies. Activist networks responded with a campaign aimed at the governments upholding *TRIPS*,
attempting to coerce them into compliance with another norm – the
human right to health.

Indeed, this clash of norms nicely illustrates the difficulty with framing the discussion around the *responsibility* to the human right to health.
The access campaign story concerns not simply a question of a breach

of one international norm but a clash between a conflictual norm – the emerging human right to health – and its evolution in a contested normative space dominated by a cooperation norm, the one granting monopoly to intellectual property rights holders. To the extent that South Africa and Brazil were in violation of WTO law, it was regime-specific law which arguably stands in conflict to international human rights law.

The adoption of *TRIPS* came at the end of negotiations involving the WTO members and with a strong presence of business networks. Human rights activists, who might have had a critical view on *TRIPS* and its founding principles, were not given voice during this process. Countries that are primarily on the receiving end of intellectual property, in turn, are typically marginalized in WTO negotiations, and their ability to voice their concerns was very limited here as well.[49] For this reason, the process through which current intellectual property norms were adopted may be seen as deeply flawed from the deliberative perspective outline above, and the resultant norms lack the kind of legitimacy that generates adherence to norms. While *TRIPS* was adopted by a consensual decision of all WTO member states at the end of lengthy deliberations, it was far from being a power-free, inclusive debate among all affected participants.

The way in which the access campaign has unfolded since is a direct outcome of this flawed lawmaking process. Activist networks launched an attack on intellectual property norms because they view them as illegitimate. The tactics they used involved acts of shaming and social sanctioning of states, and they have done so successfully because their power is grounded in their moral authority and their ability to sway public opinion through the media. These networks took aim at wealthy intellectual-property-producing countries, pharmaceutical companies, and the WTO. Interestingly, while in most cases of transnational activism studied so far, civil society groups acted to *strengthen* international institutions at the cost of eroding national sovereignty, the access campaign is an example of activism aimed at *weakening* an international institution by defending the sovereign right of states to protect the health of their publics.[50] The considerable success of activist networks in defending the rights of South Africa and Brazil to ensure access to essential drugs, and the *Doha* process that followed, all suggest that social sanctioning is an effective tool in bringing about normative change, as predicted by the constructivist studies reviewed above.[51] The access campaign, therefore, seems to confirm the first hypothesis regarding the emergence of norms – that significant normative shifts are often driven by non-state entities, and that through a focused campaign involving the mobilization of public support, shaming, and sanctioning, international norms may come into being. The question remains, however, how the kind of input offered by the networks of activists into the lawmaking process can be further channelled into institutional settings in the continuous lawmaking that follows. The second hypothesis considered above suggested that this may be done through the establishment of an inclusive discourse, where all stakeholders may partake in the lawmaking. Such an inclusive discourse, we have seen, has not been taking place in the context of *TRIPS*, and the discussion below asks whether it should become so in the future.

Enhancing Corporate Responsibility by Making International Institutions More Inclusive: Some Second Thoughts

There is a growing body of literature exploring the legal mechanisms through which human rights, environmental rights, and labour rights may be linked to global trade lawmaking forums.[52] Some legal scholars insist that such linkage is not needed, since economic liberalization is broadly supportive of human rights and consequently there is no need to impose formal restraints on free trade to deal with conflicts that arise between the two regimes.[53] Other scholars, who are rightly more concerned with the shorter-term, devastating impact of human rights violations, have advanced proposals on how to effectively link the international trade and human rights regimes, including constitutional integration of these two regimes within the WTO,[54] the amendment of GATT and other WTO agreements,[55] and interpretive linkage via the WTO dispute-resolution body.[56]

There appears to be a general agreement that one of the most effective ways to channel human rights discourse into the WTO is increased transparency and openness of this institution to civil society groups.[57] The WTO is notorious for its lack of openness and the secrecy of its negotiations. The member states' approach is based on the problematic assumption that 'closer consultation and cooperation with NGOs can also be met constructively through appropriate processes at the national level.'[58] However, as Steve Charnovitz contends, the assumption that accountability of governments may be achieved at the national level can no longer hold.[59] In this view, opening the WTO to NGO input in its decision-making would have an equalizing effect on the institution. It would give voice to civil society groups in non-democratic states (for whom transnational participation is the only open channel of influence), to individuals in states who have not joined the WTO yet but are affected by its decisions, and to activists in non-powerful states that are routinely marginalized in the institutional deliberations.[60]

Other institutions of global governance, it is claimed, have successfully incorporated stakeholder and civil society input into their decision-making processes (the climate-change regime mentioned above is a case in point), and this experience supports the argument that consultation with non-state actors in negotiation and rulemaking in the WTO will ensure that broader perspectives will be represented in the institutional dialogue.[61] This can be achieved through permitting non-state actors to observe WTO negotiations, address delegates at the hearings, submit position papers to state delegations, and submit amicus briefs to the dispute-settlement bodies.[62] In this view, then, by reforming the opportunity structure of the political system and its level of openness we may be able to produce the kind of inclusive discourse that is evident in other regimes. These calls to open up institutional deliberation forums appear to support the second hypothesis discussed earlier, regarding the advantages of adopting a deliberative approach to international institutional lawmaking. As noted earlier, corporate entities are arguably also a part of this conceptual schema, and their participation in the ongoing dialogue should be equally encouraged. The participation of corporations in the production and reproduction of international norms, it was suggested, is part of the process of generating the legitimacy of norms and would therefore guarantee their adherence to the norms in the future. Before concluding that such institutional reform is the way forward, however, we must also consider the prospects of implementing this reform in a meaningful way: setting aside the political feasibility of such reform, we must also ask whether such reform is desirable, given the potential effect of what I would like to call the 'institutional imperatives.'

John Dryzek defines a *state imperative* as 'any function that governmental structures must perform if those structures are to secure longevity and stability.'[63] These imperatives usually include all significant matters relating to national security and foreign policy, fiscal, monetary and trade policy, the welfare state, civil and criminal justice, and environmental policy. State imperatives are stable in the sense that they define the very need for the state and may override government preferences. For example, if a government is elected that is committed to income redistribution, there may be very little it could actually do in face of the need not to frighten the markets and avoid economic crisis. In other words, very often an elected government is unable to implement the policies it wishes to adopt because it is constrained by the institutional logic within which it operates. Are there any systemic *global* imperatives that similarly constrain international institutions? As illustrated by the access campaign, since different international legal regimes operate on different logics (and therefore may often clash), it may be more appropriate to consider the *institutional* imperatives in question.

International economic institutions operate on the logic of market liberalism. Free trade is the norm against which all policies are measured, and any consideration of non-trade issues is exception based.[64] As noted above, *TRIPS* has managed to create an exception to the principle of free trade, which is an institutional imperative in itself – a global intellectual-property-protection system based on long-term monopoly on patent rights rather than competition and diffusion of rights. Any challenge to this imperative from within the WTO would be based on piecemeal amendments, creating exceptions that would still be interpreted by the WTO dispute-settlement body, headed by trade experts who are bound by this institutional logic.[65] This casts some doubt on the soundness of the proposals to open up this institution to the input of non-state groups.

To understand why this is so, consider again the realm of global environmental governance, which is often brought as an exemplary implementation of inclusive lawmaking processes. The difference there is that both environmental and business actors could be assimilated at least partly into the emerging imperative of environmental conservation dominating international environmental regimes. The very logic behind the discourse of 'sustainable development,' upon which international environmental agreements are often founded, is that it is possible to restructure the capitalist political economy along environmentally defensible lines. In other words, rather than challenging capitalist production, it aims to 'sell' the idea that a clean and healthy environment is good for business, and that there is money to be made from ecological modernization.[66] Moderate green civil society groups, as well as corporate actors, which could identify with this emerging imperative, could best promote their agenda by seeking inclusion in international environmental institutions. Other groups, such as green radicals (who aim for a future beyond capitalism), would stay outside of the institutional framework and employ contentious tactics to promote their agendas.

The diversity of the global environmental movement would guarantee a continued vitality of the green public sphere as well as healthy challenge to the dominant discourses. This may be distinguished from the evolution of the right to health, in that civil society groups involved in the access campaign appear to be unified by a codified set of international human rights standards that are sometimes incorporated into national law and policy as well.[67] This network of activists aims to illuminate the cause–effect relationship between high drug prices that are protected by *TRIPS* and the death caused by diseases that such drugs may prevent or treat. Their common goal is to defend the rights of governments to take measures to improve people's access to essential medicines by devising strategies to significantly reduce their prices. The strategies and tactics of these civil society groups may differ, but they all appear to share the language of international human rights discourse, with its underlying philosophical foundations.[68]

The difficulty, of course, is that the human rights discourse shared by these actors faces an institutional imperative prioritizing the economic gain associated with patent rights protection, and this has implications for the prospects of deliberative lawmaking in the WTO. Other authors have recognized that reframing intellectual property rights as a public health issue may indeed be unthinkable in institutions such as the WTO, given its pro-market philosophy.[69] Lawrence Helfer has made one of the most thoughtful attempts to explore the alternatives to using the WTO as a lawmaking forum addressing public health concerns.[70] NGOs (as well as developing countries), he maintains, can successfully use other international forums that are more receptive to their input: the regimes regulating biodiversity, plant genetic resources, public health, and human rights. Admittedly, standards created in other regimes will not have the same binding effect that *TRIPS* has, given the hard-edged enforcement provided by the WTO dispute-settlement procedure, but Helfer suggests that soft laws created in the biodiversity or human rights regimes may have considerable influence on WTO jurisprudence and act as progenitors of proposals to revise WTO rules.[71] The regained faith in the ability of this pro-market institution to revise its standards through judicial interpretation, however, ultimately presents us with a curious proposition: that rules that were unthinkable in the WTO – the reason why NGOs and states decided to shift their attention to other regimes in the first place – will become thinkable in the WTO only because they were successfully negotiated elsewhere. The idea that a collision between conflicting norms created in different international regimes could be a creative clash is indeed worth studying, but it is doubtful that WTO jurisprudence, which has consistently championed immutable trade principles, can serve as a vehicle for such attempts at normative harmonization.[72]

This is not to suggest that using alternative institutional platforms is not a good strategy, but only to highlight the limited utility of such strategies. I suggested earlier that a power-free, inclusive deliberation that produces legitimate international norms is a regulative ideal that should be aspired to, even though it may never be entirely reached. The prospects of coming any closer to this ideal in the international institutions in charge of implementing the *TRIPS* agreement, however, appear particularly dim, given the institutional imperatives that define the very need for these institutions. For this reason, the opening up of institutional settings to both corporate and NGO input should proceed with much caution. In instrumental terms, it may well be that a more effective way to enhance the responsibility of corporations to the right to health would be to provide several more 'shocks to the system' that the access campaign has been responsible for until now, through maintaining an oppositional stance towards both states and international institutions, and through mobilizing support for the cause in the public sphere.

Conclusion

The relative success of the campaign to improve access to essential medicines so far confirms the hypothesis that major ideational and normative shifts often begin through a process of international socialization initiated by non-state actors, involving a form of social influence that is essentially coercive. The second hypothesis suggested that international norms may continue to evolve in deliberative frameworks developed within institutional settings. Deliberative lawmaking processes that are fair and inclusive, it was argued, will produce norms that are legitimate in the eyes of their addressees and will be more effective for that reason. This implies that the key to enhancing the responsibility of corporations for the right to health lies with the openness of institutions such as the WTO to the input of both corporate and activist groups in the decision-making processes. While from the perspective of legitimacy, deliberative approaches to lawmaking are generally superior to protest-based ones, I suggested that deliberation may not always produce the best outcomes when the preconditions for discursive engagement are not likely to be met within the lawmaking institution. State actors may be open to be persuaded and change their preferences, but they are sometimes constrained by institutional imperatives that prevent them from accepting the better argument in a genuine discourse. When this is the case, the stepping in of a lively and oppositional civil society that would engage in contentious political action may be more likely to produce the desired effect.

NOTES

1 See the contributions to J.L. Goldstein, Miles Kahler, Robert O. Keohane, and Anne-Marie Slaughter, eds., *Legalization and World Politics* (Cambridge, MA: MIT Press, 2001). A notable example for treating *ratification* as the defining moment of lawmaking is the comprehensive studies on compliance with human rights and environmental treaties conducted by Oona A. Hathaway, 'Between Power and Principle: An Integrated Theory of International Law,' *Chicago Law Review* 72 (2005): 469–536.

2 Ryan Goodman and Derek Jinks, 'Measuring the Effects of Human Rights Treaties,' *European Journal of International Law* 14 (2003): 174.

3 Martha Finnemore and Stephen J. Toope, 'Alternatives to "Legalization": Richer Views of Law and Politics,' *International Organization* 55 (2001): 750.

4 Harold Koh's formulation of the 'transnational legal process' has been especially influential. International legal obligation is created, he maintains, in a series of continuous repeated interactions in which a legal rule is constructed, interpreted, clarified, internalized, and enforced. Harold H. Koh, 'Transnational Legal Process,' *Nebraska Law Review* 75 (1996): 181–207.

5 A term coined by Robert M. Cover, 'Forward: Nomos and Narrative,' *Harvard Law Review* 97 (1983): 40; and later employed by Harold H. Koh, 'The 1998 Frankel Lecture: Bringing International Law Home,' *Houston Law Review* 35 (1998): 641.

6 Jutta Brunnée and Stephen J. Toope, 'International Law and Constructivism: Elements of an Interactional Theory of International Law,' *Columbia Journal of Transnational Law* 39 (2000): 47–8.

7 In the area of international environmental law, see generally Edith Brown Weiss, 'International Environmental Law: Contemporary Issues and the Emergence of a New World Order,' *Georgetown Law Journal* 81 (1993): 687–8. In the area of biotechnology, see Sean D. Murphy, 'Biotechnology and International Law,' *Harvard International Law Journal* 43 (2001): 47–139.

8 See Robert O. Keohane, 'International Organizations: Two Approaches,' *International Studies Quarterly* 32 (1998): 379.

9 For a discussion of this literature, see Lisa L. Martin and Beth A. Simmons, 'Theories and Empirical Studies of International Institutions,' *International Organization* 52 (1998): 729–57, 742–7.

10 For a discussion, see Asher Alkoby, 'Non-State Actors and the Legitimacy of International Environmental Law,' *Non-State Actors and International Law* 3 (2003): 66–7.

11 For a useful review, see Emanuel Adler, 'Seizing the Middle Ground: Constructivism in World Politics,' *European Journal of International Relations* 3 (1997): 319–63; and Martha Finnemore, *National Interests in International Society* (Ithaca: Cornell University Press, 1996), 1–33.

12 See James G. March and Johan P. Olsen, 'The Institutional Dynamics of International Political Orders,' *International Organization* 52 (1998): 943–69.

13 For a comprehensive review of this literature, see Richard Price, 'Transnational Civil Society and Advocacy in World Politics,' *World Politics* 55 (2003): 579–606.

14 See Martha Finnemore and Kathryn Sikkink, 'International Norm Dynamics and Political Change,' *Int'l Org.* 52 (1998): 896.

15 Ibid., 898–904.

16 See Sebastian Oberthür, Matthias Buck, Sebastian Müller, Stefanie Pfahl, and Richard G. Tarasofsky, *Participation of Non-Governmental Organisations in International Environmental Governance: Legal Basis and Practical Experience* (Berlin: Ecologic & FIELD 2002), and the vast empirical literature that they review. See also Alkoby, 'Non-State Actors'; Karen T. Liftin, *Ozone Discourses, Science and Politics in Global Environmental Cooperation* (New York: Columbia University Press, 1994); David Tolbert, 'Global Climate Change and the Role of International Non-Governmental Organizations,' in *International Law and Global Climate Change*, ed. Robin Churchill and David Freestone, 95–108 (London: Graham & Troman / M. Nijhoff, 1991).

17 In Asher Alkoby, 'Global Networks and International Environmental Lawmaking: A Discourse Approach,' *Chicago Journal of International Law* 8 (2008): 377–407. For other Habermasian analyses, see Christian Reus-Smith, 'The Constitutional Structure of International Society and the Nature of Fundamental Institutions,' *International Organization* 51 (1997): 564–6; and also Thomas Risse, 'Let's Argue! Communicative Action in World Politics,' *International Organization* 54 (2000): 1–39, and the references there.

18 Jürgen Habermas, *Structural Transformation of the Public Sphere*, trans. Thomas Burger (Cambridge, MA: MIT Press, 1989), 99.

19 Ibid., 82.

20 See the recent restatement of the rules of argumentation, as applied to the international realm, in Andrew Linklater, 'Dialogic Politics and the Civilising Process,' *Review of International Studies* 31 (2005): 141–54.

21 Jeffery Checkel argued that state elites engage in argumentative persuasion, defined as 'an activity or process in which a communicator attempts to induce a change in the belief, attitude, or behaviour of another person … through the transmission of a message in a context in which the persuadee has some degree of free choice.' Jeffrey T. Checkel, 'Why Comply? Social Learning and European Identity Change,' *International Organization* 55 (2001): 553–88. He demonstrated, for example, how a pattern of discursive engagement was found in the adoption of the Council of Europe's citizenship rights norms in the Ukraine, through an interaction of state officials with regional experts. (574–8). Similarly, Thomas Risse, drawing on studies of German unification, suggested that 'social learning' is what brought Soviet leadership to agree to German unification within NATO at the end of the Cold War. Soviet leaders were convinced by the arguments made by German and U.S. officials, through 'true dialogue of mutual persuasion,' which included the legitimacy of the principle of self-determination. Risse, 'Let's Argue!' 23. For an extended discussion, see Thomas Risse, 'The Cold War's Endgame and German Unification (A Review Essay),' *International Security* 21 (1997): 178–9.

22 See Alkoby, 'Non-State Actors,' 47–50, and the citations there.

23 See my discussion in Alkoby, 'Global Networks,' 399–405.

24 See Randall L. Schweller, 'Fantasy Theory,' *Review of International Studies* 25 (1999): 147 (arguing that discursive approaches to international relations argue 'by fiat rather than by the weight of hard evidence, which is in scant supply here').

25 Ilan Kapoor, 'Deliberative Democracy or Agonistic Pluralism? The Relevance of the Habermas–Mouffe Debate for Third World Politics,' *Alternatives* 27 (2002): 462.

26 See Alkoby, 'Global Networks,' 396–9.

27 See, for example, David P. Fidler, 'Constitutional Outlines of Public Health's "New World Order,"' *Temple Law Review* 77 (2004): 264–9. In his earlier work, attempting to locate global health jurisprudence in broader theoretical discussions, Fidler is quick to dismiss discourse ethics as a framework for global health governance for lack of prescriptive appeal. David P. Fidler, *International Law and Infectious Diseases* (Oxford: Clarendon, 1999), 301–2.

28 See James Orbinski, 'Global Health, Social Movements, and Governance,' in *Governing Global Health: Challenges, Response, Innovation*, ed. Andrew F.

Cooper, John J. Kirton, and Ted Schrecker (Aldershot, UK: Ashgate, 2007), 29. A similar analysis is offered by Zacher and Keefe, who observe that NGOs 'have moved from a contained role of agents of advocacy into the realm of hard science, where they are formulating groups of medical experts and actually creating new drugs.' Mark W. Zacher and Tania J. Keefe, *The Politics of Global Health Governance: United by Contagion* (New York: Palgrave Macmillan, 2008), 124.

29 With the exception of the contributions cited in the following section.

30 On the centrality of legitimacy in international lawmaking, see Thomas M. Franck, *The Power of Legitimacy among Nations* (Oxford: Oxford University Press, 1990).

31 Brunnée and Toope, 'International Law and Constructivism,' 66.

32 See Obijiofor Aginam, 'Between Life and Profit: Global Governance and the Trilogy of Human Rights, Public Health and Pharmaceutical Patents,' *North Carolina Journal of International Law and Commercial Regulation* 31 (2006): 905–7; and Thomas Keith Mirabile, 'AIDS, Africa and Access to Medicines,' *Michigan State University – D.C.L. Journal of International Law* 11 (2002): 218. For a more detailed discussion, see Lisa Forman, 'A Transformative Power? The Role of the Human Right to Medicines in Accessing AIDS Medicines – International Human Rights Law, TRIPS and the South African Experience' (SJD diss., University of Toronto, 2006), chap. 1, and the references there.

33 *Agreement on Trade-Related Aspects of Intellectual Property Rights*, Annexure 1C to the Marrakesh Agreement Establishing the World Trade Organization, signed in Marrakesh, Morocco, on 15 Apr. 1994.

34 Susan. K. Sell, 'Structures, Agents and Institutions: Private Corporate Power and the Globalisation of Intellectual Property Rights,' in *Non-State Actors and Authority in the Global System, ed.* Richard Higgott, Geoffrey Underhill, and Andreas Bieler (London: Routledge, 2000), 91.

35 Ibid., 94. For the historical background of private-sector involvement in U.S. IP policy, see also Susan K. Sell, 'The Origins of a Trade-Based Approach to Intellectual Property Protection,' *Science Communication* 17 (1995): 163–85.

36 Sell, 'Structures and Agents,' 94, 100.

37 Sell, 'Structures and Agents.'

38 Ibid., 97–103.

39 United Nations, *Human Development Report 1999: Globalization with a Human Face*, 74, http://hdr.undp.org/reports/global/1999.

40 John Braithwaite and Peter Drahos, *Global Business Regulation* (Cambridge, UK: Cambridge University Press, 2000), 202.

41 See Susan K. Sell, 'Post-TRIPS Developments: The Tension between Commercial and Social Agendas in the Context of Intellectual Property,' *Florida Journal of International Law* 14 (2002): 210–11.

42 The Pharmaceutical Manufacturer's Association and Others v. The President of the Republic of South Africa case no. 4183/98, Trans. Prov. Div. For a detailed analysis of the case, see Forman, 'Transformative Power,' chap. 5.

43 Zacher and Keefe, *Politics of Global Health Governance*, 115–18.

44 World Trade Organization, Ministerial Conference Fourth Session, Doha, 9–14 Nov. 2001, *Declaration on the TRIPS Agreement and Public Health*, WT/MIN(01)/DEC/2 (2001).

45 Helene Cooper, 'U.S. Drops WTO Claim against Brazilian Patent Law,' *Wall Street Journal*, 26 June 2001.

46 Forman, 'Transformative Power,' 81. Since then, the WTO General Council reached a decision in December 2005 to amend TRIP to explicitly permit the compulsory licensing of drugs under certain circumstances. Member states had until 1 December 2007 to consent to this amendment, which requires the consent of two-thirds of WTO members for entry into force. See World Trade Organization General Council, *Amendment to the TRIPS Agreement*, WT/L/64 (2005).

47 Amit Gupta, 'Patent Protection Rights on Pharmaceutical Products and Affordable Drugs: Can TRIPS Provide a Solution?' *Buffalo Intellectual Property Law Journal* 2 (2004): 147. And compare Tei-Heng Cheng, 'Power, Norms and International Intellectual Property Law,' *Michigan Journal of International Law* 28 (2006): 142 (arguing that the Declaration is a significant move towards the harmonization of IP protection with human rights norms).

48 Gupta, 'Patent Protection Rights,' 151. See also Forman, 'Transformative Power,' 85 (arguing that 'despite these flexibilities, the danger posed by TRIPS is lack of balance between intellectual property protection and the right to medicines'). For a critique of the cumbersome procedures required in order to use the *TRIPS* exceptions, see Anthony P. Valach, 'TRIPS: Protecting the Rights of Patent Holders and Addressing Public Health Issues in Developing Countries,' *Chicago Kent Journal of Intellectual Property* 4 (2005): 167–8.

49 See United Nations, *Human Development Report*, and more generally, on the power asymmetries in the WTO, see B.S. Chimni, 'International Institutions Today: An Imperial Global State in the Making,' *European Journal of International Law* 15 (2004): 19–20.

50 Paul Nelson and Ellen Dorsey, 'New Rights Advocacy in a Global Public Domain,' *European Journal of International Relations* 13 (2007): 187–216.

51 As observed by Forman, 'Transformative Power'; Orbinski, 'Global Health'; Sell, 'Post-TRIPS Developments'; and Zacher and Keefe, *Politics of Global Health Governance*.

52 See Symposium, 'The Boundaries of the WTO,' *American Journal of International Law* 96 (2002): 1–158.

53 See, for example, Mark A.A. Warner, 'Globalization and Human Rights: An Economic Model,' *Brooklyn Journal of International Law* 25 (1999): 99–112.

54 Ernst-Ulrich Petersmann, 'Time for a United Nations "Global Compact" for Integrating Human Rights into the Law of Worldwide Organizations: Lessons from European Integration,' *European Journal of International Law* 13 (2002): 621–50.

55 As is currently done in the context of *Amendment to the TRIPS Agreement*.

56 Salman Bal, 'International Free Trade Agreements and Human Rights: Reinterpreting Article XX of the GATT,' *Minnesota Journal of Global Trade* 10 (2001): 62–108.

57 See, for example, Robert Howse, 'From Politics to Technocracy – and Back Again: The Fate of the Multilateral Trade Regime,' *American Journal of International Law* 96 (2002): 114–16; Maura B. Jeffords, 'Turning the Protester into a Partner for Development: The Need for Effective Consultation between the WTO and NGOs,' *Brooklyn Journal of International Law* 28 (2003): 937–88; Richard Shell, 'The Trade Stakeholder Model and Participation by Non-State Parties in the World Trade Organization,' *University of Pennsylvania Journal of International Law* 17 (2004): 703–24; Special Symposium, 'Citizen Participation in the Global Trading System,' *Rutgers Law Review* 56 (2004): 877–1010.

58 World Trade Organization, *Guidelines for Arrangements with Non-Governmental Organizations*, WT/L/162 (1996), para. VI.

59 Steve Charnovitz, 'Transparency and Participation in the World Trade Organization,' *Rutgers Law Review* 56 (2004): 927–59.

60 Ibid., 948–50. Charnovitz, who has been studying WTO engagement with civil society groups for over a decade, sees some promising developments in the level of openness of the WTO, but maintains that two factors will continue to stand in the way: the de facto consensus decision-making rule, and the fact that many WTO member states are not democratic and therefore do not share the values of participation and transparency. Steve Charnovitz, 'The WTO and Cosmopolitics,' *Journal of International Economic Law* 7 (2004): 682.

61 See Jeffords's review of institutional cooperation with NGOs in 'Turning the Protester,' 967–77.

62 See Charnovitz, 'Transparency and Participation,' 985–8. Currently, under the WTO dispute settlement rules, NGOs do not have the right to submit briefs to the adjudicative bodies. Rather, panels may seek amicus briefs from NGOs and may also accept unsolicited briefs if they choose to. In the current practice, even when panels accept NGO submissions, they do not always find it necessary to take the arguments made in briefs into account in their rulings. See Charnovitz, *supra* note at 957.
63 John S. Dryzek, *Deliberative Democracy and Beyond: Liberals, Critics, Contestations* (Cambridge, UK: Cambridge University Press, 2000), 83.
64 See Aginam, 'Between Life and Profit,' 914–17.
65 For a proposal to include non-trade experts in WTO panels, see Shell, 'Trade Stakeholder Model,' 721.
66 Steven Bernstein has termed this discourse 'liberal environmentalism.' See *The Compromise of Liberal Environmentalism* (New York: Columbia University Press, 2001).
67 See Forman's discussion, 'Transformative Power,' chaps 2 and 3 (tracing the evolution of the right to health in international human rights law and its incorporation into post-apartheid South African law).
68 This seeming lack of diversity within the movement raises another concern that by partnering with states and international institutions NGOs may lose their critical edge and become imbued with the values and logic of the institution. See the discussion in Dryzek, *Deliberative Democracy*, chap. 2.
69 Aginam, 'Between Life and Profit'; and also Susan K. Sell, 'The Quest for Global Governance in Intellectual Property and Public Health: Structural, Discursive and Institutional Dimensions,' *Temple Law Review* 77 (2004): 363–99.
70 Lawrence R. Helfer, 'The TRIPs Agreement and New Dynamics of International Intellectual Property Lawmaking,' *Yale International Law Journal* 29 (2004): 1–83.
71 See ibid., 75–9.
72 As Sell rightly maintains, the 'regime shifting' strategy offered by Helfer also risks the injection of further uncertainty and incoherence into the governance of global health. Instead, Sell proposes to institutionalize expertise and support for developing country delegations and the pursuit of competition legislation at the national level.

REFERENCES

Adler, Emanuel. 'Seizing the Middle Ground: Constructivism in World Politics.' *European Journal of International Relations* 3 (1997): 319–63.

Aginam, Obijiofor. 'Between Life and Profit: Global Governance and the Trilogy of Human Rights, Public Health and Pharmaceutical Patents.' *North Carolina Journal of International Law and Commercial Regulation* 31 (2006): 901.

Agreement on Trade-Related Aspects of Intellectual Property Rights. Annexure 1C to the Marrakesh Agreement Establishing the World Trade Organization, signed in Marrakesh, Morocco on 15 Apr. 1994, LT/UR/A-1C/IP/1.

Alkoby, Asher. 'Global Networks and International Environmental Lawmaking: A Discourse Approach.' *Chicago Journal of International Law* 8 (2008): 377–407.

– 'Non-State Actors and the Legitimacy of International Environmental Law.' *Non-State Actors and International Law* 3 (2003): 23.

Bal, Salman. 'International Free Trade Agreements and Human Rights: Reinterpreting Article XX of the GATT.' *Minnesota Journal of Global Trade* 10 (2001): 62–108.

Bernstein, Steven. *The Compromise of Liberal Environmentalism*. New York: Columbia University Press, 2001.

Braithwaite, John, and Peter Drahos. *Global Business Regulation*. Cambridge, UK: Cambridge University Press, 2000.

Brown Weiss, Edith. 'International Environmental Law: Contemporary Issues and the Emergence of a New World Order.' *Georgetown Law Journal* 81 (1993): 675–710.

Brunnée, Jutta, and Stephen J. Toope. 'International Law and Constructivism: Elements of an Interactional Theory of International Law.' *Columbia Journal of Transnational Law* 39 (2000): 19–74.

Charnovitz, Steve. 'Transparency and Participation in the World Trade Organization.' *Rutgers Law Review* 56 (2004): 927–59.

– 'The WTO and Cosmopolitics.' *Journal of International Economic Law* 7 (2004): 675–82.

Checkel, Jeffrey T. 'Why Comply? Social Learning and European Identity Change.' *International Organization* 55 (2001): 553–88.

Cheng, Tei-Heng. 'Power, Norms and International Intellectual Property Law.' *Michigan Journal of International Law* 28 (2006): 109–155.

Chimni, B.S. 'International Institutions Today: An Imperial Global State in the Making.' *European Journal of International Law* 15 (2004): 1–37.

Cooper, Helene. 'U.S. Drops WTO Claim against Brazilian Patent Law.' *Wall Street Journal*, 26 June 2001.

Cover, Robert M. 'Forward: Nomos and Narrative.' *Harvard Law Review* 97 (1983): 4–68.

Dryzek, John S. *Deliberative Democracy and Beyond: Liberals, Critics, Contestations*. Cambridge, UK: Cambridge University Press, 2000.

Fidler, David P. 'Constitutional Outlines of Public Health's "New World Order."' *Temple Law Review* 77 (2004): 247–90.

– *International Law and Infectious Diseases* (Oxford: Clarendon, 1999).

Finnemore, Martha. *National Interests in International Society*. Ithaca: Cornell University Press, 1996.

Finnemore, Martha, and Kathryn Sikkink. 'International Norm Dynamics and Political Change.' *International Organization* 52 (1998): 887–917.

Finnemore, Martha, and Stephen J. Toope. 'Alternatives to "Legalization": Richer Views of Law and Politics.' *International Organization* 55 (2001): 743–58.

Forman, Lisa. 'A Transformative Power? The Role of the Human Right to Medicines in Accessing AIDS Medicines – International Human Rights Law, TRIPS and the South African Experience.' SJD diss., University of Toronto, 2006.

Franck, Thomas M. *The Power of Legitimacy among Nations*. Oxford: Oxford University Press, 1990.

Goldstein, J.L., Miles Kahler, Robert O. Keohane, and Anne-Marie Slaughter, eds. *Legalization and World Politics*. Cambridge, MA: MIT Press, 2001.

Goodman, Ryan, and Derek Jinks. 'Measuring the Effects of Human Rights Treaties.' *European Journal of International Law* 14 (2003): 171–83.

Gupta, Amit. 'Patent Protection Rights on Pharmaceutical Products and Affordable Drugs: Can TRIPS Provide a Solution?' *Buffalo Intellectual Property Law Journal* 2 (2004): 127–53.

Habermas, Jürgen. *Structural Transformation of the Public Sphere*. Translated by Thomas Burger. Cambridge, MA: MIT Press, 1989.

Hathaway, Oona A. 'Between Power and Principle: An Integrated Theory of International Law.' *University of Chicago Law Review* 72 (2005): 469–536.

Howse, Robert. 'From Politics to Technocracy – and Back Again: The Fate of the Multilateral Trade Regime.' *American Journal of International Law* 96 (2002): 94–117.

Jeffords, Maura B. 'Turning the Protester into a Partner for Development: The Need for Effective Consultation between the WTO and NGOs.' *Brooklyn Journal of International Law* 28 (2003): 937–88.

Kapoor, Ilan. 'Deliberative Democracy or Agonistic Pluralism? The Relevance of the Habermas–Mouffe Debate for Third World Politics.' *Alternatives* 27 (2002): 459–89.

Keohane, Robert O. 'International Organizations: Two Approaches.' *International Studies Quarterly* 32 (1998): 379–96.

Koh, Harold H. 'The 1998 Frankel Lecture: Bringing International Law Home.' *Houston Law Review* 35 (1998): 623–81.

– 'Transnational Legal Process.' *Nebraska Law Review* 75 (1996): 181–207.

Liftin, Karen T. *Ozone Discourses, Science and Politics in Global Environmental Cooperation.* New York: Columbia University Press, 1994.

Linklater, Andrew. 'Dialogic Politics and the Civilising Process.' *Review of International Studies* 31 (2005): 141.

March, James G., and Johan P. Olsen. 'The Institutional Dynamics of International Political Orders.' *International Organization* 52 (1998): 943–69.

Martin, Lisa L., and Beth A. Simmons. 'Theories and Empirical Studies of International Institutions.' *International Organization* 52 (1998): 729–57.

Mirabile, T.K. 'AIDS, Africa and Access to Medicines.' *Michigan State University – D.C.L. Journal of International Law* 11 (2002): 175–230.

Murphy, Sean D. 'Biotechnology and International Law.' *Harvard International Law Journal* 43 (2001): 47–139.

Nelson, Paul, and Ellen Dorsey. 'New Rights Advocacy in a Global Public Domain.' *European Journal of International Relations* 13 (2007): 187–216.

Oberthür, Sebastian, Matthias Buck, Sebastian Müller, Stefanie Pfahl, and Richard G. Tarasofsky. *Participation of Non-Governmental Organisations in International Environmental Governance: Legal Basis and Practical Experience.* Berlin: Ecologic & FIELD, 2002.

Orbinski, James. 'Global Health, Social Movements, and Governance.' In *Governing Global Health: Challenges, Response, Innovation*, edited by Andrew F. Cooper, John J. Kirton, and Ted Schrecker, 29–40. Aldershot, UK: Ashgate, 2007.

Petersmann, Ernst-Ulrich. 'Time for a United Nations "Global Compact" for Integrating Human Rights into the Law of Worldwide Organizations: Lessons from European Integration.' *European Journal of International Law* 13 (2002): 621–50.

The Pharmaceutical Manufacturer's Association and Others v. The President of the Republic of South Africa, case no. 4183/98, Trans. Prov. Div.

Price, Richard. 'Transnational Civil Society and Advocacy in World Politics.' *World Politics* 55 (2003): 579–606.

Reus-Smith, Christian. 'The Constitutional Structure of International Society and the Nature of Fundamental Institutions.' *International Organization* 51 (1997): 555–89.

Risse, Thomas. 'The Cold War's Endgame and German Unification (A Review Essay).' *International Security* 21 (1997): 159–85.

– 'Let's Argue! Communicative Action in World Politics.' *International Organization* 54 (2000): 1–39.

Schweller, Randall L. 'Fantasy Theory.' *Review of International Studies* 25 (1999): 147–50.

Sell, Susan K. 'The Origins of a Trade-Based Approach to Intellectual Property Protection.' *Science Communication* 17 (1995): 163–85.
– 'Post-TRIPS Developments: The Tension between Commercial and Social Agendas in the Context of Intellectual Property.' *Florida Journal of International Law* 14 (2002): 193–216.
– 'The Quest for Global Governance in Intellectual Property and Public Health: Structural, Discursive and Institutional Dimensions.' *Temple Law Review* 77 (2004): 363–99.
– 'Structures, Agents and Institutions: Private Corporate Power and the Globalisation of Intellectual Property Rights.' In *Non-State Actors and Authority in the Global System,* edited by Richard Higgott, Geoffrey Underhill, and Andreas Bieler, 91–106. London: Routledge, 2000.
Shell, Richard. 'The Trade Stakeholder Model and Participation by Non-State Parties in the World Trade Organization.' *University of Pennsylvania Journal of International Law* 17 (2004): 703–24.
Special Symposium. 'Citizen Participation in the Global Trading System.' *Rutgers Law Review* 56 (2004): 877–1010.
'Symposium: The Boundaries of the WTO.' *American Journal of International Law* 96 (2002): 1–158.
Tolbert, David. 'Global Climate Change and the Role of International Non-Governmental Organizations.' In *International Law and Global Climate Change,* edited by Robin Churchill and David Freestone, 95–108. London: Graham & Troman / M. Nijhoff, 1991.
United Nations. *Human Development Report 1999: Globalization with a Human Face.* http://hdr.undp.org/reports/global/hdr1999/.
Valach, Anthony P. 'TRIPS: Protecting the Rights of Patent Holders and Addressing Public Health Issues in Developing Countries.' *Chicago Kent Journal of Intellectual Property* 4 (2005): 156–84.
Warner, Mark A.A. 'Globalization and Human Rights: An Economic Model.' *Brooklyn Journal of International Law* 25 (1999): 99–112.
World Trade Organization. *Guidelines for Arrangements with Non-Governmental Organizations.* WT/L/162 (23 June 1996).
World Trade Organization General Council. *Amendment to the TRIPS Agreement.* WT/L/64 (2005).
World Trade Organization, Ministerial Conference Fourth Session, Doha, 9–14 Nov. 2001. *Declaration on the TRIPS Agreement and Public Health.* WT/MIN(01)/DEC/2 (2001).
Zacher, Mark W., and Tania J. Keefe. *The Politics of Global Health Governance: United by Contagion* (New York: Palgrave Macmillan, 2008).

4 Corporate Social Responsibility and the Right to Essential Medicines

PATRICIA ILLINGWORTH[1]

Introduction

When the House of Gucci designs a dress that the global fashionista would just 'die for,' there is no obligation on the House to distribute the garment to the fashion set. Though coveted by many, fashionable attire does not target a basic human need. The same is not true for essential medicines, for lack of which people in the developing world would die. When it comes to medicines, people in the developed world have obligations to those in the developing world.[2] In this essay, I am going to assume that organizations have moral obligations to the distant needy. The question I am going to tackle here is whether or not pharmaceutical companies are for some reason exempt from these obligations.[3] I will argue that, although pharmaceutical companies do indeed have an obligation of loyalty to shareholders,[4] that obligation does not override the obligations they have to respect the right to essential medicines of people in the developing world. Pharmaceutical companies are not exempt from the obligations shared both by individuals and by organizations in the developed world. If anything, they have a special duty to provide aid in the way of essential medicines, by virtue of (1) the moral character of health-care needs, (2) health as a human right, and (3) the unique capacity of pharmaceutical companies to render aid.

Corporate social responsibility is the obligation of corporations to do good and to confer benefits on the community – to give back to the community.[5] It implies a duty of corporations to give, even when satisfying that duty may be inconsistent with profit maximization. Corporate social responsibility can be justified on a number of different moral bases. It can, for example, be justified on the grounds of beneficence, the duty to do good, and to avoid or prevent harm.[6] It could also be justified on a utilitarian basis – that corporate social responsibility will maximize good consequences. It has been justified on the basis of stakeholder obligations.[7] An important justification can also be found in the idea of corporate citizenship and the obligations that follow from it.[8] This grounding for corporate social responsibility takes into account the fact that many organizations, such as multinational organizations, have greater social and economic influence than do some countries. They are part of local and global communities, and as such have citizenship obligations. Michael Blowfield and Jedrzej George Frynas stress the voluntary nature of corporate social responsibility in contrast to regulation.[9]

There are a number of ways to approach the question of what obligations, if any, pharmaceutical companies have to essential medicines. Although I will briefly review the justification in support of health as a human right, for the most part, I am going to assume that there is a right to health and that the provision of essential medicines is a part of that.

Health as a Human Right

Given the right to health, and the corresponding right to essential medicines, upon whom does the duty to meet the right fall? The United Nations Educational, Scientific, and Cultural Organization (UNESCO) answers that, according to its *Universal Declaration on Bioethics and Human Rights*, the *Declaration* is addressed not only to states, but also to 'individuals, groups, communities, institutions, and corporations, public and private'[10] It states, 'The promotion of health and social development for their people is a central purpose of governments, [which] all sectors of society share.'[11] The *Declaration* also states that 'solidarity among human beings and international cooperation towards that end are to be encouraged.'[12] Although a full analysis of this document is beyond the scope of this essay, the *Declaration* clearly states that the duty to meet the right to health falls on all sectors of society, not just on state agencies. It also states that we have duties not only domestically, but also internationally.

In the report of United Nations special representative of the secretary-general on human rights and transnational corporations, John Ruggie, a similar point is made when Ruggie states that multi-national corporations, even though they are non-state actors, have an obligation to respect human rights, especially when they undertake state-like functions.[13] This obligation, though complicated, may impose certain due diligence responsibilities on corporate actors and thus transform the voluntary nature of corporate social responsibility to include human rights obligations of respect.

These enhanced corporate obligations for human rights could not be more evident than with respect to pharmaceutical companies and the right to health. Indeed, Paul Hunt, the special rapporteur on the right to health, in his mission to GlaxoSmithKline, makes clear that pharmaceutical companies have right-to-health responsibilities that exceed those dictated by the ethics and law implicit in shareholder primacy[14] – a position that GlaxoSmithKline explicitly rejects. In the special rapporteur's concluding words, in which he comments on the use by GlaxoSmithKline of the metaphor 'family jewels' to refer to pharmaceutical patents, Mr Hunt has the following to say:

The image was revealing. In one sense the image is legitimate – patents are immensely valuable. In another sense, the image reflects a profound misunderstanding of the role of a company that develops a life-saving medicine … such a company has performed a critically important social, medical, public health and right-to-health function. While the company's 'reward' is the grant of a limited monopoly over the medicine, enabling it to enhance shareholder value and invest in further research and development, the company also has a right-to-health responsibility to take all reasonable steps to make the life-saving medicine as accessible as possible, as soon as possible, to all those in need. For a limited period, the company holds the patent for society – but the patent must be worked, so far as possible, for the benefit of all those who need it.[15]

The special rapporteur is suggesting that when pharmaceutical companies serve these public health functions, they incur right-to-health duties to ensure that the medicines reach the people who need them. Although there is still work to be done in specifying what exactly those obligations might be, the special rapporteur has taken an important step in imposing greater responsibility for the right to health on pharmaceutical companies. Thus as managers in pharmaceutical companies begin to formulate their social responsibility obligations, it would behove them to include their right-to-health obligations.[16]

In order to determine what obligations pharmaceutical companies have, it is helpful to consider these basic rights from the perspective of the moral and political reasoning that underlies them. Elizabeth Ashford provides a good explanation of the moral significance of these rights:

The distinctive features of the duties of basic justice imposed by human rights are that they are particularly morally urgent and basic and enforced by minimally just institutions, and that they are owed to every human being in virtue of their universal moral status. If the duty of aid were understood as a duty of basic justice, there would be a collective obligation to ensure that each person has reasonably secure access to basic necessities all of the time. Just institutions would specify and enforce the duties that must be implemented in order to achieve this, and so to guarantee each person's access to basic necessities to a reasonable level of security; and in the meantime, as long as any individuals lacked reasonable secure access to basic necessities, those individuals could justifiably complain that they were being deprived of what they were entitled to as a matter of basic justice.[17]

The world's poor and sick, often children, seem to have a moral right to essential medicines. Ashford states that this right is owed 'as a duty of basic justice' to 'every human being in virtue of their universal human status.'[18] The UNESCO provisions suggest that there is also a set of basic *international* human rights.

Once the claim to essential medicines is elevated to the status of a right, the nature of the duty to provide them is more perspicuous. When rights are at issue, considerations of justice demand enforcement of the rights.[19] A right to essential medicines would seem to require that pharmaceutical companies set aside some of their property rights (patents) for the sake of those in the developing world by distributing essential medicines to those who need them. Moreover, rights to life-saving medicines may require that pharmaceutical companies undertake research and development on orphan diseases in order to identify treatment for them.

The Moral Importance of Medical Needs and the Duties Generated by Them

The duty to help the developing world falls on many, including pharmaceutical companies.[20] There are many reasons why pharmaceutical companies are obligated to meet these rights, many of which have been stated elsewhere.[21] Pharmaceutical companies not only share the same duty to help as all members of the global community do, but they have an even greater responsibility than others. As organizations with a focus on human health, pharmaceutical companies have the duty to render aid to the sick. Health-care needs impose heightened responsibilities on the people and organizations that can meet them and thus have been uniformly recognized as special.[22] In part, they are morally special because of the role they play in sustaining the lives of humans,[23] and in maintaining the security, value, and integrity of those lives. Arguably, individuals and entities involved in the medical field incur certain unique responsibilities because of the moral importance of medical needs.

Physicians, for example, are expected to meet medical needs, such as providing emergency care, even when it is inconvenient, and they may be required to put themselves at risk in order to help others, as with contagions or bioterrorism. These duties are reflected in various professional ethics codes. For example, according to the American Medical Association (AMA), although physicians are in general free to choose their patients, this principle does not apply in the case of emergencies.[24] Physicians are expected to help in the case of an emergency. Furthermore, the AMA's Declaration of Professional Responsibilities states, 'We, the members of the world community of physicians, solemnly commit ourselves to ... apply our knowledge and skills when needed, though doing so may put us at risk.'[25] The declaration also states, 'Humanity is our patient.'[26] Put differently, the declaration implies that patient 'need' is the basis on which physicians treat patients and that 'humanity,' the world's people, is the community of patients to be served.

Health-care providers, unlike the common bystander, are presumed to be in a position to render reasonable aid. Physicians are under a duty to render aid not only because they are well positioned to do so, but because medical needs are morally important. There is not, for example, an analogous duty for IT technicians to render their services in the event of an emergency computer crash. The moral quality of health-care needs and their status as a right impose multiple obligations on numerous parties. Arguably, just as health-care providers are required to render aid in an emergency, so, too, are pharmaceutical companies. Pharmaceutical companies, like physicians, have the knowledge and skills needed to meet morally important health-care needs and rights.

The dire need of the afflicted and dying in a global community alone is a sufficiently compelling reason to have pharmaceutical companies act for the benefit of them. Of course, this reasoning could also be applied to other organizations with the unique wherewithal and skill set to render aid. Farmers, grocery stores, and other food purveyors, for example, are likely to have a duty to provide food to the global hungry. Indeed, such a duty was enacted in the United States at the national level with the federal *Bill Emerson Good Samaritan Food Donation Act*, the express purpose of which is to 'encourage the donation of food and grocery products ... for distribution to needy individuals by giving the Model Good Samaritan Food Donation Act the *full force and effect of law.'*[27]

With respect to saving lives, the moral expectations that we have of pharmaceutical companies should not differ significantly from those we have of physicians or food purveyors. Just as physicians are expected to help the sick, and to put themselves at risk in order to do so, and as food purveyors are expected to donate food and forfeit some profit in order to do that, it is reasonable to expect pharmaceutical companies to risk some profits in order to provide essential medicines to those in the developing world who will die without them.

One important counter-argument to this is based on the idea that shareholders in pharmaceutical companies have a claim to the profits by agreement, and by the duty of loyalty. It is difficult to imagine, however, that the duty to maximize shareholder profits could override the duty to save lives, especially in the face of a *right*. Rights, after all, trump considerations of utility.[28] Typically, the claim of shareholders to profits has been justified on a utilitarian basis: those shareholders who would not be willing to risk their money in the presence of *excessive* managerial discretion, and in the absence of the duty of loyalty, were it not for the promise of a significant return on investment. But since rights trump utility, and the claim of shareholders to pharmaceutical profits is utility based, the right of people in the developing world to essential medicines trumps the mere utility-based 'claim' of shareholders to corporate dividends.

It may also be argued, following deontological ethics, that pharmaceutical companies and their shareholders are entitled to these profits because of an implicit or explicit agreement between shareholders and pharmaceutical companies. But surely, if an implication of this agreement is that some people die unnecessarily while others line their pockets with corporate dividends, it is unconscionable. Although agreements are in general respected, in the case of necessities the courts have been more flexible, as they should be, and have set aside signed contracts that impair the 'right' to necessities. See *Henningsen v. Bloomfield Motors.*[29]

In addition, although shareholders may protest the intrusion on their profit margin, arguing that they are being denied what is rightfully theirs, given the moral urgency of those in need of essential medicines, and importantly, the forseeability of that moral claim, shareholders may be said to consent to less than maximum profits. Shareholders and potential shareholders should know that when they invest in medicines, an investment sphere that implicates the right to health, they may be required to accept less profit than if they were investing in Gucci, Prada, or IBM. Put differently, shareholders have implicitly consented to the moral strings that are attached to an investment in pharmaceuticals.

Moreover, the characteristic that gives rise to the moral strings – the morally important status of health – is one and the same characteristic that gives rise to the high profits enjoyed by pharmaceutical companies and their shareholders. The universal value placed on human health and well-being can explain why people are willing to pay the high costs for medicines. The industry targets a basic human need. From the perspective of the industry, the upside of that need is the robust profits enjoyed by shareholders; the downside is the moral strings that are inevitably attached to basic human needs. These strings should come as no surprise to anyone.

Practically speaking, it is also necessary to impose on pharmaceutical companies a duty to give in order to avert a moral loophole. If not required by pharmaceutical companies, as well as other organizations, to meet moral obligations to give, we would inadvertently be inviting shareholders to skirt their moral obligations to give, as individuals, by investing their money and thereby mitigating their obligations. From a public policy perspective, the point of shareholder status, and the attending entitlements and protections it enjoys, is to stimulate investment. It is not to create a moral loophole that invites shareholders to avoid their personal obligations.

Organizational Hybrid

Pharmaceutical companies should be regarded as organizational hybrids. They are unlike other organizations, such as the House of Gucci, that are subject primarily to market principles, insofar as they implicate two distinct sets of fiduciary duties: those of managers to shareholders, and indirectly, the fiduciary duties of physicians to their patients. In addition, the human right to health is implicated. Because of this combination, even if the ethics of business entities is in general straightforward, the ethics of organizational hybrids, such as pharmaceutical and managed-care companies, is not straightforward.[30]

For a variety of reasons, the shareholder primacy view, underlying the duty to shareholders, is not as strong as the argument characterizing it with respect to organizations that are hybrids. Shareholder primacy holds that the primary duty of the corporation is to shareholders. On some theories of the firm, there are obligations to others, including the community. These theoretical views have been encapsulated in some of the corporate constituency statutes.[31] But even if we were to accept the strong view of shareholder primacy, it does not settle the question of what obligations shareholders themselves have. It might be the case that shareholders have ethical obligations to assist the distant needy, as shareholders, in addition to the duties they have as individuals. According to shareholder primacy, managers have obligations to shareholders, but there is no reason to think that shareholders are similarly obligated: they are, after all, owners. Shareholders have greater latitude to determine what moral principles they act on. It is difficult to see how shareholders in pharmaceutical companies could justify not committing significant resources to providing essential medicines to the developing world, even when it is somewhat detrimental to the organization. The main reason why managers are obligated to shareholders is that it is arguably the only way to ensure that they don't act opportunistically to steal from shareholder owners, and that shareholders have a decent incentive to invest. These same limitations do not apply to shareholders.

Even if shareholders have a duty to the organization to support its continued existence, there is no reason to think that they have a *duty* to seek for themselves the maximum profits possible. Although we might quibble with the idea that they could reduce the organization's profitability, whether shareholders together decide to direct 'profits' to the distant needy is their decision. Corporations that do give generously and meet their obligations enhance the moral culture of the corporation and thereby enrich the quality of community. This contribution is not to be underestimated. In fact, if we understand corporations through the lens of corporate character theory, our moral expectations of corporations may change.

Corporate character theory holds corporations responsible for their wrongdoing. At the heart of corporate character theory is the idea that corporations can be held responsible for wrong actions. This theory may also justify the principle that corporations are responsible for their failure to do good. According to corporate character theory, 'corporations shape and control the behaviour of their agents not only through direct supervision by high managerial officials, but also through the use of such devices as standard operating procedures, hierarchical structures, decisions rules and disciplinary sanctions.'[32] The effect of these various procedures and policies is to create 'a corporate character which endures over time and which channels behaviour in ways that are in the interest of the corporation.'[33] In the end, the corporate character theory provides grounds for holding corporations liable for the illegal acts of the corporation. If corporate character theory can justify holding corporations responsible for their wrong actions, why not also hold them responsible for their omissions?[34] One of the important points to surface from this notion of corporate social responsibility is that the various policies and procedures of a corporation affect the conduct of the organization. Corporations that go above and beyond the minimum are good corporate citizens; they exemplify good corporate character. Just as we can argue that individuals have duties to others, so corporations, understood as possessing corporate character, have similar responsibilities. Acts of giving can influence corporate character. One implication of corporate character theory is that a corporation's character affects everyone's character and can create a climate that reflects the corporate culture. This has important implications for the well-being of society.

Ethics by Association

The ethics of a corporation are important because they establish responsibilities for the corporation and define the nature of the relationship among the corporation and other stakeholders. The well-known phrase 'guilty by association' expresses the idea that the company we keep can reflect our own guilt. For example, associating with members of the Nazi party can imply a shared commitment to Nazi values. The principle 'guilty by association' is obviously based on a fallacy. Nevertheless, in the real world, it is inevitable that people judge us by the company we keep. When we collaborate with others either indirectly or side-by-side, the values of our collaborators can affect our own actions and how we appear to others. If physicians collaborate with people and organizations that follow principles conflicting with medical values, then they risk compromising their capacity to act ethically and may create the appearance of unethical conduct, even where there is none. Creating the impression of high moral standards and a commitment to universalism is the core of medical professionalism. Moreover, the success of medicine itself depends on maintaining the impression of a commitment to medical service – not to profit maximization. By looking at the values of the physician, we can identify the values that those who work with her need to endorse.

Professions are by their very nature moral entities, and medicine is no exception. Although the presence of a fiduciary duty is not typically classified as a characteristic of a profession, it often is. Lawyers, doctors, and accountants are fiduciaries with special obligations to those whom they serve. One reason why fiduciary duties are invoked in these relationships is because there is a power imbalance between the person served and the professional. According to Robert Clarke, duties of fidelity can act as a substitute for the monitoring mechanism that might otherwise inform the conduct of the person who holds power. In view of the vulnerability of patients, because they are sick and fragile, and also given the difference in expertise between patient and physician, the duty of fidelity serves as a substitute for the inability of patients to properly and effectively monitor the performance of their physicians.[35]

To this view of professionalism, Matt Wynia adds insight about the social role of professionals: 'We think of professionalism as an activity that involves both the distribution of a commodity and the fair allocation of a social good but that is uniquely defined according to moral relationships. Professionalism is a structurally stabilizing, morally protective force in society. Along with private-sector and public or government activities, it is a cornerstone of a stable society.'[36]

Wynia points out that professions protect not only vulnerable people, but also vulnerable values, such as respect for human worth and trustworthiness.[37] According to these authors, there are three core elements to professionalism: professionalism requires (1) a moral commitment to the ethic of medical service, (2) public profession of that ethic, and (3) negotiation in which medical professionals advocate for health-care values in the context of other possibly conflicting values.[38]

These characteristics have implications for pharmaceutical companies. Just as patients are dependent on physicians because of their overwhelming knowledge, they are also dependent on pharmaceutical companies for the medicines they need. Arguably, pharmaceutical companies are coming to play the same role in people's health that physicians once played. In some specialties, they may now play a more important role than do physicians. Psycho-pharmacologists, for example, dispense psychiatric medicines primarily. In terms of improving health outcomes, the medicines are at least as important as the physician prescribing them. Patients are dependent on pharmaceutical companies for their life, security, and welfare, at least as much as they depend on the physician. Thus, the two characteristics that are key in identifying the fiduciary duties of physicians to patients, and lawyers to clients, (vulnerability and power imbalance) are present between pharmaceutical companies and patients.

It is a mistake to treat pharmaceutical companies as if they were in the same morally neutral sphere as the House of Gucci, as if essential medicines are in no way different from the 'It' dress of the season. As with the field of medicine, pharmacy is morally special. Medicines have the capacity to affect life and death, and as suggested earlier, this is even more so today than in the past, and perhaps more with respect to pharmaceutical companies than with respect to physicians. Furthermore, if pharmaceutical companies continue to choose profits over the right to essential medicines, they compromise the medical values that inform physicians' conduct.

The *UN Declaration* calls for solidarity among human beings and the *Declaration of Professional Responsibility* with its announcement that 'humanity is our patient' calls for 'acting together across geographic and ideological divides.' Perhaps it is time for pharmaceutical companies and their shareholders to join this call for solidarity, setting aside the value of profit maximization in the name of the right to health and global good will.

NOTES

1 I wish to thank Nela Suka for providing me with helpful comments and assistance with manuscript preparation. I am also grateful to Lisa Forman for helpful suggestions. This paper also benefited from comments at the Toronto conference, 'Corporate Social Responsibility and the Right to Essential Medicines.'

2 Thomas Pogge, '"Assisting" the Global Poor,' in *The Ethics of Assistance*, ed. Dean K. Chatterjee (Cambridge, UK: Cambridge University Press, 2004), 260–88; Peter Singer. *One World: The Ethics of Globalization* (New Haven, CT: Yale University Press, 2004).

3 Milton Friedman, 'The Social Responsibility of Business Is to Increase Its Profits,' in *Ethical Theory and Business*, ed. Tom L. Beauchamp and Norman E. Bowie (Upper Saddle River, NJ: Pearson Prentice Hall, 2004), 50–5.

4 Ibid.

5 R. Edward Freeman, 'A Stakeholder Theory of the Modern Corporation,' in *Ethical Theory and Business*, ed. Tom L. Beauchamp and Norman E. Bowie (Upper Saddle River, NJ: Pearson Prentice Hall, 2004), 55–64.

6 William Frankena, *Ethics* (Englewood Cliffs, NJ: Prentice Hall, 1973).

7 Freeman, 'Stakeholder Theory.'

8   Elizabet Garriga and Domenec Mele, 'Corporate Social Responsibility Theories: Mapping the Territory,' *Journal of Business Ethics* 53 (2004): 57.

9   Michael Blowfield and Jedrzej George Frynas, 'Setting New Agendas: Critical Perspectives on Corporate Social Responsibility in the Developing World,' *International Affairs* 81, no. 3 (2005): 502.

10 United Nations Educational, Scientific, and Cultural Organization (UNESCO), *Universal Declaration on Bioethics and Human Rights*, SHS/EST/BIO/06/1 (Paris: United Nations Educational, Scientific, and Cultural Organization, 2006), Article 1.

11 Ibid., Article 14.

12 Ibid., Article 13.

13 United Nations Human Rights Council, *Report of the Special Representative of the Secretary General on the Issue of Human Rights and Transnational Corporations and Other Business Enterprises – Protect, Respect and Remedy: A Framework*, UN Doc. A/HRC/8/5 (2008).

14 Special Rapporteur of the Commission on Human Rights on the Right to the Enjoyment of the Highest Attainable Standard of Physical and Mental Health, *Mission to GlaxoSmithKline*, UN Doc. A/HRC/11/12/ADD.2 (2009).

15 Ibid., Paragraph 107.

16 Isabelle Maignan and O.C. Ferrel, 'Corporate Social Responsibility and Marketing: An Integrative Framework,' *Journal of the Academy of Marketing Science* 32, no. 3 (2004): 3–19.

17 Elizabeth Ashford, 'The Duties Imposed by the Human Right to Basic Necessities,' In *Freedom from Poverty as a Human Right: Who Owes What to the Very Poor?*, ed. T. Pogge (Oxford: Oxford University Press, 2007), 201.

18 Ibid.

19 Ibid.

20 *The Montréal Statement on the Human Right to Essential Medicines*, International Workshop on Human Rights and Access to Essential Medicines / Université de Montréal, Montreal, 2005.

21 Jillian Cohen, Patricia Illingworth, and Udo Schuklenk, eds., *The Power of Pills: Social, Ethical, and Legal Issues in Drug Development, Marketing, and Pricing* (London: Pluto, 2006).

22 *Universal Declaration of Human Rights*, GA Res. 217 (III), UNGAOR, 3d Sess., Supp. No. 13, UN Doc. A/810 (1948) World Health Organization, 'The Declaration of Alma-Ata,' 1978, http://www.who.int/publications/almaata_declaration_en.pdf.

23 *Montréal Statement*.

24 American Medical Association, *Code of Medical Ethics: Current Opinions 2002–2003* (Chicago: AMA, 2002), xii.

25 Ibid., 145.
26 Ibid.
27 U.S. Congress, *The Federal Bill Emerson Good Samaritan Food Donation Act of 1996*. Pub. L. No. 104-210 (Washington: Government Printing Office, 1996).
28 Ronald Dworkin, *Taking Rights Seriously* (Cambridge, MA: Harvard University Press, 1977).
29 *Henningsen v. Bloomfield Motors, Inc.* 32 N.J. 358, 161 A.2d 69 (1960).
30 Patricia Illingworth, *Trusting Medicine* (Oxford: Routledge, 2005).
31 Brett H. McDonnell, 'Corporate Constituency Statutes and Employee Governance,' *William Mitchell Law Review* 30, no. 4 (2004): 1228.
32 Jennifer Moore, 'Corporate Culpability under the Federal Sentencing Guidelines,' in *Ethical Theory and Business*, ed. Tom L. Beauchamp and Norman E. Bowie (Upper Saddle River, NJ: Pearson Prentice Hall, 2004), 102.
33 Ibid.
34 Thomas Pogge, 'World Poverty and Human Rights,' *Ethics & International Affairs* 19 (2005): 1–7.
35 Robert Clark, 'Agency Costs versus Fiduciary Duties,' in *Principals and Agents: The Structure of Business*, eds. John W. Pratt and Richard J. Zeckhauser, 55–80 (Boston: Harvard Business School Press, 1985).
36 Matthew Wynia, 'Medical Professionalism in Society,' in *Ethical Healthcare*, ed. Patricia Illingworth and Wendy Parmet (Englewood Cliffs, NJ: Prentice Hall, 2005), 174.
37 Ibid., 175.
38 Ibid.

REFERENCES

American Medical Association. *Code of Medical Ethics: Current Opinions 2002–2003*. Chicago: AMA, 2002.

Ashford, Elizabeth. 'The Duties Imposed by the Human Right to Basic Necessities.' In *Freedom from Poverty as a Human Right: Who Owes What to the Very Poor?* edited by T. Pogge. Oxford: Oxford University Press, 2007.

Blowfield, Michael, and Jedrzej George Frynas. 'Setting New Agendas: Critical Perspectives on Corporate Social Responsibility in the Developing World.' *International Affairs* 81, no. 3 (2005): 502.

Clark, Robert. 'Agency Costs versus Fiduciary Duties.' In *Principals and Agents: The Structure of Business*, edited by John W. Pratt and Richard J. Zeckhauser, 55–80. Boston: Harvard Business School Press, 1985.

Cohen, Jillian, Patricia Illingworth, and Udo Schuklenk, eds. *The Power of Pills: Social, Ethical, and Legal Issues in Drug Development, Marketing, and Pricing.* London: Pluto, 2006.

Dworkin, Ronald. *Taking Rights Seriously.* Cambridge, MA: Harvard University Press, 1977.

Frankena, William. *Ethics.* Englewood Cliffs, NJ: Prentice Hall, 1973.

Freeman, R. Edward. 'A Stakeholder Theory of the Modern Corporation.' In *Ethical Theory and Business,* edited by Tom L. Beauchamp and Norman E. Bowie, 55–64. Upper Saddle River, NJ: Pearson Prentice Hall, 2004.

Friedman, Milton. 'The Social Responsibility of Business Is to Increase Its Profits.' In *Ethical Theory and Business,* edited by Tom L. Beauchamp and Norman E. Bowie, 50–5. Upper Saddle River, NJ: Pearson Prentice Hall, 2004.

Garriga, Elizabet, and Domenec Mele. 'Corporate Social Responsibility Theories: Mapping the Territory.' *Journal of Business Ethics* 53 (2004): 57.

Henningsen v. Bloomfield Motors, Inc. 32 N.J. 358, 161 A.2d 69 (1960).

Illingworth, Patricia. *Trusting Medicine.* Oxford: Routledge, 2005.

Maignan, Isabelle, and O.C. Ferrel. 'Corporate Social Responsibility and Marketing: An Integrative Framework.' *Journal of the Academy of Marketing Science* 32, no. 1 (2004): 3–19.

McDonnell, Brett H. 'Corporate Constituency Statutes and Employee Governance.' *William Mitchell Law Review* 30, no. 4 (2004): 1228.

The Montréal Statement on the Human Right to Essential Medicines. Montréal: International Workshop on Human Rights and Access to Essential Medicines / Université de Montréal, 2005.

Moore, Jennifer. 'Corporate Culpability under the Federal Sentencing Guidelines.' In *Ethical Theory and Business,* edited by Tom L. Beauchamp and Norman E. Bowie. Upper Saddle River, NJ: Pearson Prentice Hall, 2004.

Pogge, Thomas. '"Assisting"' the Global Poor.' In *The Ethics of Assistance,* edited by Dean K. Chatterjee, 260–88. Cambridge, UK: Cambridge University Press, 2004.

– 'World Poverty and Human Rights.' *Ethics & International Affairs* 19 (2005): 1–7.

Singer, Peter. *One World: The Ethics of Globalization.* New Haven, CT: Yale University Press, 2004.

Special Rapporteur of the Commission on Human Rights on the Right to the Enjoyment of the Highest Attainable Standard of Physical and Mental Health. *Mission to GlaxoSmithKline.* UN Doc. A/HRC/11/12/ADD.2 (2009).

United Nations Educational, Scientific, and Cultural Organization (UNESCO). *Universal Declaration on Bioethics and Human Rights.* SHS/EST/BIO/06/1. Paris: UNESCO, 2006.

United Nations Human Rights Council. *Report of the Special Representative of the Secretary General on the Issue of Human Rights and Transnational Corporations and Other Business Enterprises – Protect, Respect and Remedy: A Framework.* UN Doc. A/HRC/8/5 (2008).

Universal Declaration of Human Rights. GA Res. 217 (III), UNGAOR, 3d Sess., Supp. No. 13, UN Doc. A/810 (1948).

U.S. Congress. *The Federal Bill Emerson Good Samaritan Food Donation Act of 1996.* Pub. L. No. 104-210. Washington: Government Printing Office, 1996.

World Health Organization. 'The Declaration of Alma-Ata.' 1978. http://www.who.int/publications/almaata_declaration_en.pdf.

Wynia, Matthew. 'Medical Professionalism in Society.' In *Ethical Healthcare*, edited by Patricia Illingworth and Wendy Parmet, 174. Englewood Cliffs, NJ: Prentice Hall, 2005.

PART TWO

Social versus Business Responsibilities

5 Benchmarking and Transparency: Incentives for the Pharmaceutical Industry's Corporate Social Responsibility

MATTHEW LEE AND JILLIAN CLARE KOHLER[1]

Introduction: The Pharmaceutical Industry and Corporate Social Responsibility

Medicines save lives, reduce suffering, and improve health. The need for increased global access to medicines is undeniable, as exemplified by over two billion people lacking access to medicines or vaccines for treatable diseases – which equates to approximately one-third of the world's population. This number can rise to 50 per cent in areas of Africa and Southeast Asia. Also, with 15 per cent of the world's population consuming over 90 per cent of pharmaceuticals,[2] there is inequality between the developing and undeveloped world in the access to medicines. The World Health Organization (WHO) estimates that if there were a scaling up of medicinal interventions, over ten million lives could be saved per year. However, the two main challenges to increasing global access to medicines, as reported by the United Nations (UN), are making more affordable existing medications, and the development of new medications to treat diseases of the poor.[3] The issues surrounding these challenges are multifaceted, and their solutions require involvement of governments, international organizations, and non-governmental organizations (NGOs) – and participation from the pharmaceutical industry.

The pharmaceutical industry's role in the global economy is to research, develop, and produce innovative medicines to save sick people's lives. At the same time, as corporations, they have a duty to increase profits. Further, the industry faces a diverse group of stakeholders including patients, health professionals, the media, regulators, political authorities, and the general public when integrating corporate social responsibility (CSR) into its business – and unequivocally faces the scrutiny of each of them when doing so.[4] Thus, there is a special pressure placed on the pharmaceutical industry and the level of its engagement in CSR. Oxfam, one of the world's foremost NGOs, writes, 'Society expects pharmaceutical companies – with their privileged access to a global market – to develop necessary products at prices that are affordable … The pharmaceutical industry is expected to fulfill these requirements reliably and sustainably, and by so doing, play its part in the wider responsibilities to improve the health of all.'[5]

The foundation of the pharmaceutical industry's CSR is in the WHO's 1946 constitution, stating the 'right to the highest attainable standard of health … as a fundamental right of every human being.' This right is continually affirmed within the realm of international agencies. The UN's General Comment 14 says that, although states are ultimately accountable for the right to health, 'private business … [also] have responsibilities regarding the realization of the right to health.' The UN Millennium Development Goal 8 (Develop a Global Partnership for Development), Target 17, states, 'In cooperation with pharmaceutical companies, provide access to affordable essential drugs in developing countries.'[6] However, international agencies' policies cannot be enforced by law. Rather, companies are meant to implement them by voluntary efforts, which are often insufficient and lead to meaningless CSR policies.[7]

From an ethical point of view, pharmaceutical companies should give back to society in addition to performing their regular roles – to research, develop, and produce medicines profitably. The industry is criticized for tolerating excessive prices for life-saving medicines for those in the developed world. Is it morally acceptable to put corporate profits before a human life?[8] The five most common reasons pharmaceutical companies bear the moral obligation to aid the global poor are outlined by Chang.[9] Although he questions these generally held principles, they still hold as the current arguments of support:

1. Pharmaceutical companies produce life-saving drugs with a relatively low production cost, and this alone holds them morally responsible to help those in need.
2. Because pharmaceutical companies benefit heavily from both governmental and public support (for example, patent protection or university research), they must reciprocate this support to the public in need.
3. Pharmaceutical companies are able to share their intellectual property rights on products that can save lives in the developing world (for example, by allowing countries to generically produce

these drugs themselves), without affecting their for-profit products. This puts them in a distinct position over other types of companies, as their financial bottom line would not be affected.

4. In the Western world's industry, the impoverished world is often a neglected stakeholder. If this is true, why should it be required to follow the procedures of the Western world, and, moreover, be restricted access to medicines based on Western intellectual property rights?

5. Pharmaceutical companies consistently produce larger profit margins than any other, and thus they have a moral duty to help those who have less.

Resnik also argues on the moral basis for the pharmaceutical industry to aid the global poor: 'Corporations are like moral agents in that they make decisions that have important effects on human beings. In making these decisions, corporations can decide to either accept or ignore social values, such as respect for the environment, public safety, and so on … In particular, corporations have obligations to avoid causing harm and to promote social welfare and justice … Since pharmaceutical companies are corporations, they also have social responsibilities.'[10]

Further, on the basis of this argument and on the principles of beneficence and justice, he argues that pharmaceutical companies have a social obligation to promote the welfare of humankind.

Human rights and ethical arguments have traditionally formed the basis for urging the pharmaceutical industry to improve its CSR involvement. This paper argues that, in addition, companies can compete to achieve superior socially responsible investment (SRI) ratings to improve access to medicines, thereby saving millions of lives. The idea of creating an inter-business competitive CSR environment, through SRI ratings, recognizes and takes advantage of pharmaceutical companies being driven primarily to increase their financial bottom line – just as any other business. The key to realizing this potential is through accurate benchmarking and transparency of pharmaceutical CSR practices. Paul Hunt, former UN special rapporteur on the right to health, said of benchmarking, 'Pharmaceutical companies have a profound impact – both positive and negative – on Governments' ability to realise the right to the highest attainable standard of health. It is time to identify what pharmaceutical companies should do to help realize the human right to medicine. How can we expect pharmaceutical companies to respect human rights if we fail to explain what they are expected to do?'[11]

This paper demonstrates the importance of benchmarking and transparency in creating inter-business competition through analysing how companies have responded to current benchmarking efforts, and the translation of these responses to actual access to medicine.

Benchmarking the Pharmaceutical Industry

With the continual criticism the pharmaceutical industry faces, there is an unequivocal need for proper assessments of what exactly is being done – to justify the current criticisms and to provide the transparency necessary for further assessments. This can be accomplished through appropriate benchmarks applied to performance in access to medicines. Persistent scrutiny from civil society will lead to increased transparency of pharmaceutical companies' performance, putting pressures on the industry to end secrecies around its price-setting.[12] While the industry has made some advancement in access to medicines, the actual amount of progress made can be contested, so it is crucial to establish objective parameters to measure progress.[13] The tying of health to human rights is a relatively new concept, and so too are the ways to measure health decisions and their effectiveness. There needs to be a way to measure the effectiveness of assessment methods and indicators of human rights concerns, and the extent to which these indicators need to change.[14] In comparison to mature fields, such as environmental CSR, which have been benchmarking outcomes for several decades, the pharmaceutical industry is in its infancy. There is a lack of significant literature in the pharmaceutical industry about reporting to its stakeholders.[15]

Only recently have there been attempts to benchmark the pharmaceutical industry's efforts in access to medicines. Three recent pharmaceutical benchmarking reports are The Interfaith Centre of Corporate Responsibility's (ICCR) *Benchmarking AIDS*,[16] Oxfam's *Investing for Life*, and the *Access to Medicines* index,[17] released in 2006, 2007, and 2008 respectively. The motive for benchmarking can be best explained by the authors themselves, and each has outlined its purpose in its introduction. *Benchmarking AIDS* states that the 'report will measure how effectively companies are addressing these two fundamental problems (failure to develop new medicines, and lack of access to existing medicines) by comparing actual pharmaceutical responses against industry best practices.'[18] They further wish to determine which companies are more effectively involved in these best practices. In comparison, *Investing for Life* 'seeks to establish how far companies have gone in demonstrating their commitments in the five years since [our last report],'[19] and to advance ideas as to why pharmaceutical companies have resisted meeting their responsibilities. And finally, it hopes to encourage companies towards a progressive approach with the provided outline. The *Access to Medicines* index has three goals: (1) to supply all stakeholders with impartial and accurate information regarding pharmaceutical companies and access to medicines, (2) to increase transparency in pharmaceutical companies in order to assess, monitor, and improve their performance, including public and investor profiles, and (3) to provide a platform for all stakeholders to discuss best practices.[20]

The mission statements of Oxfam and of ICCR may further provide some understanding about why these benchmarking reports target the pharmaceutical industry's involvement in access to medicines: 'Oxfam International is an international group of independent non-governmental organizations (NGO) dedicated to fighting poverty and related injustice around the world … Oxfam believes that … [p]overty and powerlessness are avoidable and can be eliminated by human action and political will … that basic human needs and rights can be met.' And 'Through the lens of faith, ICCR builds a more just and sustainable world by integrating social values into corporate and investor actions.'[21]

NGOs and pharmaceutical companies share a dynamic relationship. For instance, NGOs and media are often the broadcasters of negative news about a company.[22] Also, they often make critically evident the gaps between corporate values and its actual practices. Meanwhile, companies underestimate their irresponsible actions and overstate responsible ones. These differences are expected, as the internal values and roles of each organization are inherently different. The role of an NGO can include 'activities to relieve suffering, promote the interests of the poor, protect the environment, provide basic social services, or undertake community development.'[23] In contracts, a corporation's role, as defined by economist Milton Freidman, is to increase its profits.[24] Tensions between the two are due to their differences in purpose and a lack of knowledge and mutual understanding, causing mistrust.[25] Organizations such as Oxfam or the ICCR that criticize pharmaceutical companies act as interest groups against which companies must often defend themselves.

Intrigued by the potential for an increase in socially responsible investing, a new mutually beneficial relationship is arising. The benefits for this form of alliance for the NGO are that it gains a broadened range of people it can influence, the ability to learn new skills and disciplines, and increased financial support. In turn, corporations receive the good reputation and moral influence of the NGO, contacts with leaders and countries to which the NGO has ties, expertise in the area of the NGO's interest, and the tax benefits of working with the NGO.[26] Our paper further explores this developing relationship and benefits that may arise from it, through a qualitative analysis of company attitudes and feedback on current benchmarking standards of pharmaceutical CSR. This is based on two major publications: the ICCR *Benchmarking AIDS* and Oxfam's *Investing for Life*.

The term corporate public discourse (CPD) is defined by separating it into its three component terms. First, the term *corporate* is a 'social entity that possesses the power to affect and change whole societies.' Next, *public* is 'open, visible, and available to all to accept or refuse.' Finally, *discourse* is 'language as meaningful social action: a key instrument of individuals' and groups' participation in social roles, social contexts, social situations, and social processes.'[27] Examples of CPD include a corporation's mission statement, annual report, news bulletin, or web-page, or a CEO's media interview or media address. The significance of corporate discourses and their ability to affect a corporation's public image has been debated. For instance, a corporation's rhetoric often differs from its values and actions,[28] and this difference can be demonstrated by companies eagerly releasing discourse about their 'fine values,' while defending against accusations from different interest groups on company actions. This discrepancy may be due largely to the increasing essentiality of image to corporations, leading to established methods for firms to prevent or restore any image problems they face.[29]

The Business and Human Rights Resource Centre[30] invited each of the companies benchmarked to respond to the reports, which are now available for public access. The documents posted on the Internet then act as a corporate public discourse. Eighteen statements were made directly in response to benchmarking guidelines. The ICCR *Benchmarking AIDS* report received ten company responses, and the Oxfam *Investing for Life* report received eight (see tables 5.1, 5.2, 5.3). Our report identifies and groups the responses in these statements.

Results Seen in Feedback

Tables 5.1 and 5.2 display the results of a qualitative analysis on company feedback on the two benchmarking publications. Five responses commonly given when analysing the discourses included the tendency for companies to

1. Be disappointed or claim the report is inaccurate.
2. Identify the company's own CSR practices.

Table 5.1 Company responses to Oxfam *Investing for Life*

Responses	Disappointment or inaccuracies seen	Identifies its own CSR practices	Dissatisfaction with input reflected in report	Shared responsibility of all stakeholders	Companies not being acknowledged
Abbot	V	V	V	V	V
Astra Zeneca	V	V	V	V	
GSK	V	V	V	V	V
Johnson and Johnson	V				
Merck	V	V	V	V	V
Novartis		V		V	
Pfizer	V	V	V	V	V
Sanofi Aventis	V	V		V	V

Table 5.2 Company responses to ICCR *Benchmarking AIDS*

Responses	Disappointment or inaccuracies seen	Identifies its own CSR practices	Dissatisfaction with input reflected in report	Shared responsibility of all stakeholders	Companies not being acknowledged
Abbot		V			
Astra Zeneca					V
Brystol-Myers Squibb		V			
Boehringer Ingleheim		V			
GSK	V	V	V	V	
Merck	V	V	V	V	V
Novartis		V		V	
Pfizer	V		V	V	V

3. Be dissatisfied with the amount of input reflected in the benchmarking report that companies provided.
4. Emphasize that increasing access to medicines is a multi-stakeholder
issue and not the responsibility of the pharmaceutical industry
alone.
5. Feel the pharmaceutical industry is not receiving proper acknowledgment for its current CSR practices.

Table 5.3 Company feedback

Company	Included in Benchmarking AIDS	Benchmarking AIDS feedback provided	Included in Oxfam's Investing for Life	Oxfam's Investing for Life feedback provided
Abbott Laboratories	Y	Y	Y	Y
Astra Zeneca PLC	Y	Y	Y	Y
Boehringer-Ingelheim	Y	Y	N	N
Bristol-Myers Squibb	Y	Y	Y	N
Eli Lilly & Company	Y	N	Y	N
Gilead Sciences Inc.	Y	N	Y	N
GlaxoSmithKline	Y	Y	Y	Y
Johnson & Johnson	Y	Y (Tibotec)	Y	Y
Merck and Company Inc	Y	Y	Y	Y
Novartis AG	Y	Y	Y	Y
Pfizer Inc	Y	Y	Y	Y
Roche Holdings Ltd	Y	N	Y	N
Sanofi-Aventis	Y	N	Y	Y
Schering-Plough Corp				
Teva Pharmaceutical Ind. Ltd	Y	N	N	N
Wyeth	Y	Y	Y	N

Note: The ICCR *Benchmarking AIDS* report received ten company responses, while the Oxfam *Investing for Life* report received eight.

First Response: Be Disappointed or Claim the Report Is Inaccurate

Companies have employed 'technocracy' to gain leverage against critiques. Here 'trained experts rule by virtue of their specialised knowledge.'[31] Built on this concept is 'technocratic rationality,' the 'policy legitimation which is dependent on specialisation, expertise, and professionalization.'[32] This means that, in order to have any grounds of influence on companies, lobbyists need expertise and specialization, and must be representative of specific groups with knowledge. Thus, any NGOs, lay people, or community groups who wish to influence CSR are not taken seriously, unless they are equipped with proper credentials. Industry members often suggest that only they are 'expert' enough to develop appropriate regulatory criteria, because they alone are specialists in their particular operations and processes. The business argument claims, 'Only business has adequate experience of the technologies and economics of its "real world" operations, so only business can know the "true" situation and potential for amelioration; moreover, if regulators do not take business advice, then they will set impossible standards far beyond current technological or economic capability, and therefore compliance will be poor. This sets up an asymmetry of knowledge between regulator and regulated, in which it is argued that the regulator cannot simply tell companies what to do and be sure of the outcome.'[33]

This concept can be applied to pharmaceutical companies. Their responses included language indicating disappointments, inaccuracies, or wrongfulness in the benchmarks. For instance, GSK says about Oxfam's benchmarks, 'We do not believe [intellectual property] benchmarks used in the report are realistic or meaningful.'[34] They make this claim on the classic basis that IP is necessary in order to provide the research industry with incentive. Merck responds to the same Oxfam paper by stating, 'Oxfam has created an unrealistic set of measures by which to assess industry efforts – most of which aren't directly related to improving access to medicines,' And concludes by saying Oxfam has 'published inaccurate and unbalanced reports.'[35] Pfizer, in response to ICCR's benchmarking AIDS report, says, 'Limited assessments of best practices are not a useful method to benchmark pharmaceutical companies.'[36] This statement concurs with their response to Oxfam as they compellingly write in opposition to it,

> The Oxfam paper does not engage in any substantive discussion of the obstacles that continue to prevent poor patients from accessing [essential drugs] and other medicines. Rather, it rests its dubious conclusion on the proposition that IP is a considerable barrier to access, and it provides no evidence that this premise has any basis in fact. We accept that Oxfam may neither like nor agree with some of the legitimate enforcement mechanisms necessary to ensure that the IP system actually works. However, we would respectfully submit that Oxfam should acknowledge at least some benefits that patients past, present and future derive from this paradigm. In its refusal to do so, or to present a single evidentiary point for its distorted conclusions about the barriers to access presented by IP, the Oxfam paper is unbalanced, unsubstantiated, and conclusory, representing a tract that exalts political rhetoric over scientific rigor and analysis.[37]

These examples of company responses demonstrate the pharmaceutical industry's attitudes towards NGOs. In their view, NGOs are not appropriately knowledgeable enough to create standards and benchmarks. Rather, companies believe their practices are correct and sufficiently match the standards required of them.

Second Response: Identifying the Company's Own CSR Practices

In response to benchmarking, companies have highlighted their own specific practices while explaining their importance and significance. In some cases, they further question why these practices were left out of the report and validate them. In GSK's response to *Benchmarking AIDS*, it defends itself in categories where it received a score of one or two out of five. For instance, GSK received a score of two in the fixed-dose combinations (FDC) category. In response, GSK explains the difficulties in combining active ingredients, and showcases its willingness to collaborate and its current collaboration with Boehringer-Ingelheim to develop a co-pack of Combivir with nevirapine. Further, in the category of patent relaxation in which GSK received a score of one, the report penalizes the company proceeding with a patent application in India for Combivir. Still, GSK strongly states that it believes the role of IP in access to medicines is 'overstated' and that this 'best practice' is overvalued as a mechanism for access to medicines and thus is not appropriate. It concludes its report by stating that it believes its practices are 'appropriate for GSK, and do not represent a barrier to access or threat to our reputation.'[38]

Another example is found in Merck's response to the Oxfam paper, in which its Mectizan Donation Program for the treatment of river blindness is profiled. Merck responds that its Mectizan program is not only an example of *some* success in eradicating disease but also *exemplifies* it as a model of public–private partnership in the fight against eradication. It claims, 'Oxfam has chosen to *downplay* the major advances that have been made in the fight against river blindness,'[39] then goes on to showcase some of its successes, which include the millions in Africa who receive treatment for river blindness, or the forty thousand cases of river blindness prevented each year. When companies respond by justifying why their actions are correct in comparison to the benchmarks, it raises questions about the significance these benchmarks have for them. In other words, if benchmarks are intended to provide ratings for companies, but they are not in agreement with the standards, the benchmarks lose meaning.

*Third Response: Be Dissatisfied with the Amount of Input Reflected
in the Benchmarking Report That Companies Provided*

Benchmarking reports are meant to evaluate real practices accurately. To accomplish this goal, Oxfam and ICCR individually interviewed companies for deeper insight, rather than relying upon external publications. Appendix 2 of the Oxfam report outlines the dates each company was interviewed, and the ICCR explains it had constant dialogue with companies. Nevertheless, companies responded that much of what they said during these interviews and the comments they made were excluded from final publications. Astra Zeneca is 'disappointed that the final report does not reflect the extensive dialogue we have had with Oxfam.'[40] GSK responds to the ICCR report by stating that 'GSK had an opportunity in March 2006 to provide comments on an early draft of the ICCR report. Some of these are reflected in the final report, however the fundamental point that improving healthcare in the developing world requires a global partnership is not well reflected in the final report. We did not see the methodology for the scoring or GSK's scores until the final report was published so were unable to comment on these.'[41] Another powerful example of this type of response can be seen in Merck's reply: 'Relatively little of the information we provided in our conversations and correspondence with the ICCR seems to have made its way into the final publication. Instead, the ICCR study relies heavily on reports, often outdated, by those who have been critical in the past of Merck and the pharmaceutical industry, without updating the information or making use of the relevant and readily available reports from such organizations.'[42]

This type of response displays the discordance between the NGOs and pharmaceutical companies. The lack of cooperation exemplifies the potential difficulty in the application of proper benchmarking processes. For benchmarking to achieve its purpose, there must be improvement objectives and an action plan made in collaboration between the firm and the partner performing the benchmarking. Partnership is required in the benchmarking process; however, as seen in this response, it is absent. With this fragile association between the two, it is difficult to foresee the significance of current benchmarking practices. If there is no partnership between pharmaceutical companies and the organizations benchmarking, under what accord should companies be under their influence?

*Fourth Response: Access to Medicines Is a Multi-Stakeholder Issue
and Not the Responsibility of the Pharmaceutical Industry Alone*

The majority of companies make clear the importance of a multi-stakeholder approach to improving access to medicines. For instance, Abbott Laboratories criticizes the Oxfam paper for suggesting that there are simple solutions for solving a very complex problem. They claim that the paper 'does not acknowledge that fighting the HIV epidemic requires the shared responsibility and shared commitment of all stakeholders in global health, but it rather places a strong focus on the pharmaceutical industry.'[43] Abbott then suggests that other stakeholders, such as developed countries and NGOs play a role similar to that of the companies themselves. Sanofi Aventis also strongly suggests the need for other stakeholders: 'Importantly, in our opinion, the report does not sufficiently recognize the fact that "access to health" cannot be limited to "access to medicines." Of course, medicines play a critical role in improving health, but "access to health" depends on many other stakeholders than the pharmaceutical industry alone, in particular governments and public agencies. Confusing the two issues leads to pointing at the pharmaceutical industry as the main culprit for insufficient access to health in developing countries, which we believe is just not true.'[44]

There are strong grounds for this response, for access to medicines is built on the contributions of all stakeholders, and surely it is beyond the scope of the pharmaceutical industry alone. This fact is made evident repeatedly in documents outlining solutions to access to medicines. Is it natural for companies to respond in this manner when both the Oxfam and ICCR publications are directed at the industry, and not other stakeholders? Their responses are available to the public, which may influence pharmaceuticals' feedback, in order to maintain a good image. However, each stakeholder has a unique position to improve access to medicines, and each requires specific guidelines laid out for it.

*Fifth Response: Proper Acknowledgment Is Not Being Received
for Current CSR Practices*

The importance of providing business incentives for corporations that strive to be a part of alleviating the global health problem is paramount. The term reputation capital applies to companies rewarded for their actions. There is growing emphasis on the need for reputation capital in order to help facilitate a change in corporate attitudes towards helping the global poor. Leisinger provides insight on this topic:

> Assuming that the 'value set' of mainstream managers is unlikely to change overnight, the prospects for more companies becoming engaged in the fight against extreme poverty are therefore sobering ... This perspective could change if there were more positive feed-back from society for those managers and companies who are doing 'the right thing' from a global development point of view. If the individuals and organizations (i.e., NGOs, churches, and the political world) who most audibly advocate poverty alleviation went on record in support of the most active corporations, thereby 'donating' reputation capital to companies most deserving it, the media would probably follow in making such corporate deeds an issue for public debate. Is it too much to ask that credit be given to those corporate leaders who engage in the fight against misery?[45]

With this argument in mind, why are these benchmarking reports exceedingly critical of the pharmaceutical companies? The pharmaceutical industry demonstrates this lack of acknowledgment in its response to the benchmarking reports, as GSK's statement on the Oxfam paper strongly demonstrates: 'The industry is making significant contribution to improving healthcare in the developing world, and there have been significant improvements in the past 5 years. We believe this contribution is understated in the Oxfam paper ... [It] fails to acknowledge the significant improvements in investments in R&D by GSK and others in the industry as a whole.'[46]

With the growing movement for investors to put their money into socially responsible companies, this is now a new driving force for society to impose upon the pharmaceutical industry.

Discussion

Background Information

CSR is a business practice concept that has become increasingly important to companies in the past decade. It has been described as a broad, complex, and evolving concept, which is ambiguous and subjective, with unclear boundaries.[47] Other definitions in the literature include one by McWilliams and Siegel, who define CSR as 'actions that appear to further some social good, beyond the interest of the firm and that which is required by law ... CSR means going *beyond* obeying the law,'[48] while Hemingway and Maclagon define it as the 'extent to which companies should promote human rights, democracy, community improvement and sustainable development objectives through the world.'[49] Because the definition of CSR is not universally agreed upon, it can be seen as a vague and intangible term that is open to individual interpretation,[50] and the lack of a clear definition has made it difficult to produce guidelines for companies to follow.

Companies now devote more of their resources to CSR practices. A survey conducted in 2007 by the Economist Intelligence Unit shows that over the past three years, more than 20 per cent of corporations have been giving 'high' priority to CSR.[51] A 2008 study concludes that CEOs plan to further increase their CSR investments by over 25 per cent over the next three years.[52] This change can be attributed to regulatory frameworks placing new demands on corporations, corporate actors mobilizing to aid in state development, and managerial trends,[53] as well as companies having to work to protect their reputations, nongovernmental organizations watching over corporate activities, and new rankings and rating systems putting pressure on companies to report their non-financial performance in addition to their financial results.[54] With this increase in CSR practices, companies have been striving to achieve a favourable performance rating, which can often result in awards, applause, sales, and enhanced reputation.[55] However, it has been heavily debated whether companies with elaborate CSR programs benefit, either financially or strategically. In literature analysing correlations between a company's CSR performance and their financial performance, three main outcomes have been found:[56]

1. There is a negative correlation: companies are at a competitive disadvantage by spending resources on CSR.[57]
2. There is a neutral correlation: there is no relationship between CSR and financial performance.[58]
3. There is a positive correlation: companies are at a competitive advantage by engaging in CSR activities.[59]

Renneboog, Ter Horst, and Zhang[60] conclude that it is a 'puzzle' whether investing in socially sound companies produces superior returns. McWilliams, Siegel, and Wright review empirical papers on CSR, and show outcomes of studies for each of the three possible correlations. However, Burke and Logsdon[61] suggest it is fundamentally understood that those companies that support CSR benefit themselves, their stakeholders, and society in general.

Regardless of the mixed evidence for the correlation of corporate returns to CSR practice, socially responsible investing has been an escalating practice over the past decade.[62] From 2005 to 2007, assets controlled under socially responsible investing increased by more than 18 per cent, as reported by the Forum for Sustainable and Responsible Investment.[63] In addition, from 1995 to 2007, the total SRI-controlled assets rose from $639 billion to $2.5 trillion – an increase of 324 per cent, versus a 260 per cent increase of normally controlled investments. In the United States, 11 per cent of all professionally managed funds are now tied to corporate social responsibility.

The broadest definition of SRI is investing in companies based on both financial and social performance. A company's social performance, for example, can include its practices in the environment, workplace safety, adopting labour standards, or contributing to its local communities.[64] With both profits and social performance in mind, SRI is an investment that – in addition to generating profits – aims to do good, implying that a primary objective is to achieve social objectives.[65] However, this investing concept is evolving, as both companies and investors know that improving their social practices could be a competitive advantage over companies in the same industry. Investors practise this 'value-seeking' when judging how much a company's social and environmental performance can positively affect a company's stock price. Although these investors do practise SRI, their main purpose is to increase profits by using a company's social performance as a screening method to determine where to invest.[66] Several indexes to help investors with this assessment, including the popular Domini 400 Social Index (DS400), which is a benchmark of socially responsible companies based on criteria such as community relations, diversity, and human rights.[67] For some companies, SRI has compelled them to consider the potential financial benefits that socially responsible investors would bring.

Discussion of Results

In the relationship between the pharmaceutical industry and NGOs, 'sweeping negative judgements' are made on the industry as a whole,[68] as confirmed in response 5 above, in which companies claim they failed to receive proper acknowledgment for their contributions. In order to gauge where the pharmaceutical industry stands in facing criticisms from the ICCR and Oxfam, the matrix of responses created by Swajkowski[69] was applied to the five identified responses. This matrix outlines a company's possible 'psychological defences' when facing accusations:

1. *Refusals* or denials – an organization admits neither net harm nor responsibility for misconduct;
2. *Excuses* – an organization admits net harm, but not responsibility · for the misconduct;
3. *Justifications* – an organization admits responsibility for misconduct, but does not admit that its misconduct has caused harm; and
4. *Concessions* – an organization admits both net harm and responsibility for misconduct.

In this chapter, misconduct is defined as the lack of substantiation, as reported by the benchmarking reports, that pharmaceutical companies display in their CSR towards access to medicines. Our analysis of feedback displays the pharmaceutical industry as predominantly in the excuses phase of its psychological defence. In almost all discourses, companies admit that lack of access to medicines is a major global health issue and that the industry does and can play a role in alleviating it – *admitting net harm*. However, as in response 4 of the analysis, these same companies also insist that access to medicines is a multistakeholder issue in which the pharmaceutical industry is only one player among many.

Zadek describes the five stages an organization must learn and pass through in order to appropriately handle corporate responsibility,[70] and he uses them to explain the struggle between the social activists and NGOs versus Nike that occurred during the nineties over sweatshop conditions. In the 'defensive' stage, a company is faced with unexpected criticism and responds by denying practices and negative accusations. In the 'compliance' stage, corporations create value by doing only as much as they have to. They protect the company's reputation by creating corporate policy that is visible to society's scrutiny. In the 'managerial' stage, companies realize problems cannot be solved simply through public relations, and that managers at the core business level must deal with them. In the 'strategic' stage, companies learn that a socially responsible business strategy can give it a competitive advantage over others and contribute to long-term success. Finally, in the 'civil' stage of response, companies become promoters in the advancement of society's concerns.

This same framework can be used to describe the pharmaceutical industry and its response to criticisms about access to medicines. Pharmaceutical companies have sophisticated CSR programs devoted to ensuring societal sustainability. These values and practices are often already implemented in the company's core values. They partner themselves with NGOs and international organizations, and they deserve much credit for the increased access to medicines available today. Their actions are showcased through annual CSR reports, which are advanced and transparent in their accomplishments. These activities would classify the industry beyond the early stages of organizational learning, and within the realm of the strategic and civil stages. As discovered by our analysis of the feedback discourses, however, their responses display the defensive and excusatory attitude of the industry when benchmarked. This is in sync with the idea that companies respond to criticism by providing evidence that inappropriate standards were used in evaluating company actions.[71] These types of responses place pharmaceutical companies in an earlier stage defensive stage of organizational development, according to Zadek's learning stages. Ketola observes that 'managerial and organizational psychological defences have an important role in the slow, and often painful, change process towards a more responsible corporation,'[72] and Zadek confirms this view: 'Organizations' learning pathways are complex and iterative. Companies can make great strides in one area only to take a few steps back when a new demand is made of them.' In the same way, 'the exercise of corporate social responsibility can be viewed in practice as a dynamic negotiation, an interaction between multiple actors.'[73] These statements allow one to better understand the path the pharmaceutical industry is taking. Corporations must undergo stages in their attitudes towards corporate responsibility before they can arrive at the 'civil' stage of responsibility.

However, there are barriers to Zadek's learning stages, and the six fundamental paradoxes outlined by Frankental must be addressed before CSR can have real substance.[74] One paradox is the 'systematic denial of wrongdoing.' According to Frankental, 'Any company that aspires to be socially responsible must be prepared to admit to its shortcomings and mistakes.' He concludes, 'Denial is a function of crisis management, news management and public relations. It serves as a barrier to corporate social responsibility, which requires openness, transparency, a critical faculty and a willingness to learn lessons from past mistakes.'

Flanagan and Whiteman identify two potential major weaknesses of a firm's CSR program: 'lack of meaningful participation by external stakeholders in policy development' and 'lack [of] effective processes for ensuring and measuring the implementation of their CSR policy.'[75] Further, 'Monitoring and sanctions are the most important test for the seriousness of a code's implementations.'[76] These statements highlight the practical importance of company participation in benchmarking for the meaningfulness of its CSR activities. Successful benchmarking proceeds through five phases: (1) the need for an initial diagnosis of company performance, (2) a defined benchmark framework as well as the companies it will be applied to, (3) analysis of the firms selected, (4) improvement objectives, and (5) application of the benchmarking results.[77] The fourth phase is of particular interest: 'the definition of improvement objectives by partners, with the action plan which allows them to be reached.' The five responses found in the company feedback to benchmarking clearly indicate the discordance between the ICCR and Oxfam, and the pharmaceutical companies. Responses 1, 3, and 5 particularly demonstrate this absence of a partnership. For instance, response 1 indicates that companies, in general, do not believe the benchmarking standards laid out for them are meaningful, and therefore lead to inaccurate reports. Or the companies and NGOs are in disagreement with the measuring standards for CSR policy. Along similar lines, response 3 displays this discordance through the companies' dissatisfaction with the amount of input from the interviews that NGOs conducted with them. On the other hand, response 5 illustrates overcriticism of the industry by NGOs, which may be overwhelming and detrimental to a healthy development of a partnership.

This type of relationship can in part be explained by Kallio, who writes on the 'political nature' taboo of CSR, which is the 'promotion of the actors' own interests, and the pursuit of social legitimacy for business in particular.'[78] This explains a company's need for legitimation from its surrounding society in order to be successful, which has led to pursuit of a responsible image. Relating this to environmental CSR, 'greenwashing' is now a common practice, in which corporations take the 'easy' path, having 'artificially tried to construct their image to be as green and responsible.' Levy shows that businesses now strive to be politically sustainable over environmentally sustainable, or in other words, they strive to maintain their image towards the public.[79] Kallio further cites Crook[80] on this matter, stating that, on the intellectual level, 'the corporate world has surrendered' and started to praise CSR, while at the level of action, 'when commercial interests and broader social welfare collide, profit comes first ... [Thus] for most companies, CSR does not go very deep.'[81] This difference is often referred to as corporate rhetoric versus reality of CSR practice – the gap between actual corporate practices and the ethical commitments they have made.[82] This concept is directly applicable to the pharmaceutical industry as he seeks to find the connection between core business practices and ethical standards. Initially, pharmaceutical companies have been comfortable with the fact that they produce life-saving medicines as evidence of their CSR. However, in the face of the global AIDS crisis, the pharmaceutical industry has been relieved of this comfort and accused of 'undermining poor people's access to medicines' through stubbornly defending their patents rights and pricing drugs beyond the reach of the under-developed world.[83] He argues that pharmaceutical companies have attempted to mitigate these accusations through actions such as drug donations, yet very few have chosen to meet the challenge 'head on.' Drug donations, for example, gain publicity for the donating company but offer an unsustainable solution for the continued support of access to medicines for the global poor. The industry has failed to 'address the health crisis in a meaningful way.'[84] As a result, the inability to apply core business operations to access to medicines has concerned investors. Dhanaragan outlines the four potential risks connected to the lack of meaningful progress the pharmaceutical companies have made in their CSR actions: (1) damage to company reputation, whose harm to profits can outweigh the benefits of holding patents; (2) damage to relationships with regulatory bodies that control the pricing of drugs; (3) restrictions to the ability to access to markets; and (4) damage to staff morale.[85] With these factors in mind, socially responsible investing is an alternative route for companies to gain a competitive advantage.

The main tool to facilitate this process is increasing transparency through benchmarking to reveal both individual companies' shortfalls and successes. It has been suggested that public exposure of a company's behaviour is the most effective mechanism to police its actions.[86] Benchmarking continuously and systematically assesses a company's products, services, and methods in comparison to those of its most serious competitors or industry leaders.[87] Maire defines it as 'a process of identifying, sharing, and using knowledge of best practices.'[88] It is a way to negate discrepancies between corporate practices and image, or NGOs being overly critical of them. In a neutral fashion, it increases the transparency of companies to the public by releasing information that normally would be inaccessible, and it is important, because CSR is a relationship between societal actors – business, state, and civil society. This relationship is the foundation for a new direction in CSR, because the 'dynamic negotiations between multiple actors' improves CSR outcomes.[89] Economic markets and public opinion can pressure businesses to behave in a manner favourable to the public eye, encouraging companies by positively affecting their attitudes and actions that normally would be free from public scrutiny. If the best-performing corporations receive positive feedback from members of society who most audibly advocate the alleviation of poverty (such as NGOs and political organizations), and these members publicly support companies, they 'donate' reputation capital to those who most deserve it. Public recognition then leads to increased availability of philanthropic resources.[90]

When there is transparent communication between companies and stakeholders, companies' reputations fall under appropriate public scrutiny, leading to accurate representations of their CSR programs. This opens the potential for civil society to have major influence on companies' image, which, with the growing SRI trend, directly affects their financial bottom line. In the *Human Rights Guidelines for Pharmaceutical Companies in Relation to Access Medicines*,[91] a portion of the publication is devoted to recognizing pharmaceutical companies' responsibility to enhance shareholder value. Building partnerships and affording reputation capital towards pharmaceutical companies would entice investors and increase profits – the eventual goal for all business. This is a sensible method that could be synergistic for the company, the NGO, and the socially responsible investor. Parker writes, 'Efficiency and/or profit constitute the "bottom line" for individual action, and this is a line that defines what lies inside business ethics and what is assumed to be outside it … So, if ideology is concerned with what is made visible, what do (and don't) we see within business ethics?'[92]

The 'pro-business ideological stance of the [CSR] field' is a taboo that is part of what we 'don't' see in business ethics.[93] In other words, CSR scholars have never seriously discussed the CSR relation to the capitalist market economy. As found in the corporate discourse responses, pharmaceutical companies are making excuses and being defensive to benchmarking. With increasing SRI and benchmarking practices, this demonstrates the competitive nature of corporations, because no corporation wants to be singled out from others in their CSR efforts. Thus, these initial discourses can be seen as part of gaining ground in the 'dynamic negotiations' to improve CSR. Once a profit-driven company faces a threat to its financial performance, it will take matters seriously. CSR moves from being a company side sector or philanthropy project to being incorporated into its core business practices.

The significance of this new potential synergy becomes paramount when relating it to the effect it can have on the global inequality in access to medicines. Médecins sans frontières report that infectious diseases kill over fourteen million people per year – over thirty-eight thousand per day – with nine out of ten deaths occurring in developing countries.[94] The WHO estimates that a scaling up of access to medicines practices can save up to ten million lives per year.[95] However, one-third of the world's population remains without medications to cure diseases of the developing world. There is undoubtedly room for improvement, and we believe benchmarking – a process that vigorously and accurately portrays actual company practices with the global poor – could be a key step in initiating true changes in pharmaceutical companies' core values.

Conclusions and Future Research

Benchmarking of CSR actions can be the key to improve pharmaceutical CSR performance by creating inter-company competition, by increasing transparency of CSR to the public investor, whose choices are ultimately the primary motivator of corporate behaviour. Review of the literature shows an increasing trend in corporate social responsibility, which could be continually stimulated by the demands for companies to achieve higher SRI ratings. Benchmarking can facilitate this trend by providing suitable standards for CSR assessment, thereby providing the public with a neutral means to choose a company in which to invest. Proper benchmarking would offer companies tangible measures for the appropriate reputation capital they deserve, providing further incentive for improved CSR performance.

NGOs are often regarded as a third party representative of 'civil society.'[96] Despite the responses the pharmaceutical industry has directed towards Oxfam and ICCR, one cannot automatically assume that benchmarks are not influencing the industry. Benchmarking helps to reveal the discrepancies between corporate practices and rhetoric, and makes clear any public relations acts the industry may exercise. In doing so, it allows for a transparent forum facilitating further criticism and pressuring of CSR. Societal pressures can act as the starting point for true changes in the way corporations respond to CSR concerns. In response to societal criticism, it is natural for a company to initially resist change and act defensively. It is then expected that pharmaceutical companies will continue to progress through the organizational learning stages Zadek has outlined. The five trends identified in pharmaceutical company feedback discourses demonstrate defensive attitudes, and this can be seen as preserving the company image to the public. This is crucial with the increasing trend in socially responsible investments. With this, it is anticipated that the pharmaceutical industry will also strive towards a true change in their attitude towards access to medicines.

A limitation to our study is that literature provides us with mixed results on the relationship between CSR and financial performance;[97] some reports show evidence of a positive correlation between CSR performance and stock price, others negative, while others show no correlation at all. Regardless, the overwhelming increases in raw numbers of SRI are undeniable, thus allowing us to draw conclusions. The current benchmarking of the pharmaceutical industry is heading in a positive direction with the release of the Access to Medicines Index (ATM index) in 2008 by the Access to Medicines Foundation. What makes this index unique is that it encompasses a multi-stakeholder approach to the benchmarking process, including the industry, NGOs, academics, investors, consultants, and the government. In doing so, it provides a broader approach to benchmarking, allowing for real discussion, rather than only that from an NGO's point of view. Indeed, the investors tied to the ATM index, representing over US1.2 trillion dollars of SRI funds, believe access to medicines is linked to long-term shareholder value creation. With the commitment of the ATM index to update the CSR ratings of pharmaceutical companies, there is now opportunity to further study the impact that inter-company rating systems can have in creating true changes to their core business practices. Transparency through benchmarking is a powerful tool that reveals the industry's shortfalls to the public. Further, the transparency of companies is listed as one of the cardinal principles for the right to the highest attainable standard of health.[98] If enough pressure from the public is applied, socially responsible investors may choose companies on the basis of these benchmarks, creating a financial incentive for companies to perform in CSR, leading to the potential to save millions of lives. Thus, transparency to investors can effectively influence the CSR actions of pharmaceutical companies, and further research in this area is warranted.

NOTES

1   Reprinted with kind permission from Springer Science+Business Media: *Journal of Business Ethics* (2010), Matthew Lee and Jillian Kohler.

2   United Nations, 'Human Rights Guidelines for Pharmaceutical Companies in Relation to Access to Medicines, Draft for Consultation,' *Report of the UN Special Rapporteur on the Right to Health* (19 Sept. 2007).

3   Beryl Leach, Joan E. Paluzzi, and Paula Munderi, UN Millennium Project. *Prescription for Healthy Development: Increasing Access to Medicines.* 2005, http://www.unmillenniumproject.org/documents/TF5-medicines-Complete.pdf., 2.

4   D. Esteban, 'Strengthening Corporate Social Responsibility in the Pharmaceutical Industry,' *Journal of Medical Marketing* 8, no. 1 (2008): 77–9.

5   Oxfam, *Investing for Life: Meeting Poor People's Needs for Access to Medicines through Responsible Business Practices*, Briefing Paper No. 109 (London: Oxfam, 2007).

6   Leach, Paluzzi, and Munderi, *Prescription for Healthy Development*.

7   W. Flanagan and G. Whiteman, '"Aids Is Not a Business": A Study in Global Corporate Responsibility – Securing Access to Low-cost HIV Medications,' *Journal of Business Ethics* 73 (2007): 66.

8   K.M. Leisinger, 'The Corporate Social Responsibility of the Pharmaceutical Industry: Idealism without Illusion and Realism without Resignation,' *Business Ethics Quarterly* 15, no. 4 (2005): 579.

9   L.B. Chang, 'Who's in the Business of Saving Lives?' *Journal of Medicine and Philosophy* 31, no. 5 (2006): 461–82.

10   D.B. Resnik, 'Developing Drugs for the Developing World: An Economic, Legal, Moral, and Political Dilemma,' *Developing World Bioethics* 1, no. 1 (2001): 11–32.

11   United Nations, 'UN Independent Expert Launches Draft Human Rights Guidelines for Pharmaceutical Companies,' news release, 19 Sept. 2007, http://www.unhchr.ch/huricane/huricane.nsf/view01/497E81A16B31B9C8C125735B0059D7B0?opendocument.

12   Oxfam, *Investing for Life*, 26.

13   S.F. Musungu, 'Benchmarking Progress in Tackling the Challenges of Intellectual Property, and Access to Medicines in Developing Countries,' *Bulletin of the World Health Organization* 84, no. 5 (2006): 369.

14   S. Gruskin, E.J. Mills, and D. Tarantola, 'History, Principles, and Practice of Health and Human Rights,' *Lancet* 370, no. 9585 (2007): 453.

15   L. Sweeney and J. Coughlan, 'Do Different Industries Report Corporate Social Responsibility Differently? An Investigation through the Lens of

Stakeholder Theory,' *Journal of Marketing Communications* 14, no. 2 (2008): 117.

16 K. Hartsough, D.E. Rosan, and L. Sachs, 'Benchmarking AIDS: Evaluating Pharmaceutical Company Responses to the Public Health Crisis in Emerging Markets,' *Corporate Examiner* 34, nos. 6–7 (2006): 1–88.

17 V. Menou, A. Hornstein, and E. Lipton-McCombie, *Access to Medicines Index: Ranking Access to Medicines Practices* (Haarlem, The Netherlands: Access to Medicines Foundation, 2008).

18 Hartsough, Rosan, and Sachs, 'Benchmarking AIDS,' 7.

19 Oxfam, *Investing for Life*, 5.

20 Menou, Hornstein, and Lipton-McCombie, *Access to Medicines Index*, 11.

21 Oxfam mission statement available at http://www.oxfam.org/en/about/what/purpose-and-beliefs. ICCR mission statement available at http://www.iccr.org/about/.

22 T. Ketola, 'A Holistic Corporate Responsibility Model: Integrating Values, Discourses and Actions,' *Journal of Business Ethics* 80 (2007): 429.

23 World Bank, 'Involving Nongovernmental Organizations in World Bank–Supported Activities,' *World Bank Operational Manual*, Operational Directive 14.70, 28 Aug. 1989.

24 M. Friedman, 'The Social Responsibility of Business Is to Increase Its Profits,' *New York Times Magazine*, 13 Sept. 1970.

25 K.M. Leisinger, 'Corporate Philanthropy: The "Top of the Pyramid,"' *Business and Society Review* 112, no. 3 (2007): 333.

26 T. Fox, 'Relationships with NGOs Have Been Fundamental to Many Corporations' Social Responsibility Programs,' *Monday Developments* 19, no. 17 (2001): 5–14.

27 R. Fox and J. Fox, *Organizational Discourse: A Language-Ideology-Power Perspective* (Westport, CT: Praeger, 2004).

28 Ketola, 'Holistic Corporate Responsibility Model,' 423.

29 W.L. Benoit, 'Image Repair Discourse and Crisis Communication,' *Public Relations Review* 23, no. 2 (1997): 177.

30 See www.business-humanrights.org.

31 Fischer cited in S. Eden, '"We Have the Facts": How Business Claims Legitimacy in the Environmental Debate,' *Environment and Planning A* 31 (1999): 1297.

32 Ibid.

33 Ibid., 1298.

34 GlaxoSmithKline, 'GlaxoSmithKline Response to Oxfam's Report, "Investing for Life."' 2007. http://www.reports-and-materials.org/GSK-response-Oxfam-11-Dec-2007.doc, 2.

35 Merck, 'Benchmarking AIDS: Evaluating Pharmaceutical Company
    Responses to the HIV-TB-Malaria Pandemics,' 2006, 1, http://www.
    reports-and-materials.org/Merck-response-re-ICCR-Benchmarking-AIDS-
    11-Sep-2006.pdf.
36 Pfizer, 'Benchmarking AIDS: Evaluating Pharmaceutical Responses to the
    Public Health Crisis in Emerging Market,' 2006, 1, http://www.reports-
    and-materials.org/Pfizer-response-re-ICCR-Benchmarking-AIDS-12-
    Sep-2006.pdf.
37 Pfizer, 'Pfizer Response to Oxfam's Report "Investing for Life,"' 2008, 4,
    http://www.reports-and-materials.org/Pfizer-response-Oxfam-15-
    Feb-2008.doc.
38 GlaxoSmithKline, 'GlaxoSmithKline Response to Interfaith Center on
    Corporate Responsibility's Report "Benchmarking AIDS,"' 2006, http://
    www.reports-and-materials.org/GSK-response-re-ICCR-Benchmarking-
    AIDS-6-Sep-2006.doc.
39 Merck, 'Response to "Investing for Life" Briefing Paper,' 2007, 1, http://
    www.business-humanrights.org/Documents/Merck-response-to-Oxfam-
    11-Dec-2007.pdf.
40 AstraZeneca, 'AstraZeneca Response to Oxfam's report "Investing for
    Life,"' 2007, 1, http://www.business-humanrights.org/Documents/
    AstraZeneca-response-Oxfam-26-Nov-2007.doc.
41 GlaxoSmithKline, 'GlaxoSmithKline Response to Interfaith Center on
    Corporate Responsibility's Report "Benchmarking AIDS,"' 2006, 1,
    http://www.reports-and-materials.org/GSK-response-re-ICCR-
    Benchmarking-AIDS-6-Sep-2006.doc.
42 Merck, 'Benchmarking AIDS', 1.
43 Dirk Van Eeden, 'Abbott Laboratories Response to Oxfam's Report
    "Investing for Life,"' 2007, 1, http://www.business-humanrights.org/
    Documents/Abbott-response-Oxfam-18-Dec-2007.doc.
44 Sanofi Aventis, 'Sanofi Aventis Statement on the Oxfam International's
    Response to the Pharmaceutical Industry's Reflections on Oxfam's
    Briefing Paper, "Investing for Life,"' 2008, 1, http://www.business-
    humanrights.org/Documents/Sanofi-Aventis-response-to-Oxfam-12-
    Feb-2008.pdf.
45 Leisinger, 'Corporate Philanthropy,' 333.
46 GlaxoSmithKline, 'GlaxoSmithKline Response to Oxfam's Report,' 1.
47 L. Sweeney and J. Coughlan, 'Do Different Industries Report Corporate
    Social Responsibility Differently? An Investigation through the Lens of
    Stakeholder Theory,' *Journal of Marketing Communications* 14, no. 2 (2008):
    113.

48 A. McWilliams and D. Siegel, 'Corporate Social Responsibility: A Theory of the Firm Perspective,' *Academy of Management Review* 26, no. 1 (2001): 117.

49 C.A. Hemingway and P.W. Maclagan, "Managers' Personal Values as Drivers of Corporate Social Responsibility,' *Journal of Business Ethics* 50 (2004): 33.

50 P. Frankental, 'Corporate Social Responsibility: A PR Invention?' *Corporate Communications* 6, no. 1 (2001): 18–23.

51 Economist Intelligence Unit, 'Global Business Barometer,' 2007, http://www.economist.com/media/pdf/20080116CSRResults.pdf.

52 BusinessAssurance.com, 'CEOs Plan to Increase CSR Investments by 25 Percent,' 2008, http://businessassurance.com/ceos-plan-to-increase-csr-investments-by-25-percent.

53 K. Sahlin-Andersson, 'Corporate Social Responsibility: A Trend and a Movement, but of What and for What?' *Corporate Governance* 6, no. 5 (2006): 595–6.

54 D. Franklin, 'Just Good Business,' *Economist*, 17 Jan. 2008, http://www.economist.com/node/10491077.

55 A. Márquez and C.J. Fombrun, 'Measuring Corporate Social Responsibility,' *Corporate Reputation Review* 7, no. 4 (2005): 304–8.

56 A. McWilliams, D.S. Siegel, and P.M. Wright, 'Guest Editors' Introduction – Corporate Social Responsibility: Strategic Implications,' *Journal of Management Studies* 43, no. 1 (2006): 1–18.

57 S. Brammer, C. Brooks, and S. Pavelin, 'Corporate Social Performance and Stock Returns: UK Evidence from Disaggregate Measures,' *Financial Management*, Autumn (2006): 97–116.

58 A. McWilliams and D. Siegel, 'Corporate Social Responsibility and Financial Performance: Correlation or Misspecification?' *Strategic Management Journal* 21 (2000): 603–9.

59 S. Waddock and S. Graves, 'The Corporate Social Performance–Financial Performance Link,' *Strategic Management Journal* 18, no. 4 (1997): 303–19.

60 F. Renneboog, J. Ter Horst, and C. Zhang, 'Socially Responsible Investments: Institutional Aspects, Performance, and Investor Behavior,' *Journal of Banking & Finance* 32 (2008): 1723–42.

61 L. Burke and J.M. Logsdon, 'How Corporate Social Responsibility Pays Off,' *Long Range Planning* 29, no. 4 (1996): 495–502.

62 Renneboog, Ter Horst, and Zhang, 'Socially Responsible Investments,' 1723–42.

63 Social Investment Forum Foundation, *Investment Trends Report*, 2007, http://ussif.org/resources/req/?fileID=7

64 M.A. Starr, 'Socially Responsible Investment and Pro-Social Change,' *Journal of Economic Issues* 42, no. 1 (2008): 51.

65 N. Rubin, 'The Challenge of Socially Responsible Investments,' *CPA Journal* 78, no. 7 (2008): 52.

66 Ibid.

67 Ibid., 53.

68 Leisinger, 'Corporate Philanthropy,' 333.

69 E. Swajkowski, 'Accounting for Organizational Misconduct,' *Journal of Business Ethics* 11 (1992): 401–11, cited in Ketola, 'Holistic Corporate Responsibility Model,' 424.

70 S. Zadek, 'The Path to Corporate Responsibility,' *Harvard Business Review* 82, no. 12 (2004): 125–32.

71 J.L. Bradford and D.E. Garrett:, 'The Effectiveness of Corporate Communicative Responses to Accusations of Unethical Behavior,' *Journal of Business Ethics* 14 (1995): 875–92, cited in Ketola, 'Holistic Corporate Responsibility Model,' 424.

72 Ketola, 'Holistic Corporate Responsibility Model,' 424.

73 Flanagan and Whiteman, '"Aids Is Not a Business,"' 72.

74 Frankental, 'Corporate Social Responsibility,' 18–23.

75 Flanagan and Whiteman, '"Aids Is Not a Business,"' 66.

76 A. Kolk and R. van Tulder, *International Codes of Conduct: Trends, Sectors, Issues and Effectiveness* (Rotterdam: Erasmus University, 2002), 26, cited in Flanagan and Whiteman, '"Aids Is Not a Business,"' 66.

77 J. Maire, 'A Model of Characterization of the Performance for a Process of Benchmarking,' *Benchmarking* 9, no. 5 (2002): 506.

78 T.J. Kallio, 'Taboos in Corporate Social Responsibility Discourse,' *Journal of Business Ethics* 74 (2007): 165–75.

79 D.L. Levy, 'Environmental Management as Political Sustainability,' *Organization and Environment* 10, no. 2 (1997): 126–47, cited in Kallio, 'Taboos,' 170.

80 C. Crook, 'The Good Company,' *Economist*, Jan. 2005.

81 Kallio, 'Taboos,' 171.

82 S. Dhanarajan, 'Managing Ethical Standards: When Rhetoric Meets Reality,' *Development in Practice* 15, no. 3 (2005): 529–38.

83 Ibid., 535.

84 Ibid.

85 Pharmaceutical Shareowners Group, *The Public Health Crisis in Emerging Markets: An Institutional Investor Perspective on the Implications of the Pharmaceutical Industry* (London: Pharmaceutical Shareowners Group, 2004).

86 M.L. Maynard, 'Policing Transnational Commerce: Global Awareness in the Margins of Morality,' *Journal of Business Ethics* 30 (2001): 17–27.

87 D. Kearns, 'Quality Improvement Begins at the Top,' *World* 20, no. 5 (1986), cited in Maire, 'Model of Characterization,' 506.

88 J. Maire, V. Bronet, and M. Pillet, 'A Typology of "Best Practices" for a Benchmarking Process,' *Benchmarking* 12, no. 1 (2005): 47.

89 Flanagan and Whiteman, '"Aids Is Not a Business,"' 65.

90 K.M. Leisinger, 'Corporate Responsibilities for Access to Medicines,' *Journal of Business Ethics Online* (2008): 4, https://springerlink3.metapress. com/content/01011u4800734242/resource-secured/?target=fulltext.pdf&s id=tgzn1ieclscu4c55nh1ijra4&sh=www.springerlink.com.

91 R. Khosla and P. Hunt, *Human Rights Guidelines for Pharmaceutical Companies in Relation to Access to Medicines: The Sexual and Reproductive Health Context* (Colchester, Essex: University of Essex, 2009), 11.

92 M. Parker, 'Introduction: Ethics, Politics and Organizing,' *Organization* 10, no. 2 (2003): 189, cited in Kallio, 'Taboos,' 171.

93 Kallio, 'Taboos,' 171.

94 See http://www.doctorswithoutborders.co.nz/education/resources/ access-brochure.pdf.

95 WHO, 'Equitable Access to Essential Medicines: A Framework for Collective Action,' Policy Perspectives on Medicines (2004), whqlibdoc. who.int/hq/2004/WHO_EDM_2004.4.pdf.

96 R. Lambell, G. Ramia, C. Nyland, and M. Michelotti, 'NGOs and International Business Research: Progress, Prospects and Problems,' *International Journal of Management Reviews* 10, no. 1 (2008): 75–92.

97 Burke and Logsdon, 'How Corporate Social Responsibility Pays Off,' 495–502; M.E. Porter and M.R. Kramer, 'Strategy and Society: The Link between Competitive Advantage and Corporate Social Responsibility,' *Harvard Business Review* 84, no. 12 (2006): 82.

98 Khosla and Hunt, *Human Rights Guidelines*, 15.

REFERENCES

AstraZeneca. 'AstraZeneca Response to Oxfam's Report "Investing for Life."' 2007. http://www.business-humanrights.org/Documents/AstraZeneca- response-Oxfam-26-Nov-2007.doc.

Benoit, W.L. 'Image Repair Discourse and Crisis Communication.' *Public Relations Review* 23, no. 2 (1997): 177–86.

Bradford, J.L., and D.E. Garrett. 'The Effectiveness of Corporate Communi- cative Responses to Accusations of Unethical Behavior.' *Journal of Business Ethics* 14 (1995): 875–92. Quoted in Ketola 2007, 424.

Brammer, S., C. Brooks, and S. Pavelin. 'Corporate Social Performance and Stock Returns: UK Evidence from Disaggregate Measures.' *Financial Management*, autumn (2006): 97–116.

Burke, L., and J.M. Logsdon. 'How Corporate Social Responsibility Pays Off.'
    Long Range Planning 29, no. 4 (1996): 495–502.
BusinessAssurance.com. 'CEOs Plan to Increase CSR Investments by
    25 Percent.' 2008. http://businessassurance.com/ceos-plan-to-increase-
    csr-investments-by-25-percent.
Chang, L.B. 'Who's in the Business of Saving Lives?' *Journal of Medicine and
    Philosophy* 31, no. 5 (2006): 461–82.
Crook, C. 'The Good Company.' *Economist*, Jan. 2005, 4.
Dhanarajan, S. 'Managing Ethical Standards: When Rhetoric Meets Reality.'
    Development in Practice 15, no. 3 (2005): 529–38.
Economist Intelligence Unit. 'Global Business Barometer.' 2007. http://www.
    economist.com/media/pdf/20080116CSRResults.pdf.
Eden, S. '"We Have the Facts": How Business Claims Legitimacy in the
    Environmental Debate.' *Environment and Planning A* 31 (1999): 1295–1309.
Esteban, D. 'Strengthening Corporate Social Responsibility in the
    Pharmaceutical Industry.' *Journal of Medical Marketing* 8, no. 1 (2008): 77–9.
Flanagan, W., and G. Whiteman. '"Aids Is Not a Business": A Study in Global
    Corporate Responsibility – Securing Access to Low-Cost HIV Medications.'
    Journal of Business Ethics 73 (2007): 65–75.
Fox, R., and J. Fox. *Organizational Discourse: A Language-Ideology-Power
    Perspective*. Westport, CT: Praeger, 2004.
Fox, T. 'Relationships with NGOs Have Been Fundamental to Many Corporations'
    Social Responsibility Programs.' *Monday Developments* 19, no. 17 (2001): 5–14.
Frankental, P. 'Corporate Social Responsibility: A PR Invention?' *Corporate
    Communications* 6, no. 1 (2001): 18–23.
Franklin, D. 'Just Good Business.' *Economist*, 17 Jan. 2008. http://www.
    economist.com/node/10491077.
Friedman, M. 'The Social Responsibility of Business Is to Increase Its Profits.'
    New York Times Magazine, 13 Sept. 1970.
GlaxoSmithKline. 'GlaxoSmithKline Response to Interfaith Center on
    Corporate Responsibility's Report "Benchmarking AIDS."' 2006. http://
    www.reports-and-materials.org/GSK-response-re-ICCR-Benchmarking-
    AIDS-6-Sep-2006.doc.
– GlaxoSmithKline. 'GlaxoSmithKline Response to Oxfam's Report,
    "Investing for Life."' 2007. http://www.reports-and-materials.org/
    GSK-response-Oxfam-11-Dec-2007.doc.
Gruskin, S., E.J. Mills, and D. Tarantola. 'History, Principles, and Practice of
    Health and Human Rights.' *Lancet* 370, no. 9585 (2007): 449–55.
Hartsough, K., D.E. Rosan, and L. Sachs. 'Benchmarking AIDS: Evaluating
    Pharmaceutical Company Responses to the Public Health Crisis in
    Emerging Markets.' *Corporate Examiner* 34, nos. 6–7 (2006): 1–88.

Hemingway, C.A., and P.W. Maclagan. 'Managers' Personal Values as Drivers of Corporate Social Responsibility.' *Journal of Business Ethics* 50 (2004): 33–44.

Kallio, T.J. 'Taboos in Corporate Social Responsibility Discourse.' *Journal of Business Ethics* 74 (2007): 165–75.

Kearns, D. 'Quality Improvement Begins at the Top.' *World* 20, no. 5 (1986). Quoted in Maire 2002, 506.

Ketola, T. 'A Holistic Corporate Responsibility Model: Integrating Values, Discourses and Actions.' *Journal of Business Ethics* 80 (2007): 419–35.

Khosla, R., and P. Hunt. *Human Rights Guidelines for Pharmaceutical Companies in Relation to Access to Medicines: The Sexual and Reproductive Health Context.* Colchester, Essex: University of Essex, 2009.

Kolk, A., and R. van Tulder. *International Codes of Conduct: Trends, Sectors, Issues and Effectiveness.* Rotterdam: Erasmus University, 2002), 26. Quoted in Flanagan and Whiteman 2007, 66.

Lambell, R., G. Ramia, C. Nyland, and M. Michelotti. 'NGOs and International Business Research: Progress, Prospects and Problems.' *International Journal of Management Reviews* 10, no. 1 (2008): 75–92.

Leach, Beryl, Joan E. Paluzzi, Paula Munderi, UN Millennium Project. *Prescription for Healthy Development: Increasing Access to Medicines.* 2005.

Leisinger, K.M. 'Corporate Philanthropy: The "Top of the Pyramid."' *Business and Society Review* 112, no. 3 (2007): 315–42.

– 'Corporate Responsibilities for Access to Medicines.' *Journal of Business Ethics* 85 (2008): S1–S23. DOI: 10.1007/s10551-008-9944-4.

– 'The Corporate Social Responsibility of the Pharmaceutical Industry: Idealism without Illusion, and Realism without Resignation.' *Business Ethics Quarterly* 15, no. 4 (2005): 577–94.

Levy, D.L. 'Environmental Management as Political Sustainability.' *Organization and Environment* 10, no. 2 (1997): 126–47. Quoted in Kallio 2007, 170.

Maire, J. 'A Model of Characterization of the Performance for a Process of Benchmarking.' *Benchmarking* 9, no. 5 (2002): 506–20.

Maire, J., V. Bronet, and M. Pillet. 'A Typology of "Best Practices" for a Benchmarking Process.' *Benchmarking* 12, no. 1 (2005): 45–60.

Márquez, A., and C.J. Fombrun. 'Measuring Corporate Social Responsibility.' *Corporate Reputation Review* 7, no. 4 (2005): 304–8.

Maynard, M.L. 'Policing Transnational Commerce: Global Awareness in the Margins of Morality.' *Journal of Business Ethics* 30 (2001): 17–27.

McWilliams, A., and D. Siegel. 'Corporate Social Responsibility and Financial Performance: Correlation or Misspecification?' *Strategic Management Journal* 21 (2000): 603–9.

- 'Corporate Social Responsibility: A Theory of the Firm Perspective.'
  Academy of Management Review 26, no. 1 (2001): 117–27.
McWilliams, A., D.S. Siegel, and P.M. Wright. 'Guest Editors' Introduction –
  Corporate Social Responsibility: Strategic Implications.' *Journal of
  Management Studies* 43, no. 1 (2006): 1–18.
Menou, V., A. Hornstein, and E. Lipton-McCombie. *Access to Medicines Index:
  Ranking Access to Medicines Practices*. Haarlem, Netherlands: Access to
  Medicines Foundation, 2008.
Merck. 'Benchmarking AIDS: Evaluating Pharmaceutical Company Responses
  to the HIV-TB-Malaria Pandemics.' 2006. http://www.reports-and-materials
  .org/Merck-response-re-ICCR-Benchmarking-AIDS-11-Sep-2006.pdf.
- 'Response to "Investing for Life" Briefing Paper.' 2007. http://www.
  business-humanrights.org/Documents/Merck-response-to-Oxfam-11-
  Dec-2007.pdf.
Musungu, S.F. 'Benchmarking Progress in Tackling the Challenges of
  Intellectual Property, and Access to Medicines in Developing Countries.'
  Bulletin of the World Health Organization 84, no. 5 (2006): 366–70.
Oxfam. 'Investing for Life: Meeting Poor People's Needs for Access to
  Medicines through Responsible Business Practices.' 2007. http://www.
  oxfam.ca/news-and-publications/publications-and-reports/investing-
  for-life-meeting-poor-people2019s-needs-for-access-to-medicines-through.
Parker, M. 'Introduction: Ethics, Politics and Organizing.' *Organization* 10,
  no. 2 (2003): 187–203. Quoted in Kallio 2007, 171.
Pfizer. 'Benchmarking AIDS: Evaluating Pharmaceutical Responses to the Public
  Health Crisis in Emerging Market.' 2006. http://www.reports-and-materials.
  org/Pfizer-response-re-ICCR-Benchmarking-AIDS-12-Sep-2006.pdf.
- 'Pfizer Response to Oxfam's Report "Investing for Life."' 2008. http://
  www.reports-and-materials.org/Pfizer-response-Oxfam-15-Feb-2008.doc.
Pharmaceutical Shareowners Group. *The Public Health Crisis in Emerging
  Markets: An Institutional Investor Perspective on the Implications of the
  Pharmaceutical Industry*. London: Pharmaceutical Shareowners Group, 2004.
Porter, M.E., and M.R. Kramer. 'Strategy and Society: The Link between
  Competitive Advantage and Corporate Social Responsibility.' *Harvard
  Business Review* 84, no. 12 (2006): 78–92.
Renneboog, F., J. Ter Horst, and C. Zhang. 'Socially Responsible Investments:
  Institutional Aspects, Performance, and Investor Behavior.' *Journal of
  Banking & Finance* 32 (2008): 1723–42.
Resnik, D.B. 'Developing Drugs for the Developing World: An Economic,
  Legal, Moral, and Political Dilemma.' *Developing World Bioethics* 1, no. 1
  (2001): 11–32.

Rubin, N. 'The Challenge of Socially Responsible Investments.' *CPA Journal* 78, no. 7 (2008): 52–5.

Sahlin-Andersson, K. 'Corporate Social Responsibility: A Trend and a Movement, but of What and for What?' *Corporate Governance* 6, no. 5 (2006): 595–6.

Sanofi Aventis. 'Sanofi Aventis Statement on the Oxfam International's Response to the Pharmaceutical Industry's Reflections on Oxfam's Briefing Paper, "Investing for Life."' 2008. http://www.business-humanrights.org/Documents/Sanofi-Aventis-response-to-Oxfam-12-Feb-2008.pdf.

Social Investment Forum Foundation. *Investment Trends Report.* 2007. http://www.socialinvest.org/resources/pubs/documents/FINALExecSummary_2007_SIF_Trends_wlinks.pdf.

Starr, M.A. 'Socially Responsible Investment and Pro-Social Change.' *Journal of Economic Issues* 42, no. 1 (2008): 51–73.

Swajkowski, E. 'Accounting for Organizational Misconduct.' *Journal of Business Ethics* 11 (1992): 401–11. Quoted in Ketola 2007, 424.

Sweeney, L., and J. Coughlan. 'Do Different Industries Report Corporate Social Responsibility Differently? An Investigation through the Lens of Stakeholder Theory.' *Journal of Marketing Communications* 14, no. 2 (2008): 113–24.

United Nations. 'Human Rights Guidelines for Pharmaceutical Companies in Relation to Access to Medicines: Draft for Consultation.' Report of the UN Special Rapporteur on the Right to Health (19 Sept. 2007).

– 'Prescription for Healthy Development: Increasing Access to Medicines.' 2005. http://www.unmillenniumproject.org/documents/TF5-medicines-Complete.pdf.

– 'UN Independent Expert Launches Draft Human Rights Guidelines for Pharmaceutical Companies.' News release, 19 Sept. 2007. http://www.unhchr.ch/huricane/huricane.nsf/view01/497E81A16B31B9C8C125735B0059D7B0?opendocument.

Van Eeden, Dirk. 'Abbott Laboratories Response to Oxfam's Report "Investing for Life."' 2007. http://www.business-humanrights.org/Documents/Abbott-response-Oxfam-18-Dec-2007.doc.

Waddock, S., and S. Graves. 'The Corporate Social Performance: Financial Performance Link.' *Strategic Management Journal* 18, no. 4 (1997): 303–19.

World Bank. 'Involving Nongovernmental Organizations in World Bank–Supported Activities.' *World Bank Operational Manual*, operational directive 14.70, 28 Aug. 1989.

Zadek, S. 'The Path to Corporate Responsibility.' *Harvard Business Review* 82, no. 12 (2004): 125–32.

6 Social Responsibility and Marketing of Drugs in Developing Countries: A Goal or an Oxymoron?

JOEL LEXCHIN

Introduction

'I would just be talking rubbish if I were to say that the multinational companies were operating in the less developed countries primarily for the welfare of those countries ... They are not bishops, they are businessmen.'[1] This somewhat old, but still relevant quote from a representative of the British pharmaceutical industry accurately sets the stage for what will be covered in this chapter. Are the pharmaceutical companies able to achieve their economic objectives in developing countries through ethical marketing practices? The economic objectives of the industry are the same wherever it operates, but what is different about developing countries is that many of them lack a functioning drug regulatory system. According to the World Health Organization, one-third of its member states 'have no medicines regulatory authority, or at best very limited capacity for regulation of the pharmaceutical market.'[2] The absence of a regulatory oversight body means that the opportunity to exploit the market through unethical means is unlikely to be effectively controlled, contrary to the situation in developed countries.

The analysis in this chapter concentrates on the multinational pharmaceutical companies. Not only do they control the lion's share of the market but also, according to the international industry's representative body, the International Federation of Pharmaceutical Manufacturers & Associations (IFPMA), 'The fact that the pharmaceutical companies take the lead as innovative philanthropists and CSR-conscious enterprises may be regarded as a continuum of the important societal role they occupy.'[3]

In order to be able to examine the quality of marketing, it is necessary to have a definition of what constitutes ethical and unethical marketing practices. This chapter uses an operational definition consisting of two parts. First, are the medications that are made available in developing countries consistent with the health needs in those countries? That is, are they drugs of proven safety and effectiveness? Second, is the information provided with those medications accurate and objective such that it will allow practitioners to appropriately prescribe them.[4] Information is transmitted through promotion, in drug compendiums, and when doctors directly seek it from companies. The first two sections of this chapter will develop these issues of marketing and information provision. Then I will examine the attempts to regulate promotion. As the focus of this chapter is the practices of the pharmaceutical industry, I will look primarily at the effectiveness of the Code of Pharmaceutical Marketing Practices developed by the IFPMA.[5] The chapter will conclude by exploring new possibilities for helping to ensure ethical marketing behaviour.

Rationality of Medications Sold in Developing Countries

While most studies that have looked into the question of whether medications used in developing countries are rational are relatively old, they all tell a remarkably similar picture: a large number of products that are sold in developing countries are irrational, dangerous, or just useless. Health Action International (HAI), a coalition of 150 consumer, health, development action, and other public interest groups, analysed the availability of vitamin preparations in 1985 in Indonesia, India, the Middle East, Africa, and the Caribbean. Out of a total of 888 products, over 75 per cent were classified as 'not recommended' on the basis that they contained non-essential ingredients, they were irrational formulations, or they contained excessive dosages.[6] The marketing of cough/cold remedies was no better than that of vitamin preparations. HAI has also examined the contents of 2,198 of these products that were available in twelve Third World countries or regions during 1987–8. Over 50 per cent contained potentially harmful ingredients, and 86 per cent had ineffective ingredients.[7] A survey of 464 anti-diarrhoeal products in the same twelve countries and regions revealed that 224 (48.3 per cent) contained antimicrobial drugs.[8] According to the World Health Organization (WHO), antibiotics should be used only for dysentery and suspected cholera. In diarrhoea of any other etiology, antibiotics are of no practical value and should not be given.[9]

Drugs marketed in six major regions of the developing world, Mexico, Brazil, French- and English-speaking Africa, the Middle East, and India, by the twenty largest European pharmaceutical companies were categorized as essential or non-essential on the basis of the 1988 WHO Model List of Essential Drugs. Out of a total of 3,021 drugs, only 482 (16 per cent) were essential or equivalent to an essential drug. The proportion for each company ranged from a low of 5.4 per cent to a high of 39.0 per cent. Over 40 per cent of the 2,539 non-essential drugs were combinations of two or more active ingredients, as compared to only 9.5 per cent of the essential drugs.[10]

An ongoing series of surveys from the German development group BUKO-Pharma-Kampagne demonstrates that the practice of marketing poor-quality drugs in developing countries is continuing. German companies are the world's largest exporters of medications, and since the mid-1980s BUKO has been looking at the drugs that these companies export to developing countries. The most recent study was done in 2003 and covered over 2,500 drugs in forty-six countries.[11] Drugs were given a negative evaluation for a number of reasons: they were provided in irrational combinations, less risky alternatives were available, their efficacy was disputed or non-existent, more effective alternatives were available, or they were insufficiently tested, in the wrong form, and wrong dosage. All told, 39 per cent of the drugs were deemed irrational. While this figure represents an improvement since the initial survey of 1984–5, which found that 67 per cent of exports were irrational, the downward trend seems to have levelled off since 1997–8 when the number was 42 per cent. Moreover, there is a serious double standard applied to those drugs that these companies sell in Germany and those they export. Seventy-seven per cent of the irrational drugs exported are not available in Germany.

Finally, BUKO notes that there is often a significant time lapse between when drugs are removed from the market in Germany for safety reasons and when the same companies stop selling these drugs in developing countries. As one example, according to BUKO, 'Aventis ... kept offering its lipid-lowering drug Lesterol® in Brazil until May 2004 although the drug had been withdrawn from the market in Germany ever since 1998.'[12] As recently as 2005, ten of the top twenty-five selling brands of medicines in India were irrational, non-essential, or hazardous. These products were being sold by both domestic and multinational firms, but the latter group was responsible for seven out of the ten products.[13]

Information Provision about Medications in Developing Countries

It would be unfair to claim that all drugs sold in developing countries are irrational. Drug companies also market products of proven effectiveness in Third World countries, but, like any medicine, they are useful only if they are used appropriately – for the right conditions, at the right doses, for the right length of time, and for people without any known contraindications. A key element in being able to use drugs correctly is getting scientifically valid information about the drugs to the doctors who are going to be prescribing them. If doctors are given the wrong information about medicines, they will prescribe them inappropriately.

The 2002 report for the WHO on drug regulation commented that 'the budget for disseminating independent drug information is often very small compared with the budgets for drug advertising and promotion of the pharmaceutical industry. The amount, frequency and reach of independent information are therefore usually no match for the drugs advertising and promotion which the industry can afford.'[14] This observation is especially true in developing countries, where a lack of professional sources for continuing medical education (CME) means that doctors rely heavily on pharmaceutical companies for their prescribing information.

Two examples illustrating this observation come from major hospitals in Nigeria and Kenya. Almost 90 per cent of Nigerian doctors in a teaching hospital had attended drug promotion forums within a six-month period, and over two-thirds agreed that drug promotional material was an incentive to prescribe promoted drugs in preference to their alternatives.[15] The chief pharmacist at the Kenyatta National Hospital in Nairobi described how companies organize CME courses in his country: 'Sponsorship of CMEs at institutional/professional organizational level (they get a guest speaker, topic of their choice, pay for coffee/tea and snacks), this partnering with an institution/professional association endorses the company. Development of resource centres (rent for space, purchase of computers and necessary software, subscriptions for journals) for professional association – quite a noble idea, but …?'[16]

Promotion

Pharmaceutical promotion takes many forms, including visits from sales representatives, the provision of samples, gifts to doctors, support of continuing medical education, and advertising in medical journals.

Doctors in developing countries are not different from their colleagues in developed countries in that they frequently interact with drug companies through visits by sales representatives, receiving drug samples, gifts, meals, invitations to meetings, and financial sponsorship of CME events.[17] While doctors often recognize that the information that they receive from the pharmaceutical industry may be biased, only a relatively small minority believe that they are vulnerable to these biases, again mirroring the pattern seen in industrialized countries. Although half of Argentinian specialists believed that benefits from the pharmaceutical industry had an effect on prescribing, only 27 per cent thought that they would be personally affected.[18] When an Indian audience of medical students, practitioners, and health-care administrators was asked if going on a drug company–sponsored cruise would affect their prescriptions of the company's product, the overwhelming majority said no. When asked if a sponsored cruise influenced the prescription practices of at least one doctor they knew, an overwhelming majority said yes.[19]

A Nepalese medical student observed that 'medical conferences … are strongly dominated by the pharmaceutical industry. Often, companies organize parties for doctors in which a continuing medical education topic is followed by a lavish cocktail dinner – but often the educational part is absent … Pharmaceutical companies also sponsor the activities of medical students (such sponsoring can take the form of sports matches, publications, and parties).'[20] This type of activity is not unique to Nepal. Similar reports come from Argentina, India, Kashmir, Kenya, Malaysia, Pakistan, and Senegal.[21] A group of Pakistani researchers gathered promotional pamphlets and brochures that were distributed to 122 general practitioners by sales representatives and then analysed the claims in these advertisements.[22] There were 345 distinct advertisements for 182 drugs, and sixty-two (18 per cent) of the advertisements were judged misleading or unjustifiable because they were exaggerated, ambiguous, false, or controversial. Although the material came from both local and multinational companies, the authors made it clear that both groups were responsible for the misleading advertisements. Promotional brochures collected in Brazil were just as bad. None of 127 that were collected from private clinics and hospitals in southern Brazil complied with all of the criteria specified by Brazilian legislation; only 43 per cent provided information on precautions, and three-quarters of the time that this information was present it was printed in a type size that was difficult to read.[23] Thai researchers collected 207 ads to health professionals that appeared in three leading medical journals and two tabloid magazines in 2003. Only a quarter of the ads contained safety information, fewer than one in five had a balance of information about benefits and risks, and between 11 per cent and 25 per cent were judged misleading. In addition, some ads were not easy to read because the type was too small, the text was too crowded, or the same colour was used for both the background and the text.[24]

A comparative analysis was undertaken of advertisements for psychoactive drugs that appeared in psychiatry journals in Brazil, the United Kingdom, and the United States.[25] The Brazilian advertisements presented the least amount of information, especially in relation to safety, including contraindications, adverse reactions, interactions, and precautions. American advertisements presented five times as many examples of adverse reactions, compared to Brazilian advertisements. When such information was included at all, it was incomplete and in a print size that was smaller than for the items favouring the use of the drug. A second comparison study looked at medical journal ads in Australia, Malaysia, and the United States for the same drugs and showed that safety information (side effects, contraindications, warnings, interactions, and precautions) was mentioned significantly less often in the Malaysian ads.[26]

While these results are disturbing enough, it is sales representatives who have the greatest effect on the prescribing habits of doctors because of the one-on-one interaction that takes place. Eighty-four per cent of Tunisian general practitioners considered sales representatives an efficient source of information, and 31 per cent said they might change their therapeutic prescribing following visits from these reps.[27] Pakistani doctors saw an average of seven sales representatives per day and received from them a variety of personalized gifts and incentives such as air conditioners, cars, cash, home appliances, and domestic cattle.[28]

In a qualitative study of drug promotion in Mumbai, Indian doctors stated that they received information on new drugs primarily through visits by sales representatives. According to the doctors, representatives rarely mentioned drug interactions and adverse reactions, but they were otherwise generally satisfied with the information provided and accepted the representative's role. On the other hand, representatives said they received cursory training in drug information. The flip chart was their main presentation aid, which was not given to doctors, even if requested. Furthermore, the representatives noted that often there were inconsistencies between what they had been told to tell the doctor, what was written in the flip charts, and what was in the detailed literature. Many representatives also remarked that they were under pressure to meet sales targets, failing which they could be transferred to a remote area or even lose their jobs.[29]

Drug Compendiums

The systematic study of differences in the quality of information provided in developing countries compared to developed ones began in 1974 with a survey done by Milton Silverman.[30] Silverman looked at twenty-six different drugs, from seven major drug categories, marketed by twenty-three multinational corporations based in the United States and Europe, and compared the information on them in the U.S. *Physicians' Desk Reference* (*PDR*) to the information given in commercial drug compendiums in twelve Latin American countries. He found that in nearly all of the products investigated the differences in the promotional or labelling material were striking. In Latin America, the listed indications were far more numerous than in the United States, while the hazards were minimized, glossed over, or totally ignored. In some cases, only trivial side effects were described, but potentially lethal hazards were not mentioned. Furthermore, there were substantial differences within the Latin American countries. From country to country, the information given about individual drugs varied enormously. After that initial survey, Silverman and his colleagues did three additional ones, each one analysing more drugs in a larger number of countries. The final survey looked at forty different drugs marketed as 1,500 different products by more than four hundred companies in seventy-four developing countries.[31] This last one did find some grounds for optimism in that 'most of the multinational firms were more willing to restrict the claims of efficacy for their products to what can be substantiated by scientific evidence ... [and] to disclose the major hazards of their products.'[32]

Since Silverman and colleagues completed their work, there have been similar studies, all with roughly equivalent results – information in compendiums in developed countries is much more complete than that in compendiums in developing countries.[33]

The pharmaceutical industry has attempted to explain these differences as a function of the litigious nature of American society.[34] According to this line of reasoning, companies were forced to include copious amounts of basically irrelevant material in U.S. labelling in order to avoid being sued and to comply with the excessively legalistic nature of U.S. legislation. However, similar gaps in information have been documented when advertisements from other industrialized countries have been examined. A Dutch study released in 1994 found that out of 161 drugs that could be assessed, 42 per cent were considered problem drugs by the criteria of the report: more than 12 per cent omitted important contraindications, while almost 10 per cent left out warnings about serious interactions or side effects. The authors also noted that because smaller producers and wholesalers did not respond to their questionnaire, the problems they identified with regard to product information could be considerably underrated.[35]

The most recent study to evaluate drug information in commercial compendiums compared the listings for the forty-four best-selling drugs in the Brazilian *Dicionário de Especialidades Farmacêuticas* (DEF) with those in the *PDR*.[36] The authors used the WHO definition of information that is indispensable to prescribers and looked for the presence or absence of this information in the two different sources. In the *PDR* this information was absent about 11 per cent of the time but in the *DEF* information was missing almost two-thirds of the time.

Information Requested by Doctors

Research in Pakistan has looked at how responsive drug companies are to information requested by doctors.[37] Ninety letters were sent to twenty-three multinational companies whose promotional brochures promised to make full prescribing information available on request. Only twenty-four responses were received, taking on average thirty-four days. The additional information provided was evaluated against standards from the WHO, and very few of the responses fully met the criteria for optimal drug information.

Industry Codes of Pharmaceutical Marketing

Industry associations in some developing countries have their own domestic marketing codes. Researchers from Consumers International requested the Pharmaceutical Association of Malaysia (PhAMA) to provide them with information on complaints PhAMA received about its national marketing code of practice in 2006. 'PhAMA did not disclose which companies had been involved in the four complaints they received. The three companies against whom complaints were upheld, supposedly received fines commensurate to the severity of the violation. However the amount and type of violation were also not explained further, nor is this information made public by the organization.'[38]

The main code that governs activities in developing countries is the one introduced by the IFPMA in 1981. In that year the World Health Assembly adopted an International Code of Marketing of Breast-Milk Substitutes, and it appeared that a pharmaceutical code might follow. It was in light of these events that IFPMA introduced its Code of Pharmaceutical Marketing Practices to promote and support 'throughout the pharmaceutical industry ... ethical principles and practices.'[39] The IFPMA president, Joseph D. Williams, called the code 'the visible public declaration of the commitment of industry to ensuring that its products are marketed responsibly and on the basis of sound scientific information and principles.'[40] Harry Schwartz, an aggressive advocate of the industry, put another light on why the code was adopted. According to Schwartz, the code was an attempt to repel 'a coming WHO effort to impose unacceptable controls over all pharmaceutical commerce in the Third World.' For Schwartz, the question was whether the 'code will be adequate to defeat the forces against private enterprise within WHO.'[41]

Especially in resource-poor countries with weak regulatory systems, voluntary industry regulation seems an attractive option. It removes the need for governments to be concerned with industry activities and puts the economic burden on drug companies that are in a much better financial condition to assume that responsibility. The problem with the foregoing analysis is that industry will always be tempted to exploit the privilege of self-regulation by producing a socially sub-optimal level of compliance with regulatory goals. Experience has repeatedly shown this to be the case in the marketing of pharmaceutical products.[42]

Effective industry control over its own promotional practices in the form of voluntary self-regulation reflects a government–industry relationship termed 'clientele pluralism' in which the state actually relinquishes some of its authority to private sector actors – typically a trade association.[43] Although the state voluntarily gives up its power, in reality it actually has little choice because of the imbalance in resources between those of the state and of the private sector.

As Lexchin and Kawachi argue,[44] in these circumstances few trade associations vested with the authority to regulate drug promotion have made systematic efforts to either monitor the advertising practices of their members or to enforce compliance. The problem is that governments and pharmaceutical manufacturers' associations have different missions and goals. The mission of government is to protect public health by encouraging rational prescribing. The mission of trade associations is primarily to increase sales and profit. From the business perspective, self-regulation is concerned mostly with the control of anti-competitive practices. Therefore, when industrial associations draw up their codes of practice, they deliberately make them vague or do not cover certain features of promotion, to allow companies wide latitude. Self-regulation works well when anti-competitive promotional practices happen to coincide perfectly with government regulators' notions of misleading advertising. Most often, however, the fit is far from perfect, because far from being anti-competitive, many misleading advertising tactics are good for business. From the public health perspective, the results of voluntary self-regulation are sub-optimal.

Analyses of the initial versions of the IFPMA voluntary code showed that in practice it was largely ineffective.[45] Early on, it was criticized for systemic weaknesses, including by parts of industry itself. The Swedish Manufacturers Association, represented in IFPMA, found that 'the code is unclear, unstructured and does not go far enough.'[46]

A major shortcoming in the code is the lack of effective sanctions. IFPMA offers 'adverse publicity' as the major sanction in assuring compliance with the code, but the only concrete action that is taken is the publication of the name of the offending company and key facts about the decision on the IFPMA website. Furthermore, the entire complaints process is presided over by industry officials, with no outside presence.

The latest version of the IFPMA code came into force on 1 January 2007. This version retains adverse publicity as the only sanction and still keeps the monitoring and enforcement of the code entirely within industry. There are also clauses present that might allow companies to present exaggerated benefits or downplay safety. Clause 4.1 states, 'It is understood that national laws and regulations usually dictate the format and content of the product information communicated on labelling, packaging, leaflets, data sheets and in all promotional material. Promotion should not be inconsistent with locally approved product information.'[47] In practice, this could very well mean that if weak national regulatory systems allow claims based on dubious science or do not require detailed safety information, then companies are under no obligation as far as the code is concerned to provide this level of detail. The new version of the code also completely eliminates any mention of the activities of sales representatives, thereby providing no mechanism to monitor and regulate the activities of this group with the results seen earlier.

Conclusion

The pharmaceutical industry is not monolithic, and undoubtedly some companies are more responsible than others, but the evidence, albeit some of it old, shows that on the whole companies do not engage in socially responsible marketing in developing countries. Many of the products that they sell in these countries are irrational and would not be allowed in developed countries. They practise double standards in the information that they provide to doctors in developing and developed countries, their advertisements leave out crucial information, they respond poorly to physicians' request for further information, and the mechanisms that they have set up to monitor their promotion are weak and ineffective.

Is this conclusion surprising? In one sense it is. The share of pharmaceutical consumption by low- and middle-income countries, representing 85 per cent of the world's population, is under 9 per cent of the world market or just over US$31 billion in 2000.[48] In comparison, in that same year Canada's consumption for a population of just over thirty million was worth one-third that value.[49] There is not a great deal of money to be made in developing countries, whether or not the companies behave in a socially responsible manner. On the other hand, companies are ultimately accountable only to their shareholders and not to society at large. By law, corporations have a 'duty to put shareholders' interests above all others and no legal authority to serve any other interests.'[50] According to this point of view, corporations are neither moral nor immoral; they need to obey the law, but beyond that their obligation is to be as profitable as possible; corporate social responsibility or anything that reduces profitability in the long term is illegal.

The other point of view is expressed in the literature on corporate social responsibility (CSR). Although there are a variety of definitions of the term, according to Blowfield and Frynas CSR can be thought of 'as an umbrella term for a variety of theories and practices all of which recognize the following: (a) that companies have a responsibility for their impact on society and the natural environment, sometimes beyond legal compliance and the liability of individuals; (b) that companies have a responsibility for the behaviour of others with whom they do business (e.g., within supply chains); and (c) that business needs to manage its relationship with wider society, whether for reasons of commercial viability or to add value to society.'[51] However, the CSR literature as it pertains to the pharmaceutical industry has focused largely on access and price.[52] There is little evidence that the companies or the organizations representing them, such as the IFPMA, have embraced CSR when it comes to either the rationality of medicines that they supply to developing countries or in the way that they promote their products.

Since 1977, the WHO has been producing its model essential medicines list (EML), defined as those medicines that 'satisfy the priority health care needs of the population … [and] are selected with due regard to public health relevance, evidence on efficacy and safety, and comparative cost-effectiveness.'[53] The EML clearly represents a statement that irrational medicines have no place in the markets of developing countries' markets. From the beginning, the pharmaceutical industry has consistently opposed the concept of an EML. In 1987, the IFPMA claimed that the medical and economic arguments for an EML were fallacious and that adopting it 'could result in sub-optimal medical care and might reduce health standards.' Although the industry now accepts the EML for the public sector in developing countries, it remains opposed to implementing it in their private sectors.[54]

The IFPMA maintains that 'the industry has an obligation and responsibility to provide accurate information about its products to health care providers … Promotional activities (marketing practices) must be consistent with high ethical standards and … [t]he same high standards of ethical behaviour should apply to the marketing of pharmaceutical products in all countries, regardless of the level of development of their economic and health care systems.'[55] Within the European Union (EU), according to Consumers International (CI), companies 'have embraced the concept of corporate social responsibility … as an appropriate response to the mounting pressures to live up to their social and ethical responsibilities. Many companies proudly flaunt their CSR objectives in their annual reports, on their websites and their public relations activities.'[56]

An investigation by CI of the actual promotional practices by twenty large multinationals operating in the EU found that CSR was honoured more in the breach than in the practice. Out of twenty large multinational pharmaceutical companies operating in the EU, only two – GlaxoSmithKline and Novartis – report the number of confirmed marketing code breaches and resulting sanctions. CI could not find any information about the European marketing policies for eight companies. According to CI, 'The absence of clear marketing policies for these companies is remarkable, given that irresponsible marketing practices form a serious, persistent and widespread problem among the entire pharmaceutical industry ... A particularly worrying trend shown by our research is that the difference between policies and practices is often striking.'[57]

If CSR in promotion is absent in the EU, how likely is it to be found in developing countries? The answer is in the many examples of un-ethical promotion cited earlier in this chapter.

While drug companies are not morally obliged to behave ethically, the state and organizations like the WHO that act on behalf of states collectively do have an obligation to ensure ethical behaviour in marketing drugs. There is virtual universal recognition that drugs are not like other consumer items. Modern pharmaceuticals are essential for health needs; much of the basic research into drug discovery is paid for by public institutions; drugs have to undergo elaborate testing before they are allowed on the market; companies are protected against competition for up to twenty years in developed countries in order to encourage them to continue to invest in developing new medications; there are strict rules about who can prescribe and dispense medications; and in most developed countries drugs are considered so essential that the public sector covers 60 per cent or more of their cost.

Any impetus for change will have to come from developing countries themselves. There are examples of where countries have taken the initiative. After FRELIMO took power in Mozambique in 1975, import licenses were withdrawn for all pharmaceutical products lacking proven therapeutic value, for those representing the worst examples of poly-pharmacy, and for those with an unreasonably high profit margin. The immediate result of this move was to reduce the number of different branded products on the market from 13,000 to 2,600.[58] A similar policy in Bangladesh led to the removal of about 1,700 drugs on the grounds that they were either harmful, irrational combinations or were useless or unnecessary.[59]

Finding the political will to pass laws or develop policies is only the first, and probably easiest, step. The difficult part is in enforcing them. Even where countries want to enforce them, the resources, both human and monetary, do not exist. Least-developed countries such as Vietnam suffer from an impaired quality-control system and do not have the capacity to perform quality control for all drugs on the market. Violations of regulations are common and enforcement is weak.[60] Even middle-income countries experience resource constraints. India should have over 2,900 drug inspectors against the existing 700.[61] The lack of personnel is one reason that India's pharmaco-surveillance system is 'grossly inadequate,' along with the fact that companies can routinely violate Indian laws on reporting of adverse drug reactions without fear of being penalized. According to Dr C.J. Shishoo, of the Ahmedabad-based Consumer Education and Research Centre, in 2007 there were at least half a dozen drugs with dubious safety profiles still being marketed in India because adverse drug reactions had not been reported to the Indian authorities.[62] Similarly in Egypt, the lack of reporting of dangerous adverse drug reactions means that drugs withdrawn in other countries because they are dangerous are still available for sale.[63]

Even were developing countries to try to enforce strong regulatory measures, policies are often difficult to maintain in the face of extreme pressure from the pharmaceutical industry and some Western governments.[64] The cases of South Africa where thirty-nine companies took the government to court over changes in the *Medicines Act* to allow for compulsory licensing, and Brazil where the United States filed a complaint at the World Trade Organization over Brazil's aggressive use of generics to provide free care for its citizens with HIV/AIDS are well known. In the past, NGOs seeking to rationalize drug use in developing countries have been labelled communist sympathizers.[65]

Developing countries will need international allies to help them control marketing. NGOs such as Oxfam, HAI, and Médecins sans frontières are natural allies in this movement, but the challenge cannot be carried forward by private groups, however well intentioned. Control over the marketing of medicines is a public health issue, and the onus to ensure responsible marketing must ultimately rest with public institutions.

The logical place to begin to look for help in providing governments with advice, resources, and technical support is the WHO, which is an intergovernmental organization charged with the mission to ensure public health. The WHO has already developed the *Ethical Criteria for Medicinal Drug Promotion*,[66] although these guidelines are largely ignored, even by the WHO itself. The WHO has developed a Medicines Strategy running over the period 2004 to 2007 based on four key policy objectives: strengthening national medicines policy, improving access to essential medicines, improving the quality and safety of medicines, and promoting their rational use.[67]

The 2006 World Health Assembly meeting – the meeting that brings together delegates of all member states in the WHO – saw the initiation of debate on a renewed rational use of medicine (RUM) strategy that came forward again at the 2007 meeting. The final resolution, passed in

May 2007, calls on member states to 'enact new, or enforce existing, legislation to ban inaccurate, misleading or unethical promotion of medicines' and 'to invest sufficiently in human resources and provide adequate financing in order to ensure more appropriate use of medicines in both the public and the private sector.'[68] The original draft of the resolution urged the director-general of the WHO to 'establish mandated multi-disciplinary national bodies to monitor medicine use and to develop national programs to promote the rational use of medicines.' HAI pointed out that this clause was consistent with one of the main objectives of the resolution, that is, to provide the WHO with a new mandate to provide effective technical support to member states to implement national coordinated programs to promote RUM.[69] However, as a result of political lobbying, that clause was removed, thereby weakening the health systems approach to promoting rational use of medicines.

NOTES

1 Diana Melrose, *Bitter Pills: Medicines and the Third World Poor* (Oxford: Oxfam, 1982).
2 World Health Organization, *The World Medicines Situation* (Geneva: WHO, 2004).
3 International Federation of Pharmaceutical Manufacturers & Associations, *Corporate Social Responsibility* (Zurich: IFPMA, 2007).
4 In many developing countries, the majority of medications are not purchased by presenting a prescription from a doctor to a pharmacist but are instead bought from a 'drug pedlar,' who is often untrained. Obviously, in this situation the prospect of appropriate use of medication is highly problematic. While an extremely important topic, the use of prescription medications without the mediation by doctors and pharmacists is outside the remit of this chapter.
5 International Federation of Pharmaceutical Manufacturers & Associations, *IFPMA Code of Pharmaceutical Marketing Practices, 2006 Revision* (Zurich: IFPMA, 2007). http://www.ifpma.org/fileadmin/content/Ethics/ IFPMA_Marketing_Code/About_IFPMA_Marketing_Code/ IFPMA_Code_2006_Revision_EN.pdf.
6 Andrew Chetley and David Gilbert, *Problem Drugs* (The Hague: HAI, 1986).
7 Andrew Chetley, *Peddling Placebos: An Analysis of Cough and Cold Remedies* (Amsterdam: HAI, 1989).
8 Ibid.

9   World Health Organization, *The Rational Use of Drugs in the Management of Acute Diarrhoea in Children* (Geneva: WHO, 1990).

10 Robert Hartog, 'Essential and Non-Essential Drugs Marketed by the 20 Largest European Pharmaceutical Companies in Developing Countries,' *Social Science and Medicine* 37 (1993): 897–904.

11 Jörg Schaaber, Karsten Velbinger, Claudia Jenkes, Christian Wagner, and Eva Zettler, *Data and Facts 2004: German Drugs in the Third World* (Bielefeld: BUKO Pharma-Kampagne, 2004).

12 Ibid.

13 Consumers International, *Drugs, Doctors and Dinners: How Drug Companies Influence Health in the Developing World* (London: Consumers International, 2007).

14 Sauwakon Ratanawijitrasin and Eshetu Wondermagegnehu, *Effective Drug Regulation: A Multicountry Study* (Geneva: World Health Organization, 2002), 100.

15 T.M. Akande and S.A. Aderibigbe, 'Influence of Drug Promotion on Prescribing Habits of Doctors in a Teaching Hospital,' *African Journal of Medicine and Medical Science* 36 (2007): 207–11.

16 Consumers International, *Drugs, Doctors and Dinners*, 20.

17 A. Ben Abdelaziz, I. Harrabi, S. Rahmani, A. Ghedira, K. Gaha, and H. Ghannem, 'Attitudes of General Practitioners to Pharmaceutical Sales Representatives in Sousse [Arabic],' *East Mediterranean Health Journal* 9 (2006): 1075–83; Leonardo Castresana, Raúl Mejia, and Mireya Aznar, 'The Attitude of Physicians regarding the Promotion Strategies of the Pharmaceutical Industry,' *Medicina* 65 (2005): 247–51; Robert A. Rubinstein, '"Breaking the Bureaucracy": Drug Registration and Neocolonial Relations in Egypt,' *Social Science and Medicine* 46 (1998): 1487–94.

18 Castresana, Mejia, and Aznar, 'The Attitude of Physicians.'

19 Nobhojit Roy, 'Who Rules the Great Indian Drug Bazaar?' *Indian Journal of Medical Ethics* 12, no. 1 (2004). http://www.issuesinmedicalethics. org/121ed002.html.

20 Bishnu Rath Giri and P. Ravi Shankar, 'Learning How Drug Companies Promote Medicines in Nepal,' *PLoS Medicine* 2 (2005): e256.

21 Castresana, Mejia, and Aznar, 'Attitude of Physicians'; Nazia Akhtar, 'MRs Pay, Doctors Prescribe,' 20 July 2007, http://www.greaterkashmir.com/ news/2007/Jul/20/-mrs-pay-doctors-prescribe--17.asp; Consumers International, 'Drugs, Doctors and Dinners'; Nobhojit Roy, Neha Madhiwalla, and Sanjay A. Pai, 'Drug Promotional Practices in Mumbai: A Qualitative Study,' *Indian Journal of Medical Ethics* 15, no. 2 (2007): 57–61.

22 Dileep Kumar Rohra, Anwarul Hassan Gilani, Ismali Kamal Memon, Ghazala Perven, Muhammad Talha Khan, Hina Zafar, and Rakesh Kumar, 'Critical Evaluation of the Claims Made by Pharmaceutical Companies in Drug Promotional Material in Pakistan,' *Journal of Pharmacy and Pharmaceutical Sciences* 9 (2006): 50–9.

23 Felipe Dal Pizzol, Tatiane da Silva, and Eloir Paulo Schenkel, 'Adequacy of Drug Advertisements Distributed to Prescribers in Southern Brazil,' *Cadernos de Saúde Pública* 14 (1998): 85–91.

24 N. Kiatying-Angsulee, S. Chaisumritchoke, K. Chantapasa, and Y. Amrumpai, 'Developing Tools for Monitoring and Evaluating Unethical Drug Promotion in Thailand,' in Second International Conference on Improving Use of Medicines. Chang Mai, Thailand, 30 Mar.–2 Apr. 2004.

25 Patricia de Carvalho Mastroianni, José Carlos Fernandes Galduróz, and Elisaldo Araujo Carlini, 'Psychoactive Drug Advertising: A Comparison of Technical Information from Three Countries: Brazil, United States and United Kingdom,' *Sao Paulo Medical Journal* 123 (2005): 209–14.

26 N. Othman, A. Vitry, and E.E. Roughead, 'Medicines Information in Medical Journal Advertising in Australia, Malaysia and the United States: A Comparative Cross-sectional Study,' *Southern Medical Review* 3 (2010): 11–18.

27 Abdelaziz et al., 'Attitudes of General Practitioners.'

28 Consumers International, *Drugs, Doctors and Dinners.*

29 Roy, Madhiwalla, and Pai, 'Drug Promotional Practices.'

30 Milton Silverman, *The Drugging of the Americas* (Berkeley: University of California Press, 1976).

31 Milton Silverman, Mia Lydecker, and Philip R. Lee, *Bad Medicine: The Prescription Drug Industry in the Third World* (Stanford: Stanford University Press, 1992).

32 Ibid., 42.

33 R.K. Dikshit and N. Dikshit, 'Commercial Source of Drug Information: Comparison between the United Kingdom and India,' *BMJ* 309 (1994): 990–1.

34 G.J. Mossinghoff, 'Drug Labeling in Developing Countries,' *Lancet* 342 (1993): 556–7.

35 P.J.M. van Maaren, J.W.F. van Mil, A.P. Hardon, F.M. Haaijer-Ruskamp, and M.N.G. Dukes, *Dutch Medicines in Developing Countries: A Pharmacological Evaluation* (Groningen: WHO Collaborating Centre for Clinical Pharmacology and Drug Policy Science, 1994).

36 José Augusto Cabral de Barros, 'One More Case of the Double Standard: Discrepancies between Drug Information Provided to Brazilian and American Physicians,' *Pharmacoepidemiology and Drug Safety* 9 (2000): 281–7.

37 Assad Hafeez and Zafar Mirza, 'Responses from Pharmaceutical Companies to Doctors' Requests for More Information in Pakistan: Postal Survey,' *BMJ* 319 (1999): 547.

38 Consumers International, *Drugs, Doctors and Dinners*, 8.

39 International Federation of Pharmaceutical Manufacturers and Associations, *IFPMA Code of Pharmaceutical Marketing Practices* (Zurich: IFPMA, 1982).

40 'The International Industry Discusses Marketing Standards,' *Health Horizons*, May 1988, 18.

41 Health Action International, *Promoting Health or Promoting Drugs? A HAI Presentation on Rational Drug Use* (The Hague: HAI, 1987).

42 Ichiro Kawachi, 'Six Case Studies of the Voluntary Regulation of Pharmaceutical Advertising and Promotion,' in *For Health or Profit?* ed. Peter Davis, 269–87 (Auckland: Oxford University Press, 1992).

43 M.H. Atkinson and W.D. Coleman, *The State, Business, and Industrial Change in Canada* (Toronto: University of Toronto Press, 1989).

44 Joel Lexchin and Ichiro Kawachi, 'Voluntary Codes of Pharmaceutical Marketing: Controlling Promotion or Licensing Deception?' in *Contested Ground: Public Purpose and Private Interest in the Regulation of Prescription Drugs*, ed. Peter Davis, 221–35 (New York: Oxford University Press, 1996).

45 Peter Mansfield, 'Organon, the IFPMA Code and the WHO Ethical Criteria,' *MaLAM Newsletter*, Dec. 1992, 1.

46 United Nations Centre on Transnational Corporations, *Transnational Corporations in the Pharmaceutical Industry of Developing Countries* (New York: United Nations, 1984).

47 International Federation of Pharmaceutical Manufacturers & Associations, *IFPMA Code of Pharmaceutical Marketing Practices, 2006 Revision* (Zurich: IFPMA 2006).

48 World Health Organization, *World Medicines Situation*.

49 Canadian Institute for Health Information, *Drug Expenditure in Canada 1985 to 2005* (Ottawa: CIHI, 2006).

50 Joel Bakan, *The Corporation: The Pathological Pursuit of Profit and Power* (Toronto: Viking, 2004).

51 Michael Blowfield and Jedrzej George Frynas, 'Setting New Agendas: Critical Perspectives on Corporate Social Responsibility in the Developing World,' *International Affairs* 81 (2005): 499–513.

52 Daniel Callahan and Angela A. Wasunna, *Medicine and the Market: Equity v. Choice* (Baltimore: Johns Hopkins University Press, 2006); Michael A. Santoro, 'Human Rights and Human Needs: Diverse Moral Principles Justifying Third World Access to Affordable HIV/AIDS Drugs,' *North Carolina Journal of International Law* 31 (2006): 923–42; Patricia H. Werhane

and Michael E. Gorman, 'Intellectual Property Rights: Access to Life-Enhancing Drugs, and Corporate Moral Responsibilities,' in *Ethics and the Pharmaceutical Industry: Business, Government, Professional, and Advocacy Perspectives*, ed. Michael A. Santoro and Thomas M. Gorrie, 260–81 (West Nyack, NY: Cambridge University Press, 2005).

53 Richard Laing, Brenda Waning, Andy Gray, Nathan Ford, and Ellen 't Hoen, '25 Years of the WHO Essential Medicines Lists: Progress and Challenges,' *Lancet* 361 (2003): 1723–9.

54 Ibid.

55 International Federation of Pharmaceutical Manufacturers & Associations, *Ethical Promotion and Self Regulation* (Zurich, IFPMA, 2009).

56 Consumers International, *Branding the Cure: A Consumer Perspective on Corporate Social Responsibility, Drug Promotion and the Pharmaceutical Industry in Europe* (London: Consumers International, 2006).

57 Ibid.

58 C. Barker, 'The Mozambique Pharmaceutical Policy,' *Lancet* 2, no. 8353 (1983): 780–2.

59 D. Tiranti, *The Bangladesh Example: Four Years On* (Oxford: IOCU / New Internationalist War on Want, 1986).

60 T. Falkenberg, T.B. Nguyen, M. Larsson, T.D. Nguyen, and G. Tomson, 'Pharmaceutical Sector in Translation: A Cross Sectional Study in Vietnam,' *Southeast Asian Journal of Tropical Medicine and Public Health* 31 (2000): 590–97.

61 'Drug Inspector,' *Tribune*, 27 June 2008, http://www.tribuneindia.com/2003/20030627/career.htm.

62 C.H. Unnikrishnan, 'Drug Regulator to Monitor Side Effects,' 26 Aug. 2007. http://www.livemint.com/2007/08/27004814/Drug-regulator-to-monitor-side.html.

63 Rubinstein, '"Breaking the Bureaucracy."'

64 Andrew Chetley, *A Healthy Business? World Health and the Pharmaceutical Industry* (London: Zed Books, 1990).

65 Ibid.

66 World Health Organization, *Ethical Criteria for Medicinal Drug Promotion* (Geneva: WHO, 1988).

67 World Health Organization, *WHO Medicines Strategy: Countries at the Core, 2004–2007* (Geneva: WHO, 2004).

68 Sixtieth World Health Assembly, 'Progress in the Rational Use of Medicines,' World Health Organization, 2007, http://www.who.int/gb/ebwha/pdf_files/WHA60/A60_R16-en.pdf.

69 Health Action International, 'Rational Use,' 2006, http://www.haiweb.org/03_other.htm.

REFERENCES

Abdelaziz, A. Ben, I. Harrabi, S. Rahmani, A. Ghedira, K. Gaha, and H.
  Ghannem. 'Attitudes of General Practitioners to Pharmaceutical Sales
  Representatives in Sousse [Arabic].' *East Mediterranean Health Journal* 9
  (2006): 1075–83.
Akande, T.M., and S.A. Aderibigbe. 'Influence of Drug Promotion on
  Prescribing Habits of Doctors in a Teaching Hospital.' *African Journal of
  Medicine and Medical Science* 36 (2007): 207–11.
Akhtar, Nazia. 'MRs Pay, Doctors Prescribe.' 20 July 2007. http://www.
  greaterkashmir.com/news/2007/Jul/20/-mrs-pay-doctors-prescribe--17.asp.
Atkinson, M.H., and W.D. Coleman. *The State, Business, and Industrial Change
  in Canada*. Toronto: University of Toronto Press, 1989.
Bakan, Joel. *The Corporation: The Pathological Pursuit of Profit and Power*.
  Toronto: Viking, 2004.
Barker, C. 'The Mozambique Pharmaceutical Policy.' *Lancet* 2, no. 8353 (1983):
  780–2.
Blowfield, Michael, and Jedrzej George Frynas. 'Setting New Agendas: Critical
  Perspectives on Corporate Social Responsibility in the Developing World.'
  International Affairs 81 (2005): 499–513.
Cabral de Barros, José Augusto. 'One More Case of the Double Standard:
  Discrepancies between Drug Information Provided to Brazilian and
  American Physicians.' *Pharmacoepidemiology and Drug Safety* 9 (2000): 281–7.
Callahan, Daniel, and Angela A. Wasunna. *Medicine and the Market: Equity v.
  Choice*. Baltimore: Johns Hopkins University Press, 2006.
Canadian Institute for Health Information. *Drug Expenditure in Canada 1985 to
  2005*. Ottawa: CIHI, 2006.
Castresana, Leonardo, Raúl Mejia, and Mireya Aznar. 'The Attitude of
  Physicians regarding the Promotion Strategies of the Pharmaceutical
  Industry.' *Medicina* 65 (2005): 247–51.
Chetley, Andrew. *A Healthy Business? World Health and the Pharmaceutical
  Industry*. London: Zed Books, 1990.
– *Peddling Placebos: An Analysis of Cough and Cold Remedies*. Amsterdam: HAI,
  1989.
Chetley, Andrew, and David Gilbert. *Problem Drugs*. The Hague: HAI, 1986.
Consumers International. *Branding the Cure: A Consumer Perspective on
  Corporate Social Responsibility, Drug Promotion and the Pharmaceutical Industry
  in Europe*. London: Consumers International, 2006.
– *Drugs, Doctors and Dinners: How Drug Companies Influence Health in the
  Developing World*. London: Consumers International, 2007.

Dikshit, R.K., and N. Dikshit. 'Commercial Source of Drug Information: Comparison between the United Kingdom and India.' *BMJ* 309 (1994): 990–1.

'Drug Inspector.' *Tribune*, 27 June 2008. http://www.tribuneindia. com/2003/20030627/career.htm.

Falkenberg, T., T.B. Nguyen, M. Larsson, T.D. Nguyen, and G. Tomson. 'Pharmaceutical Sector in Translation: A Cross Sectional Study in Vietnam.' *Southeast Asian Journal of Tropical Medicine and Public Health* 31 (2000): 590–7.

Giri, Bishnu Rath, and P. Ravi Shankar. 'Learning How Drug Companies Promote Medicines in Nepal.' *PLoS Medicine* 2 (2005): e256.

Hafeez, Assad, and Zafar Mirza. 'Responses from Pharmaceutical Companies to Doctors' Requests for More Information in Pakistan: Postal Survey.' *BMJ* 319 (1999): 547.

Hartog, Robert. 1993. 'Essential and Non-Essential Drugs Marketed by the 20 Largest European Pharmaceutical Companies in Developing Countries.' *Social Science and Medicine* 37 (1993): 897–904.

Health Action International. *Promoting Health or Promoting Drugs? A HAI Presentation on Rational Drug Use*. The Hague: HAI, 1987.

– 'Rational Use.' 2007. http://www.haiweb.org/03_other.htm.

International Federation of Pharmaceutical Manufacturers & Associations. *Corporate Social Responsibility*. Zurich: IFPMA, 2007.

– *Ethical Promotion and Self Regulation*. Zurich, IFPMA, 2009.

– *IFPMA Code of Pharmaceutical Marketing Practices*. Zurich: IFPMA, 1982.

– *IFPMA Code of Pharmaceutical Marketing Practices, 2006 Revision*. Zurich: IFPMA, 2006.

'The International Industry Discusses Marketing Standards.' *Health Horizons*, May 1988, 18–19.

Kawachi, Ichiro. 'Six Case Studies of the Voluntary Regulation of Pharmaceutical Advertising and Promotion.' In *For Health or Profit?* edited by P. Davis, 269–87. Auckland: Oxford University Press, 1992.

Kiatying-Angsulee, N., S. Chaisumritchoke, K. Chantapasa, and Y. Amrumpai. 'Developing Tools for Monitoring and Evaluating Unethical Drug Promotion in Thailand.' In Second International Conference on Improving Use of Medicines, Chang Mai, Thailand, 30 Mar.–2 Apr. 2004.

Laing, Richard, Brenda Waning, Andy Gray, Nathan Ford, and Ellen 't Hoen. '25 Years of the WHO Essential Medicines Lists: Progress and Challenges.' *Lancet* 361 (2003): 1723–9.

Lexchin, Joel, and Ichiro Kawachi. 'Voluntary Codes of Pharmaceutical Marketing: Controlling Promotion or Licensing Deception?' In *Contested Ground: Public Purpose and Private Interest in the Regulation of Prescription Drugs*, edited by P. Davis, 221–35. New York: Oxford University Press, 1996.

Mansfield, Peter, 'Organon, the IFPMA Code and the WHO Ethical Criteria.' *MaLAM Newsletter*, December 1992, 1.

Mastroianni, Patricia de Carvalho, José Carlos Fernandes Galduróz, and Elisaldo Araujo Carlini. 'Psychoactive Drug Advertising: A Comparison of Technical Information from Three Countries: Brazil, United States and United Kingdom.' *Sao Paulo Medical Journal* 123 (2005): 209–14.

Melrose, Diana. *Bitter Pills: Medicines and the Third World Poor*. Oxford: Oxfam, 1982.

Mossinghoff, G.J. 'Drug Labelling in Developing Countries.' *Lancet* 342 (1993): 556–7.

Othman, N., A. Vitry, and E.E. Roughead, 'Medicines Information in Medical Journal Advertising in Australia, Malaysia and the United States: A Comparative Cross-sectional Study.' *Southern Medical Review* 3 (2010): 11–18.

Pizzol, Felipe Dal, Tatiane da Silva, and Eloir Paulo Schenkel. 'Adequacy of Drug Advertisements Distributed to Prescribers in Southern Brazil.' *Cadernos de Saúde Pública* 14 (1998): 85–91.

Ratanawijitrasin, Sauwakon, and Eshetu Wondermagegnehu. *Effective Drug Regulation: A Multicountry Study*. Geneva: World Health Organization, 2002.

Rohra, Dileep Kumar, Anwarul Hassan Gilani, Ismali Kamal Memon, Ghazala Perven, Muhammad Talha Khan, Hina Zafar, and Rakesh Kumar. 'Critical Evaluation of the Claims Made by Pharmaceutical Companies in Drug Promotional Material in Pakistan.' *Journal of Pharmacy and Pharmaceutical Sciences* 9 (2006): 50–9.

Roy, Nobhojit. 'Who Rules the Great Indian Drug Bazaar?' *Indian Journal of Medical Ethics* 12, no. 1 (2004). http://www.issuesinmedicalethics.org/121ed002.html.

Roy, Nobhojit, Neha Madhiwalla, and Sanjay A. Pai. 'Drug Promotional Practices in Mumbai: A Qualitative Study.' *Indian Journal of Medical Ethics* 4, no. 2 (2007). http://www.ijme.in/152oa57.html.

Rubinstein, Robert A. '"Breaking the Bureaucracy": Drug Registration and Neocolonial Relations in Egypt.' *Social Science and Medicine* 46 (1998): 1487–94.

Santoro, Michael A. 'Human Rights and Human Needs: Diverse Moral Principles Justifying Third World Access to Affordable HIV/AIDS Drugs.' *North Carolina Journal of International Law* 31 (2006): 923–42.

Schaaber, Jörg, Karsten Velbinger, Claudia Jenkes, Christian Wagner, and Eva Zettler. *Data and Facts 2004: German Drugs in the Third World*. Bielefeld: BUKO Pharma-Kampagne, 2004.

Silverman, Milton. *The Drugging of the Americas*. Berkeley: University of California Press, 1976.

Silverman, Milton, Mia Lydecker, and Philip R. Lee. *Bad Medicine: The Prescription Drug Industry in the Third World*. Stanford: Stanford University Press, 1992.
Sixtieth World Health Assembly. 'Progress in the Rational Use of Medicines.' World Health Organization, 2007. http://www.who.int/gb/ebwha/pdf_files/WHA60/A60_R16-en.pdf.
Tiranti, D. *The Bangladesh Example: Four Years On*. Oxford: IOCU / New Internationalist / War on Want, 1986.
United Nations Centre on Transnational Corporations. *Transnational Corporations in the Pharmaceutical Industry of Developing Countries*. New York: United Nations, 1984.
Unnikrishnan, C.H. 2008. 'Drug Regulator to Monitor Side Effects.' 2007. http://www.livemint.com/Articles/PrintArticle.aspx.
Van Maaren, P.J.M., J.W.F. van Mil, A.P. Hardon, F.M. Haaijer-Ruskamp, and M.N.G. Dukes. *Dutch Medicines in Developing Countries: A Pharmacological Evaluation*. Groningen: WHO Collaborating Centre for Clinical Pharmacology and Drug Policy Science, 1994.
Werhane, Patricia H., and Michael E. Gorman. 'Intellectual Property Rights: Access to Life-Enhancing Drugs, and Corporate Moral Responsibilities.' In *Ethics and the Pharmaceutical Industry: Business, Government, Professional, and Advocacy Perspectives*, edited by Michael A. Santoro and Thomas M. Gorrie, 260–81. West Nyack, NY: Cambridge University Press, 2005.
World Health Organization. *Ethical Criteria for Medicinal Drug Promotion*. Geneva: WHO, 1988.
– *The Rational Use of Drugs in the Management of Acute Diarrhoea in Children*. Geneva: WHO, 1990.
– *WHO Medicines Strategy: Countries at the Core, 2004–2007*. Geneva: World Health Organization, 2004.
– *The World Medicines Situation*. Geneva: WHO, 2004.

PART THREE

Case Studies for Achieving Corporate Responsibility

7 Managing the Market for Medicines Access: Realizing the Right to Health by Facilitating Compulsory Licensing of Pharmaceuticals – A Case Study of Legislation and the Need for Reform

RICHARD ELLIOTT

The Right to Health and Access to Medicines

For over half a century, most of the world's states have repeatedly recognized and affirmed their obligation, under international law, to protect and promote health as a matter of human rights. The 'enjoyment of the highest attainable standard of health' was recognized as a 'fundamental right' by the international community with the adoption in 1946 of the constitution of the newly created World Health Organization (WHO).[1] In addition, this treaty declares that 'unequal development in different countries in the promotion of health and control of disease, especially communicable disease, is a common danger.'[2] The adoption of the *Charter* of the United Nations during the previous year created a binding treaty obligation on all member states to 'take joint and separate action' to promote 'solutions of international ... health, and related problems' and universal respect for, and observance of, human rights and fundamental freedoms.[3] While the *WHO Constitution* recognized the right to health specifically, other instruments subsequently elaborated the nature and extent of UN member states' obligation to address health as a matter of human rights. The *Universal Declaration of Human Rights* (UDHR) adopted by consensus in 1948 by the UN General Assembly and intended as a first elaboration of the human rights referred to in the *UN Charter*, affirms that everyone 'has the right to a standard of living adequate for the health and well-being of himself and of his family, including ... medical care' and 'the right ... to share in scientific advancement and its benefits,' and that everyone 'is entitled to a social and international order in which the rights and freedoms set forth in this Declaration can be fully realized.'[4]

The human right to health has also subsequently found expression, in one form or another, in numerous treaties subsequently adopted within the UN system (and within the domestic legal systems of many states).[5] In particular, the *International Covenant on Economic, Social and Cultural Rights* (*ICESCR*) is one key treaty elaborating on some of the general rights stated in the UDHR. The states parties 'recognize the right of everyone to the enjoyment of the highest attainable standard of physical and mental health' and declare, as a treaty obligation, that

> the steps to be taken by States Parties to the present Covenant to achieve the full realization of this right shall include those necessary for:
> a. the provision for the reduction of the stillbirth-rate and of infant mortality and for the healthy development of the child; ...
> b. the prevention, treatment and control of epidemic, endemic, occupational and other diseases;
> c. the creation of conditions which would assure to all medical service and medical attention in the event of sickness.[6]

In addition, each state party to the *ICESCR* is treaty-bound 'to take steps, individually and through international assistance and cooperation, especially economic and technical, to the maximum of its available resources, with a view to achieving progressively the full realization of the rights recognized in the present Covenant by all appropriate means, including particularly the adoption of legislative measures.'[7]

The UN expert committee tasked with monitoring states' compliance with their *ICESCR* obligations has laid out the most authoritative interpretation of the right to health under Article 12, clarifying that 'health facilities, goods and services must be affordable for all,' that states must make 'individual and joint efforts to, *inter alia*, make available relevant technologies,' and that states must ensure 'provision of essential drugs.'[8] The committee also reaffirmed states parties' obligation of international assistance and cooperation towards fully realizing the right to health, with explicit reference to states' obligations under the *UN Charter* to take joint and separate action to solve international health problems and achieve universal observance of human rights.[9] Additional UN treaties,[10] as well as various treaties and declarations adopted within various regions,[11] also recognize a right to health in legally binding form. Access to medicines has been recognized specifically as a component of the right to health within the UN system by other expert committees,[12] programmatic agencies,[13] and member states themselves.[14] These international human rights instruments have provided the basis for a number of domestic court rulings compelling government action to address barriers to medicines access.[15]

Patent Barriers and Treatment Access: A Public Health Crisis and Human Rights Failure

Notwithstanding such legally binding human rights commitments by states, the reality, of course, is rather different, as dramatically demonstrated by the ongoing global inequity in access to medicines. In 2000, the WHO estimated that one-third of the world's population lacked access to essential drugs, with the figure rising to over 50 per cent in the poorest parts of Africa and Asia.[16] More recent estimates suggest the situation overall has not changed drastically.[17] The global HIV pandemic has thrown this global health gap into stark relief, prompting the WHO and UNAIDS to initiate in 2003 a strategy to ensure that 3 million people in the developing world were receiving antiretroviral medications (ARVs) by the end of 2005 (of the then 6 million estimated to be in need). By the end of 2006, only about 2 million people were receiving needed therapies, and the unmet need had grown to an additional 5 million people.[18] While the original target has still not been reached, the initiative did triple the total number of people on treatment by the end of 2005,[19] and the effort to scale up treatment access has generated momentum, with ongoing pressure by health and human rights advocates to take the action necessary to reach the newly agreed global target of 'universal access to treatment by 2010.'[20] By the end of 2010, an estimated 6.65 million people in low- and middle-income countries were receiving needed antiretroviral medicines, representing about 47 per cent of the estimated total number of people in need.[21] Such pressure – in the form of community mobilization, action-oriented research, media advocacy, and litigation – has been necessitated, unfortunately, by the failure of many governments, in both high-income and developing countries, to deliver on promises of action that would help realize the human right to health – be it funding for scaling up AIDS treatment or health systems more broadly, or necessary legislative or policy reform to facilitate access to medicines or other health goods and services.[22]

Central to achieving the human right of access to medicines is increasing their affordability, for patients and for government payers, particularly in resource-limited settings.[23] It follows that regard must be had for the rules of the pharmaceutical marketplace, including international and domestic legislation on intellectual property that plays a role in determining the price of medicines to alleviate suffering and save lives – such as the rules set out in the *Agreement on Trade-Related Aspects of Intellectual Property Rights* (*TRIPS* Agreement) of the WTO, binding all WTO members (153 countries as of February 2011). As observed by the WHO, poor people cannot afford patent-protected prices for medicines,[24] and both the WHO and the WTO Secretariat have made it clear that access to lower-cost, generic pharmaceuticals is critical to treatment scale-up: 'For low-income countries and poor people in particular, bringing down the cost of medicines is key to gaining access to drugs. In developing countries, 25 to 65 percent of total health expenditures is spent on pharmaceuticals, but government health budgets are too low to purchase enough medicines and poor people often cannot afford to buy them on their own.'[25]

As the United Nations Development Programme (UNDP) observed in 2003: 'Drug prices are a critical determinant of access to health care. Patented drugs are substantially more expensive than generic versions ... Several studies for developing countries have estimated the impact of patents on drug prices ... Their estimated increases range from 12 per cent to 68 per cent once TRIPS is implemented. In the case of anti-retroviral drugs for HIV/AIDS, patented drugs that cost US$10,000–$12,000 per patient per year are available for US$200–300 in their generic form.'[26]

Competition from generics has been shown repeatedly to have a significant and lasting effect in lowering ARV prices globally and in specific countries.[27] It is now not seriously disputed that developing countries, and their people, can be harmed by uncritical application of enhanced intellectual property protection on pharmaceuticals such as the rules found in the *TRIPS* Agreement.[28] Consequently, it is now widely recommended – for example, by the WHO Commission on Intellectual Property Rights, Innovation and Public Health – that developing countries take measures, among other things, to make use of *TRIPS* 'flexibilities' such as compulsory licensing to promote access to more affordable medicines.[29] Such flexibilities were recognized, at least in theory, in the 2001 *Declaration on the TRIPS Agreement and Public Health*, in which WTO members unanimously reaffirmed the right of each member 'to grant compulsory licences and the freedom to determine the grounds upon which such licences are granted.'[30] They also recognized, however, that countries with insufficient pharmaceutical manufacturing capacity 'could face difficulties in making effective use of compulsory licensing under the *TRIPS* Agreement,'[31] because of the restriction in Article 31(f) of the treaty that any use of a patented process or product under a compulsory licence 'shall be authorized predominantly for the supply of the domestic market of the Member authorizing such use,' thereby limiting the potential scope of compulsory licensing in a WTO member to produce generic pharmaceuticals for export to countries lacking sufficient domestic production capacity. As summarized in an editorial in the *Economist* at the time, 'As they stand, the WTO's rules leave the vast majority of poor, disease-ridden countries in a pickle. They cannot afford to buy the patented versions of essential drugs; they do not have the resources to make cheaper generic versions; and they cannot import generics, because the countries that make them are not allowed to export them.'[32]

After acrimonious negotiations, on 30 August 2003, WTO members agreed on an ostensible 'solution' to this problem, in the form of a decision of the WTO General Council that waives this restriction,[33] accompanied by a negotiated statement that sets out 'shared understandings' of WTO members on the interpretation and implementation 'of the waiver.[34] The WTO Decision and accompanying Chairperson's Statement have been criticized by health advocates as falling short of allowing the flexible, rapid use of compulsory licensing to address global health needs, particularly those of developing countries, and as putting in place restrictions that would lead to both market forces and political pressure by high-income countries frustrating the use of the system.[35] More than eight years after the adoption of the WTO Decision in 2003, twelve jurisdictions – including the European Union (consisting of 27 member countries) – had adopted legislation, regulations, or other instruments that implement the Decision in a fundamentally similar fashion, albeit with varying degrees of specificity and latitude on various points. The balance of this chapter presents a case study of Canada's domestic implementation of the WTO Decision – at this writing, the only regime to have been used at all, and even then only once. It demonstrates that advocates' concerns about the Decision have been well founded, and recommends significant reforms that would create a regime better suited to encouraging and permitting socially responsible action by generic pharmaceutical companies in advancing the realization of the human right to health by responding to the needs of developing countries for less-expensive medicines.

Fixing the Flaws: Remedying Canada's Access to Medicines Regime

Within weeks of the WTO Decision in August 2003, in response to calls from Canadian civil society organizations and Stephen Lewis, the UN special envoy for HIV/AIDS in Africa, the Government of Canada announced its intention to implement the Decision domestically. Following an eight-month advocacy campaign by civil society groups,[36] legislation amending the *Patent Act* and the *Food and Drugs Act* was passed unanimously in both houses of Parliament in May 2004.[37] After further pressure from NGOs, the law and accompanying regulations were brought into force one year later.[38] But over three years after its enactment, despite efforts by both the international humanitarian organization Médecins sans frontières (MSF) and the commitment of Canada's largest generic pharmaceutical manufacturer, Apotex, Inc., to develop a fixed-dose combination (FDC) antiretroviral AIDS drug requested by MSF, not a single pill had yet been exported under what the federal government has labelled 'Canada's Access to Medicines Regime' (CAMR),[39] in part because of the apparent unwillingness of any developing country eligible to import under CAMR to make the requisite notifications to the WTO or the Government of Canada. In January 2007, interested parties made submissions to the Government of Canada as part of the review of CAMR that had been mandated in its enabling legislation.[40] Further submissions with recommendations for reform were made in April 2007 to a parliamentary committee at hearings into the failure of the legislation to deliver on the pledge of greater access to affordable medicines,[41] and an international expert consultation similarly identified several features of concern in CAMR, undermining its utility.[42]

In July 2007, almost four years since the WTO Decision had been adopted, Rwanda became the first country to notify the WTO of its intention to use the Decision to import the Apotex product.[43] In August 2007, it was incorrectly reported that Apotex and the holders of the relevant Canadian patents on the constituent products of Apotex's fixed-dose combination ARV tablet had successfully negotiated voluntary licences that would permit Apotex to export its generic product to Rwanda. Full details of the supposed voluntary licences were never revealed, and it turned out that it was not possible to conclude necessary agreements with all the patent-holders in the end.[44] In early September 2007, Apotex therefore filed an application for a compulsory licensing with the commissioner of patents, in accordance with the provisions of CAMR.[45] Two weeks later, the commissioner issued the requested licence, authorizing Apotex to produce and export the quantity notified by Rwanda (and referenced in Apotex's application), amounting to 15.6 million tablets over a period of up to two years.[46] (As treatment consists of two tablets daily, this would amount to a year's course of treatment for more than 21,000 patients.) Finally, following international tendering initiated by the Government of Rwanda, it was announced in May 2008 that it had selected Apotex as the supplier; the publicly reported price was US$0.195 per tablet, meaning treatment with this regimen would cost US$146 per patient per year, significantly lower than the then-lowest price from any other generic source (US$176 per patient per year) reported publicly.[47]

In response to these developments, health advocates expressed cautious optimism at moving this important step closer to possible use of the WTO's Decision, via its Canadian implementation, but cautioned that Canada still needed to reform its legislation on compulsory licensing for export if there was to be any real likelihood of it being used beyond this one instance.[48] In particular, Canadian advocates have argued that Canada's government and Parliament should not merely tinker with a few adjustments to the regime. Rather, Canada can and should learn from its experience of the hurdles and disincentives encountered to date in the effort to use CAMR, and should legislate in its place a simpler, more streamlined process that would be more user-friendly for both developing country purchasers and generic suppliers. These recommendations, and the rationale for each, are summarized in brief below,[49] as a contribution to the ongoing national and global debates over reforming intellectual property policy to support the now internationally-agreed goal of 'universal access' to HIV/AIDS treatment.[50]

Streamline the Compulsory Licensing Process: The 'One Licence Solution'

The single most important and significant reform that is needed is to streamline the process for securing legal authorization to manufacture generic medicines for export to eligible developing countries. As enacted, CAMR embodies the basic mechanism for obtaining a compulsory licence authorizing export of generics that was agreed in the WTO Decision in 2003, but in unnecessarily restrictive form. (As noted above, this basic mechanism has also been replicated in the regimes adopted in several other legal instruments elsewhere, none of which has resulted in generic exports at the time of writing.) CAMR requires seeking a separate licence for each desired order of medicines by a single country. The would-be importing country, and the details of the anticipated product order, must be disclosed in advance as part of the process of seeking application for a licence, first to the patent-holder(s) in an effort to seek a voluntary licence and then, failing that, in the application for a compulsory licence. If obtained, the licence authorizes only the export of that predetermined quantity of the product to that single country (and for a short, arbitrary time). Such a process ignores the practical considerations facing both generic manufacturers and developing country purchasers, the two parties whose ability and willingness to use the mechanism determine its success in facilitating access to lower-cost medicines for patients.

Canada should instead grant a broader legal authorization upfront to manufacture generic medicines for export, instead of limiting the authorization to fulfilling only a single order for a single country after a cumbersome process. This could be done easily by amending the *Patent Act* to include a simple section authorizing the manufacture of generic versions of any pharmaceutical product patented in Canada for export to any eligible country specified in the legislation. Alternatively, a manufacturer could be granted a single, open-ended licence on a given drug that authorizes the export of that drug to any eligible country specified in the legislation, with the flexibility to supply the quantities requested by countries as their needs evolve. Under either approach, a generic manufacturer would still be required to remit periodically to the patent-holder(s) any royalties payable, which can be determined according to the existing formula in the regime (calculating the royalty on a sliding scale based on the importing country's ranking on the UN's Human Development Index based on proposals by civil society during the legislative process).

With either of these approaches to streamlining CAMR, the authorization would not be limited to exporting a predetermined quantity of a product to a single country (thereby facilitating economies of scale), and would not require a new application for every single (tentative) contract negotiated between a generic manufacturer and a potential purchaser (thereby further reducing transaction costs). In addition, there would be no need to reveal the name of a would-be purchaser (which exposes the country to pressure from governments or corporations opposed to compulsory licensing) before the generic manufacturer has the certainty of a licence legally authorizing it to sell and export the drug to its would-be client.

Such an approach is consistent with a flexible, purposive interpretation of the 2003 WTO Decision, as has been confirmed by international experts and outlined in submissions to Canadian parliamentary committees.[51] However, even if this were not the case, legislating such a mechanism of compulsory licensing for export would still be permissible under WTO rules – in particular, by treating it as a 'limited exception' to exclusive patent rights as permitted under *TRIPS* Article 30. In adopting the WTO Decision in 2003, WTO members explicitly stated that it is 'without prejudice to the rights, obligations and flexibilities,' and to their interpretation, that members have under other provisions of *TRIPS*.[52]

Eliminate Negotiating Requirements and Associated Delay and Obstruction

In enacting a simpler, more direct mechanism as just described, Canada should also eliminate, at least in some circumstances, the requirement to first attempt negotiating a voluntary licence from a patent-holder, another priority for reform. Again, this particular reform, dispensing with this precondition in all situations, could be considered part of the new regime creating a 'limited exception' to exclusive Canadian patent rights, permissible under *TRIPS* Article 30, although such an interpretation is certainly contested. At the very least, the more streamlined compulsory licensing process should abolish any requirement to try negotiating for a voluntary licence in cases where a Canadian generic manufacturer is supplying medicines to a developing country: (1) to address an emergency or similar circumstance, (2) for 'public non-commercial use,' or (3) as a remedy for practices by patent-holders that have been determined to be anti-competitive by an appropriate judicial or administrative process as set out in the importing country's law. It is already the case that, under *TRIPS* Article 31(b), no effort to negotiate a voluntary licence is required in these circumstances; at the very least, Canada's legislation on compulsory licensing should take full advantage of flexibilities that are already explicitly recognized in *TRIPS* and therefore almost certain to withstand challenge by a hostile WTO member. No logical reason for CAMR's failure to reflect these existing features of *TRIPS* has ever been advanced by government representatives.

Abolish Limits on Pharmaceutical Products Eligible for Export

In the negotiations that ultimately produced the WTO Decision in 2003, the brand-name pharmaceutical industry and some high-income countries pursued for months their proposals for restrictions on the scope of any mechanism of compulsory licensing for export, including attempting to limit it to only specific diseases or pharmaceutical products. Rightly condemned as unethical and unsound public health policy, such efforts were successfully resisted by developing countries and by civil society advocates. The mechanism agreed in the WTO Decision explicitly states a broad, open-ended definition of 'pharmaceutical product' and refers to addressing 'public health problems,' which category is also not limited, although explicit reference is made to HIV, tuberculosis, and malaria as problems of particular concern. Nonetheless, Canada's legislation undermines this international consensus by including a limited list of specific pharmaceutical products subject to possible compulsory licensing. It also creates an unnecessarily complicated bureaucratic process for expanding the list that requires a federal Cabinet decision following a recommendation from two ministers. Experience has shown that lobbying by the brand-name pharmaceutical industry has blocked the expansion of the list, and months of lobbying have been required in each of the two other cases in which products (including the Apotex fixed-dose combination ARV subsequently exported once to Rwanda) were added.[53] There is no need for Canada to narrow the scope of products eligible for compulsory licensing for export in this fashion, and any legislative amendments should abolish this restriction. At the same time, Canada's legislation could be amended to clarify explicitly that active pharmaceutical ingredients (APIs) of finished medicines, vaccines, and other patented products (such as test kits) are included within the definition of 'pharmaceutical products' covered by the regime. There can be no objection that this is inconsistent with agreed-upon WTO law as it reflects the wording of the 2003 Decision itself.

Treat Non-WTO Developing Countries Fairly

Under CAMR as it stands, a developing country (other than UN-recognized 'least-developed countries') that does not belong to the WTO – and therefore is not bound by *TRIPS* requirements regarding intellectual property – must meet additional, cumulative conditions in order to import Canadian-made generics. Specifically, the country must (1) be eligible for 'official development assistance' according to the Organization for Economic Cooperation and Development (OECD), (2) declare a 'national emergency or other circumstances of extreme urgency,' (3) specify the name and quantity of a specific pharmaceutical product needed for dealing with that emergency, and (4) agree that the imported product 'will not be used for commercial purposes.' The term *commercial purposes* is undefined; depending on how it is interpreted, it could interfere with the distribution of imported, Canadian-made generics through commercial actors such as private pharmacies or other distributors, which is frequently the reality for many patients in developing countries with limited public health-care systems. These conditions do not apply to similarly situated developing countries that *do* belong to the WTO; the double standard is unjustified and should be eliminated.

It is also not certain, under CAMR's current wording, that a particular feature of the WTO Decision of 2003, aimed at facilitating broader access to medicines, has been adequately reflected. The Decision states that, in the case that a developing country or LDC WTO member is party to a regional trade agreement (RTA) with other countries, at least half of whom are LDCs, it is permitted for that country, having imported generic pharmaceutical products under a compulsory licence, to re-export those products to the other developing country or LDC members of that regional trade group. However, a particular provision of Canada's law could be interpreted as prohibiting such action under a compulsory licence issued under CAMR, and there is also uncertainty about what the applicable royalty rate might be in such a circumstance. Canada's legislation requires clarification on this point, to enable, without confusion, the use of compulsory licensing to supply, under a simple process and with a single licence, a number of developing countries within a regional trade group as originally contemplated in the WTO Decision.

Facilitate NGO Purchasing of Generics

CAMR's current provisions require that a non-governmental organization providing humanitarian relief or an international agency procuring medicines for use in developing countries must get the 'permission' of a country's government to import Canadian-made generics. The term is undefined. This requirement is in addition to any applicable requirement of regulatory approval under the applicable laws of the important country. This additional hurdle to meeting the needs of patients in developing countries is not required under any WTO rule and should be easily eliminated.

Legislate Greater Flexibility in Regulatory Approval of Exported Products

Unlike any other medicines produced for export in Canada, those produced under compulsory licence under CAMR must receive the approval of Health Canada's Therapeutic Products Directorate, the country's drug regulatory authority, as a prerequisite of obtaining a compulsory licence permitting manufacture and export. Such a condition is not required by the WTO Decision. Since many developing countries will require pre-qualification of a product and its manufacturer by the WHO, requiring Health Canada approval as an absolute precondition can lead to duplication of effort and unnecessary delay. It should be within the purview of the importing country, not Canada, to determine the regulatory review process on which it wishes to base procurement decisions – including, for example, relying upon the WHO's Prequalification Programme (available for certain products) to assure the quality of a purchased product.[54] Canada's regime should be reformed to reflect this, preserving the capacity of Health Canada to provide regulatory review if called upon (as part of assisting developing countries in obtaining lower-cost medicines of reliable quality and recognizing that this known system will hold some attraction for Canadian generic manufacturers and some developing countries for a variety of reasons), but not mandating Health Canada as the *only* acceptable review mechanism for the operation of CAMR.

Eliminate Arbitrary Time Limit on Licences

CAMR arbitrarily limits any compulsory licence obtained under the regime to two years. This limits the economies of scale needed to make compulsory licensing viable for generic manufacturers whose intended purchasers are resource-limited developing countries, further undermines the ability of Canadian generic manufacturers to compete in response to international tenders issued by developing countries seeking to purchase generics, and calls into question for potential developing-country purchasers the long-term sustainability of supplies. The current two-year limit should be abolished; any compulsory licence obtained under CAMR should run for the remainder of the patent term on the originator product.

Abolish Provisions Encouraging Legal Proceedings to Deter or Delay Generic Exports

Under CAMR's current provisions, the patent-holder may apply for a court order terminating a generic manufacturer's compulsory licence, or seeking a higher royalty payment than what is required under the regime's standard formula, by alleging that the contract between a generic manufacturer and a developing-country purchaser is 'commercial' because of the price being charged. It is not clear that such intervention to prevent excessive pricing by a Canadian generic manufacturer is necessary, given likely competition in the global marketplace from either brand-name companies pressured into lowering their prices and seeking to keep a generic competitor out or from other generic manufacturers, including those in other countries who may have lower costs for some of the factors of production. However, assuming for the sake of the argument that such a control is necessary, the objective can be achieved through other, more direct means, such as conditions imposed in the compulsory licence itself when issued. Instead, patent-holders, who have obvious incentives to delay and undermine possible use of CAMR, are now granted a legal basis in the regime itself for such tactics. Such unnecessary features should be abolished from the regime.

Conclusion

As a matter of elementary economics, it is reasonable to assume that, in the case of private commercial pharmaceutical producers, the dominant driver of corporate behaviour will be profit maximization, although this is not to exclude the important (but almost certainly secondary) role that public perception, moral suasion, and humanitarian impulses may also play in shaping behaviour in specific instances. Furthermore, it should be remembered that, notwithstanding an ongoing debate about the human rights obligations of private business actors, the primary duty-bearers of human rights obligations under international law remain states – including the obligation to take legislative and policy measures to realize the highest attainable standard of health. It is, therefore, reasonable to look to governments to discharge their legal responsibility, in part, by adopting public policy that helps manage the market so as to create conditions favouring access to affordable, high-quality medicines, one of the recognized fundamental elements of realizing the right to health. This can, and should, then also be complemented by other active government efforts to support the use of the mechanisms made available so as to realize their potential benefits – in the case discussed here, the use of the option of compulsory licensing by developing countries to source good-quality, lower-cost generic medicines.

When the legislation creating Canada's Access to Medicines Regime was enacted in 2004, it passed with unanimous support in both houses of Parliament. Yet it took more than four years – and an unusual commitment from a single (privately owned) generic manufacturer and various NGOs, as well as the intervention of an international foundation playing a brokering role – factors that are difficult to replicate and sustain regularly and, in any event, should not be required – to achieve the first breakthrough of using CAMR to deliver medicines to a single patient. Furthermore, at this writing, this remains the only use to date of the 2003 WTO Decision, as no other jurisdiction's regime implementing that decision has yet been used – in part, because they too contain unnecessary inflexibility and limitations or fail to provide adequate clarity about how they can be used simply and with minimal risk or cost. Even if, as a result of years of effort, we should see a further welcome and felicitous instance of the regime delivering what was promised, there is little reason for celebration or for great optimism that such mechanisms, as currently configured, will play any significant role in scaling up access to treatment. Indeed, as of early 2012, all indications are that, absent reform, the Canadian legislation will not likely be used again by a generic manufacturer, and there is no indication of plans to use any other country's regime.

Achieving the objective of 'universal access' to medicines for diseases such as HIV/AIDS – not only a human rights and public health imperative, but also a commitment by G8 countries and all UN member states (as noted above) – will require, among other things, the widespread use of lower-cost, generic medicines. This, in turn, will require the ability of countries with limited resources to make effective use of compulsory licensing. To this end, civil society advocates in Canada have continued their effort to produce a workable regime of compulsory licensing for export – one that offers the 'expeditious solution' that WTO members agreed was needed. In 2009, those efforts led to the introduction of two virtually identical private member's bills in Canada's Parliament. Both bills would have streamlined the existing CAMR, amending the relevant provisions of the *Patent Act* and the *Food and Drugs Act* to create the 'one-licence solution' and some of the other reforms described here.[55] While the first bill, introduced in the Senate in March 2009, proceeded through to extensive committee hearings, it unfortunately died on the order paper when the Conservative government prorogued Parliament in December 2009. Fortunately, the bill in the House of Commons, introduced in June 2009, commanded a slim majority of votes at second reading in December 2009, following intense campaigning by civil society groups. In March 2011, after said groups lobbied intensively to restore key provisions stripped by amendments at the committee stage in late 2010, the bill passed at third and final reading in the House by a solid majority. Unfortunately, although it could have been passed easily and quickly in the Senate had there been cross-party consent, it was then deliberately stalled by several Conservative senators, coincident with the circulation of a memorandum from the minister of industry opposing the bill and mischaracterizing many of its features. After several days of stalling, the bill died on the Order Paper when the minority government fell on a vote of non-confidence and Parliament was dissolved for a general election. A substantially equivalent bill was reintroduced in February 2012 in the House of Commons.

A careful reading of *TRIPS* and the 2003 WTO Decision reveals that these reforms can be accommodated within a flexible interpretation of the 2003 WTO Decision – what is required is sufficient political will by Canadian decision-makers to do so, which has been lacking so far. Were it to take this approach, Canada would help demonstrate how the 2003 WTO Decision could be implemented in a way that makes its operation as simple and straightforward as possible, to the benefit of developing countries and people in need of medicines. However, as noted above, it should also be remembered that, as a matter of international law, Canada is not restricted simply to the (narrow) interpretation of the 2003 WTO Decision reflected in the current CAMR and can, instead, take advantage of other flexibility in WTO rules. In particular, should Canada not wish to characterize the streamlined system urged here as a preferred implementation of the 2003 WTO Decision, an alternative is for Canada to treat it as a 'limited exception' to exclusive patent rights, as permitted under *TRIPS* Article 30. In adopting the WTO Decision in 2003, WTO members explicitly stated that it is 'without prejudice to the rights, obligations and flexibilities,' and to their interpretation, that members have under other provisions of *TRIPS*.[56]

The amendments to CAMR proposed here would significantly simplify the use of compulsory licensing by developing countries to import from Canadian generic manufacturers and set a dramatic global precedent of using the limited 'flexibilities' of WTO rules to structure intellectual property policy with a view to promoting access to medicines in the global South through the mechanism of compulsory licensing and hence the power of market competition. As a high-income country and one of the first countries to implement the WTO Decision, which has yet to work as the promised 'expeditious solution' offering a 'rapid response' to the public health needs of developing countries, Canada is well positioned politically to exploit such opportunities within WTO law and to defend them against certain opposition from the brand-name pharmaceutical industry and its allied governments, including the United States and the European Union.[57] It is chiefly a matter of whether Canada's federal government and Parliament have the courage of their conviction, stated unanimously by all parliamentarians during the enactment of Canada's original legislation in 2004, that they wish to facilitate access to medicines in the developing world.

For regimes such as CAMR to contribute to the realization of the human right to health for those who cannot afford the price of staying alive or living with lessened suffering, they must be made much more user-friendly, thereby increasing the likelihood of routine use by both developing-country purchasers and generic suppliers. Canada helped lead the way in implementing the WTO Decision; experience suggests that 'solution' is largely illusory and will likely remain so. Canada should be among those leading the way in learning the lessons of the regime's failure and trying new approaches. The status quo represents a public health failure, and a betrayal of its human rights obligations and of patients in the developing world.

NOTES

1 *Constitution of the World Health Organization* [WHO Constitution], 14 U.N.T.S. 185 (1946).
2 Ibid., preamble.
3 *Charter of the United Nations [UN Charter]*, 26 June 1945, Can. T.S. 1945 No. 7, Articles 55, 56.
4 *Universal Declaration of Human Rights*, UN GA Res. 217 (III), UNGAOR, 3d Sess., Supp. No. 13, UN Doc. A/810 (1948), Articles 25, 27, and 28.
5 The UN special rapporteur on the right to health has reported that the right to health (or, more narrowly in some cases, a right to health care) is found in over sixty national constitutions: Paul Hunt, *The Right of Everyone to the Highest Attainable Standard of Physical and Mental Health: Report of the Special Rapporteur to the Commission on Human Rights*, UN Doc. E/CN.4/2003/58 (2003).
6 *International Covenant on Economic, Social and Cultural Rights*, 999 U.N.T.S. 3 (1976), Article 12.
7 Ibid., Article 2.

8 United Nations Committee on Economic, Social and Cultural Rights, *General Comment 14: The Right to the Highest Attainable Standard of Health (Art. 12)*, UN Doc. E/C.12/2000/4, paras 12, 16, and 17.

9 Ibid., paras 38, 43.

10 E.g., *Convention on the Elimination of All Forms of Racial Discrimination*, 660 U.N.T.S. 195 (1969), Article 5; *Convention on the Elimination of All Forms of Discrimination against Women*, 1249 U.N.T.S. 13 (1981), Article 12; *Convention on the Rights of the Child*, 1577 U.N.T.S. 3 (1990), Article 24(1).

11 *American Convention on Human Rights*, 1144 U.N.T.S. 123 (1978), Article 26; *Additional Protocol to the American Convention on Human Rights in the Area of Economic, Social and Cultural Rights ('Protocol of San Salvador')*, OAS T.S. 69 (1998), Article 10; *American Declaration on the Rights and Duties of Man*, OAS Res. XXX (1948), Article 11 (binding on all states parties to the *Charter of the Organization of American States* pursuant to the *Protocol of Buenos Aires* [1970], 721 U.N.T.S. 324); *African Charter on Human and Peoples' Rights* (1986), OAU Doc. CAB/LEG/67/rev. 5, (1982) 21 I.L.M. 58, Article 16; *African Charter on the Rights and Welfare of the Child* (1999), OAU Doc. CAB/ LEG/24.9/49 (1990), Article 14; *European Social Charter* (1965), 529 U.N.T.S. 89, E.T.S. No. 35, Part I; *Protocol to the African Charter on Human and Peoples' Rights on the Rights of Women in Africa* (2005), AU Doc. CAB/LEG/66.6 (2000), reprinted at (2001) 1 Afr. Hum. Rts. L.J. 40, Article 14.

12 For a review of some examples, see Alicia Ely Yamin, 'Not Just a Tragedy: Access to Medications as a Right under International Law,' *Boston University International Law Journal* 21 (2003): 325–71.

13 World Health Organization, *Globalization, TRIPS and Access to Pharmaceuticals*, WHO Policy Perspectives on Medicines No. 3, WHO/ EDM/2001.2 (2001), 5; World Health Organization & Joint UN Programme on HIV/AIDS, *Treating 3 Million by 2005: Making It Happen: The WHO Strategy* (Geneva: WHO & UNAIDS, 2003), 5; Office of the UN High Commissioner for Human Rights & Joint UN Programme on HIV/AIDS, *International Guidelines on HIV/ADS and Human Rights*, 2006 consolidated version, (Geneva: OHCHR & UNAIDS, 2006), Guideline 6.

14 See, e.g., United Nations Commission on Human Rights, *Access to Medication in the Context of Pandemics such as HIV/AIDS, Tuberculosis and Malaria*, CHR Res. 2001/33, UN Doc. E/CN.4/RES/2001/33 (2001); United Nations Commission on Human Rights, *Access to Medication in the Context of Pandemics such as HIV/AIDS, Tuberculosis and Malaria*, CHR Res. 2003/29, UN Doc. E/CN.4/RES/2003/29 (2003); United Nations Commission on Human Rights. *Access to Medication in the Context of Pandemics such as HIV/AIDS, Tuberculosis and Malaria*, CHR Res. 2004/26,

UN Doc. E/CN.4/RES/2004/26 (2004); United Nations Commission on Human Rights, *Access to Medication in the Context of Pandemics such as HIV/ AIDS, Tuberculosis and Malaria*, CHR Res. 2005/23, UN Doc. E/CN.4/ RES/2005/23 (2005); United Nations General Assembly, *Access to Medication in the Context of Pandemics such as HIV/AIDS, Tuberculosis and Malaria*, GA Res. 58/179, UN Doc. A/RES/58/179 (22 Dec. 2003); United Nations General Assembly, *Global Crisis – Global Action: Declaration of Commitment on HIV/AIDS*, GA Res. S-26/2, UNGAOR, 26th Spec. Session, Supp. No. 1, UN Doc. A/RES/S-26/2 (2001), paras 55, 58; United Nations General Assembly, *Political Declaration on HIV/AIDS*, GA Res. 60/262, UN GAOR, 60th Sess., Supp. No. 49, UN Doc. A/RES/60/262 (2006) at para. 12; World Health Assembly, 'WHO Medicines Strategy,' WHA Res. WHA 54.11, 54th World Health Assembly (2001), para. 1(2).

15 For summaries of some such cases, see Richard Elliott, Joanne Csete, Glenn Betteridge, and Richard Pearshouse, *Courting Rights: Case Studies in Litigating the Human Rights of People Living with HIV* (Geneva: Canadian HIV/AIDS Legal Network & UNAIDS, 2006), 49–97.

16 World Health Organization, *WHO Medicines Strategy: Framework for Action in Essential Drugs and Medicines Policy 2000–2003*. WHO/EDM/2000.1 (Geneva: WHO, 2000).

17 World Health Organization, *The World Medicines Situation* (Geneva: WHO, 2004). For more detailed and recent data, see the most recent *World Health Statistics* report produced by the WHO's Global Health Observatory, online via www.who.int/gho.

18 World Health Organization, UNAIDS, & UNICEF, *Towards Universal Access: Scaling Up Priority HIV/AIDS Interventions in the Health Sector*, 2009, http://www.who.int/hiv/pub/2009progressreport/en/index.html.

19 World Health Organization and UNAIDS, *Progress on Global Access to HIV Antiretroviral Therapy: A Report on '3 by 5' and Beyond* (Geneva: WHO and UNAIDS, 2006), http://www.who.int/hiv/fullreport_en_highres.pdf.

20 E.g., Group of Eight, 'Development and Africa,' Summit Leaders Declaration (Hokkaido Toyako, Japan, 8 June 2008), paras 40, 45, 46; Group of Eight, 'Fight against Infectious Disease' (St Petersburg: G8, 16 July 2006), para. 15; Group of Eight, 'Gleneagles Communiqué on Africa, Climate Change, Energy and Sustainable Development' (Gleneagles, Scotland: G8, 8 July 2005); Group of Eight, 'Growth and Responsibility in Africa,' Summit Declaration (Heiligendamnn, Germany: G8 8 June 2007), paras 48, 57; United Nations General Assembly, *Political Declaration on HIV/AIDS*, para. 49; United Nations General Assembly, *2005 World Summit Outcome*, GA Res. 60/1, UNGAOR, 60th Sess., Supp. No. 49, UN Doc. A/ RES/60/1 (2005), para. 57(d).

21 World Health Organization, UNAIDS & UNICEF, *Global HIV/AIDS Response: Epidemic Update and Health Sector Progress towards Universal Access – Progress Report 2011* (Geneva: WHO, UNICEF & UNAIDS, 2011), p. 97.

22 International Treatment Preparedness Coalition, *Missing the Target #6: The HIV/AIDS Response and Health Systems: Building on Success to Achieve Health Care for All* (2008); D. McIntyre, R. Loewenson, and V. Govender, 'Meeting the Promise: Progress on the Abuja Commitment of 15% Government Funds to Health,' Policy Series No. 20 (EQUINET and the Health Economics Unit, University of Cape Town, May 2008), http://www. equinetafrica.org/bibl/docs/POLBRIEF20%20Abuja.pdf; African Union, *Abuja Call for Accelerated Action towards Universal Access to HIV and AIDS, Tuberculosis and Malaria Services in Africa*, AU Doc. Sp/Assembly/ATM/2 (I), Rev. 3 (Abuja, Nigeria: African Union, 2006), http://www.africa-union. org/root/au/conferences/past/2006/may/summit/doc/en/ABUJA_ CALL.pdf; Group of Eight communiqués: 'Fight against Infectious Disease,' 'Gleneagles Communiqué on Africa,' and 'Growth and Responsibility in Africa'; UN General Assembly, *Political Declaration*.

23 It should go without saying that access must be improved to good-quality, affordable medicines, whether those products are brand-name or generic; substandard products represent a serious challenge for the health of individual patients and for public health more broadly. The World Health Organization has estimated that, in some developing countries, counterfeit medicines account for more than 10 per cent of sales of pharmaceutical products: 'Medicines: Counterfeit Medicines,' Fact Sheet No. 275 (2010), http://www.who.int/mediacentre/factsheets/fs275/en/index.html. It is also necessary to caution against incorrectly equating 'generic' with 'counterfeit' – this mischaracterization, which conflates the producer and patent status of a product with whether or not it meets regulatory standards – is commonly advanced by brand-name, patent-holding pharmaceutical companies interested in preventing competition from generic manufacturers. As the WHO explains, 'A counterfeit drug is a medicine, which is deliberately and fraudulently mislabelled with respect to identity and source. Counterfeiting can apply to both branded and generic products and counterfeit products may include products with the correct ingredients or with the wrong ingredients, without active ingredients, with insufficient active ingredients or with fake packaging': WHO, *Counterfeit Drugs: Guidelines for the Development of Measures to Combat Counterfeit Drugs*, WHO/EDM/ QSM/99.1. For further discussion, see BUKO Pharma-Kampagne, 'Counterfeit Medicines: What Are the Problems?' Pharma-brief special no. 1 (2007), http://www.bukopharma. de/Service/Archiv/E2007_01_special.pdf.

24 WHO Commission on Macroeconomics and Health, *Macroeconomics and Health: Investing in Health for Economic Development* (Geneva: WHO, 2001), 87.

25 World Health Organization and World Trade Organization Secretariat, *WHO Agreements and Public Health: A Joint Study by the WHO and WTO Secretariat* (Geneva: WHO and WTO Secretariat, 2002), 88.

26 United Nations Development Programme, *Making Global Trade Work for People* (London: Earthscan Publications, 2003), 209.

27 See, e.g., Médecins sans frontières, *Untangling the Web of Antiretroviral Price Reductions*, 14th ed. (Geneva: Médecins sans frontières, July 2011), 6.

28 WHO, *Globalization, TRIPS and Access to Pharmaceuticals*, 5–6; [U.K.] Commission on Intellectual Property Rights, *Integrating Intellectual Property Rights and Development Policy* (London: Commission, 2002), 33.

29 WHO Commission on Intellectual Property Rights, Innovation and Public Health, *Public Health, Innovation and Intellectual Property Rights* (Geneva: WHO, 2006), 139, http://www.who.int/intellectualproperty/en.

30 World Trade Organization Ministerial Conference, *Declaration on the TRIPS Agreement and Public Health*, WTO Doc. WT/MIN(01)/DEC/2 (2001), para. 5.

31 Ibid., para. 6.

32 'A WTO Deal on Drugs,' *Economist*, 1 Sept. 2003.

33 World Trade Organization, General Council, *Implementation of Paragraph 6 of the Doha Declaration on the TRIPS Agreement and Public Health* [WTO Decision], Decision of the General Council of 30 Aug. 2003, WTO Doc. IP/C/W/405 (2003).

34 World Trade Organization General Council, 'General Council Chairperson's Statement of 30 August 2003,' in WTO Doc. WT/GC/M82 (2006), 6.

35 E.g., Joint NGO Statement on TRIPS and Public Health, 'WTO Deal on Medicines: A "Gift" Bound in Red Tape,' 10 Sept. 2003, http://www.cptech.org/ip/wto/p6/ngos09102003.html.

36 For a more detailed discussion of those campaigning efforts, see Richard Elliott, 'Steps Forward, Backward, and Sideways: Canada's Bill on Exporting Generic Pharmaceuticals,' *Canadian HIV/AIDS Policy & Law Review* 9, no. 3 (2004): 15–21; Richard Elliott, 'TRIPS from Doha to Cancún … to Ottawa: Global Developments in Access to Treatment and Canada's Bill C-56, *Canadian HIV/AIDS Policy & Law Review* 8, no. 3 (2003): 1, 7–18.

37 *An Act to Amend the Patent Act and the Food and Drugs Act (Jean Chrétien Pledge to Africa)*, S.C. 2004, c. 23.

38 Government of Canada, *Food and Drugs Regulations (1402 – Drugs for Developing Countries)*, S.O.R 2005/141; Government of Canada, *Medical Devices Regulations (Developing Countries)*, S.O.R. 2005/142; Government of Canada, *Use of Patented Products for International Humanitarian Purposes*

Regulations, S.O.R. 2005/243; Industry Canada, 'Coming into Force of the *Jean Chrétien Pledge to Africa Act*,' news release, 13 May 2005.

39 For an overview of these efforts, see Médecins sans frontières, *Neither Expeditious, Nor a Solution: The WTO August 30th Decision Is Unworkable – An Illustration through Canada's Jean Chrétien Pledge to Africa*, Aug. 2006, http://utw.msfaccess.org/.

40 Government of Canada, *Report on the Statutory Review of Sections 21.01 to 21.19 of the Patent Act* (Ottawa, 14 December 2007), online via www.camr.gc.ca.

41 For the committee's summary of issues raised before it, see Government of Canada, House of Commons Standing Committee on Industry, Science and Technology, letter to Maxime Bernier, Minister of Industry, 14 May 2007, and accompanying summary, http://cmte.parl.gc.ca/Content/ HOC/committee/391/indu/webdoc/wd2967322/391_INDU_ Letter/391_INDU_RelDoc_PDF-e.pdf.

42 Canadian HIV/AIDS Legal Network and North-South Institute, *Access to Medicines and Intellectual Property: An International Expert Meeting on Canada's Access to Medicines Regime, Global Developments, and New Strategies for Improving Access – Meeting Report* (Ottawa, 19–21 Apr. 2007) (Toronto: Legal Network and NSI, 2007).

43 Government of Rwanda, 'Notification under Paragraph 2(a) of the Decision of 30 August 2003 on the Implementation of Paragraph 6 of the Doha Declaration on the TRIPS Agreement and Public Health,' WTO Doc. IP/N/9/RWA/1 (2007).

44 Lisa Priest, 'Canadian Companies Agree to Share Generic AIDS Drugs with Rwanda,' *Globe and Mail*, 9 Aug. 2007; Tanya Talaga, 'AIDS Drugs Fiasco a Tale of Red Tape,' *Toronto Star*, 9 Aug. 2007; Sheryl Ubelacker, 'Canada's Untapped Access to Medicines Program to Export First AIDS Drug,' *Canadian Press*, 8 Aug. 2007.

45 Apotex, 'Application Pursuant to Section 21.04 of the Patent Act,' 4 Sept. 2007.

46 Commissioner of Patents (Canadian Intellectual Property Office), 'Authorization under Section 21.04 of the Patent Act,' 19 Sept. 2007.

47 Apotex, 'Canadian Company Receives Final Tender Approval from Rwanda for Vital AIDS Drug,' news release, Toronto, 7 May 2008.

48 Canadian HIV/AIDS Legal Network, 'Canada Finally Poised to Deliver on Promise of Affordable Medicines to Developing Countries?' news release, Toronto, 7 May 2008; Canadian HIV/AIDS Legal Network, 'Rwanda First to Try Buying Affordable AIDS Drug from Canada Using Access to Medicines Regime,' news release, 20 July 2007. See also Richard Elliott, 'Delivery Past

Due: Global Precedent Set under Canada's Access to Medicines Regime,' *Canadian HIV/AIDS Policy & Law Review* 13, no. 1 (2008): 1, 5–12.

49 For a more detailed technical discussion of these points, and sample statutory provisions that would implement these recommendations, see Richard Elliott and Cailin Morrison, *Making CAMR Work: Streamlining Canada's Access to Medicines Regime – Legal Network's Brief to the House of Commons Standing Committee on Industry, Science and Technology regarding Bill C-393* (Toronto: Canadian HIV/AIDS Legal Network, Oct. 2010), online via www.aidslaw.ca/camr.

50 See, e.g., UN General Assembly, *Political Declaration on HIV/AIDS* (2006).

51 Elliott and Morrison, *Making CAMR Work*; Richard Elliott, *Bill C-393: Key Features and Compliance with Canada's WTO Obligations – A Submission by the Canadian HIV/AIDS Legal Network to the Standing Committee on Industry, Science and Technology* (Toronto: Canadian HIV/AIDS Legal Network, Oct. 2010); *Reforming Canada's Access to Medicines Regime (CAMR): Bill C-393 – Finding the Expeditious Solution — Conclusions of an International Expert Consultation Convened by the UN Development Programme and the Canadian HIV/AIDS Legal Network* (February 2010), all online via http://www.aidslaw.ca/camr.

52 WTO Decision, at para. 9.

53 See Elliott, 'Steps Forward, Backwards and Sideways,' 17.

54 For information about WHO's Prequalification Programme, see http://mednet3.who.int/prequal.

55 The texts of Bill S-232 and Bill C-393 and related material can be found online at http://www.parl.gc.ca/legisinfo. Additional analyses, including the text of full submissions to parliamentary committees regarding the proposed reforms, can be found online via http://www.aidslaw.ca/camr.

56 WTO Decision, para. 9.

57 It should be noted that the provisions at issue in *TRIPS* – Articles 30 and 31 – are essentially identical to those found in the intellectual property chapter of the *North American Free Trade Agreement* (*NAFTA*), from which they were simply copied into the WTO legal framework. Canada's obligations to the United States and Mexico under *NAFTA* are legally distinct from those under *TRIPS*. However, just as it may choose to treat a streamlined regime of compulsory licensing for export as a 'limited exception' under *TRIPS* Article 30, it may invoke the same provision in *NAFTA*. While a complaint to the dispute resolution mechanisms under either *TRIPS* or *NAFTA* might be pursued by another party to the treaty, such as the United States, Canada has the option to defend a different, improved compulsory licensing regime under these provisions.

REFERENCES

An Act to Amend the Patent Act and the Food and Drugs Act (Jean Chrétien Pledge to Africa). S.C. 2004, c. 23.

Additional Protocol to the American Convention on Human Rights in the Area of Economic, Social and Cultural Rights ('Protocol of San Salvador'). OAS T.S. 69 (1998).

African Charter on Human and Peoples' Rights. OAU Doc. CAB/LEG/67/rev. 5, (1982) 21 I.L.M. 58 (1986).

African Charter on the Rights and Welfare of the Child. OAU Doc. CAB/LEG/24.9/49 (1990) (1999).

African Union. *Abuja Call for Accelerated Action towards Universal Access to HIV and AIDS, Tuberculosis and Malaria Services in Africa.* AU Doc. Sp/Assembly/ATM/2 (I), Rev. 3. Abuja, Nigeria: African Union, 2006. http://www.africa-union.org/root/au/conferences/past/2006/may/summit/doc/en/ABUJA_CALL.pdf.

American Convention on Human Rights. 1144 U.N.T.S. 123 (1978).

American Declaration on the Rights and Duties of Man. OAS Res. XXX (1948).

Apotex. 'Application Pursuant to Section 21.04 of the Patent Act.' 4 Sept. 2007.

– 'Canadian Company Receives Final Tender Approval from Rwanda for Vital AIDS Drug.' News release, 7 May 2008.

BUKO Pharma-Kampagne. 'Counterfeit Medicines: What Are the Problems?' Pharma-brief special no. 1. Bielefeld, Germany: BUKO, 2007. http://www.bukopharma.de/Service/Archiv/E2007_01_special.pdf.

Canadian HIV/AIDS Legal Network. 'Canada Finally Poised to Deliver on Promise of Affordable Medicines to Developing Countries?' News release, 7 May 2008.

– 'Getting the Regime Right: Compulsory Licensing of Pharmaceuticals for Export.' Brief to the House of Commons Standing Committee on Industry, Science and Technology regarding Canada's Access to Medicines Regime. Ottawa: Legal Network, 18 Apr. 2007.

– 'Rwanda First to Try Buying Affordable AIDS Drug from Canada Using Access to Medicines Regime.' News release, 20 July 2007.

Canadian HIV/AIDS Legal Network and North-South Institute. *Access to Medicines and Intellectual Property: An International Expert Meeting on Canada's Access to Medicines Regime, Global Developments, and New Strategies for Improving Access – Meeting Report* (Ottawa, 19–21 Apr. 2007). Toronto: Legal Network & NSI, 2007.

Charter of the United Nations. 26 June 1945, Can. T.S. 1945 No. 7.

Commission on Intellectual Property Rights. *Integrating Intellectual Property Rights and Development Policy.* London: Commission, 2002.

Commissioner of Patents (Canadian Intellectual Property Office). 'Authorization under Section 21.04 of the Patent Act.' 19 Sept. 2007.

Constitution of the World Health Organization. 14 U.N.T.S. 185 (1946).

Convention on the Elimination of All Forms of Discrimination against Women. 1249 U.N.T.S. 13 (1981).

Convention on the Elimination of All Forms of Racial Discrimination. 660 U.N.T.S. 195 (1969).

Convention on the Rights of the Child. 1577 U.N.T.S. 3 (1990).

Elliott, Richard. *Bill C-393: Key Features and Compliance with Canada's WTO Obligations – A Submission by the Canadian HIV/AIDS Legal Network to the Standing Committee on Industry, Science and Technology.* Toronto: Canadian HIV/AIDS Legal Network, October 2010.

– 'Delivery Past Due: Global Precedent Set under Canada's Access to Medicines Regime.' *Canadian HIV/AIDS Policy & Law Review* 13, no. 1 (2008): 1, 5–12.

– 'Steps Forward, Backward, and Sideways: Canada's Bill on Exporting Generic Pharmaceuticals.' *Canadian HIV/AIDS Policy & Law Review* 9, no. 3 (2004): 15–21.

– 'TRIPS from Doha to Cancún to Ottawa: Global Developments in Access to Treatment and Canada's Bill C-56.' *Canadian HIV/AIDS Policy & Law Review* 8, no. 3 (2003): 1, 7–18.

Elliott, Richard, J. Csete, G. Betteridge, and R. Pearshouse. *Courting Rights: Case Studies in Litigating the Human Rights of People Living with HIV.* Geneva: Canadian HIV/AIDS Legal Network & UNAIDS, 2006.

Elliott, Richard, and Cailin Morrison. *Making CAMR Work: Streamlining Canada's Access to Medicines Regime – Legal Network's Brief to the House of Commons Standing Committee on Industry, Science and Technology regarding Bill C-393.* Toronto: Canadian HIV/AIDS Legal Network, October 2010.

European Social Charter. 529 U.N.T.S. 89, E.T.S. No. 35 (1965).

Government of Canada. *Food and Drugs Regulations (1402 – Drugs for Developing Countries).* S.O.R 2005/141, *Canada Gazette (Part II)*, vol. 139 (no. 11), 2005.

– *Medical Devices Regulations (Developing Countries).* S.O.R. 2005/142. *Canada Gazette (Part II)*, vol. 139 (no. 11), 2005.

– Use of Patented Products for International Humanitarian Purposes Regulations, S.O.R. 2005/243. *Canada Gazette (Part II)*, vol. 139 (no. 11), 2005.

Government of Canada. House of Commons Standing Committee on Industry, Science and Technology. Letter to Maxime Bernier, Minister of

Industry, 14 May 2007. http://cmte.parl.gc.ca/Content/HOC/committee/ 391/indu/webdoc/wd2967322/391_INDU_Letter/391_INDU_RelDoc_ PDF-e.pdf.

Government of Rwanda. 'Notification under Paragraph 2(a) of the Decision of 30 August 2003 on the Implementation of Paragraph 6 of the Doha Declaration on the TRIPS Agreement and Public Health.' WTO Doc. IP/N/9/RWA/1 (2007).

Group of Eight. 'Development and Africa.' Summit Leaders declaration. Hokkaido Toyako, Japan: G8, 2008.

– 'Fight against Infectious Disease.' St Petersburg, Russia: G8, 2006.

– 'Gleneagles Communiqué on Africa, Climate Change, Energy and Sustainable Development.' Gleneagles, Scotland: G8, 2005.

– 'Growth and Responsibility in Africa.' Summit declaration. Heiligendamn, Germany: G8, 2007.

Hunt, Paul. *The Right of Everyone to the Highest Attainable Standard of Physical and Mental Health: Report of the Special Rapporteur to the Commission on Human Rights.* UN Doc. E/CN.4/2003/58 (2003).

Industry Canada. 'Coming into Force of the *Jean Chrétien Pledge to Africa Act.*' News release and backgrounder, 13 May 2005.

International Covenant on Economic, Social and Cultural Rights. 999 U.N.T.S. 3 (1976).

International Treatment Preparedness Coalition. *Missing the Target #4: Time Is Running Out to End AIDS: Treatment and Prevention for All!* 2007.

– *Missing the Target #6: The HIV/AIDS Response and Health Systems: Building on Success to Achieve Health Care for All.* 2008.

Joint NGO Statement on TRIPS and Public Health. 'WTO Deal on Medicines: A "Gift" Bound in Red Tape.' 10 Sept. 2003. http://www.cptech.org/ip/ wto/p6/ngos09102003.html.

McIntyre, D., R. Loewenson, and V. Govender. 'Meeting the Promise: Progress on the Abuja Commitment of 15% Government Funds to Health.' Policy Series no. 20. EQUINET and the Health Economics Unit, University of Cape Town, May 2008. http://www.equinetafrica.org/bibl/docs/ POLBRIEF20%20Abuja.pdf.

Médecins sans frontières. *Neither Expeditious, Nor a Solution: The WTO August 30th Decision Is Unworkable: An Illustration through Canada's Jean Chrétien Pledge to Africa, August 2006.* http://www.msfaccess.org/resources/ key-publications/key-publication-detail/?tx_ttnews[tt_news] = 1256&cHash=eef08f968b.

– *Untangling the Web of Antiretroviral Price Reductions.* 11th ed. Geneva: Médecins sans frontières, 2008.

Office of the UN High Commissioner for Human Rights & Joint UN
    Programme on HIV/AIDS. *International Guidelines on HIV/ADS and Human
    Rights.* 2006 consolidated version. Geneva: OHCHR & UNAIDS, 2006.
Priest, Lisa. 'Canadian Companies Agree to Share Generic AIDS Drugs with
    Rwanda.' *Globe and Mail,* 9 Aug. 2007.
*Protocol to the African Charter on Human and Peoples' Rights on the Rights of
    Women in Africa.* AU Doc. CAB/LEG/66.6 (2000) (2005). Repr. *African
    Human Rights Law Journal* 1 (2001): 40.
*Reforming Canada's Access to Medicines Regime (CAMR): Bill C-393 – Finding the
    Expeditious Solution — Conclusions of an International Expert Consultation
    Convened by the UN Development Programme and the Canadian HIV/AIDS Legal
    Network,* Feb. 2010. http://www.aidslaw.ca/camr.
'The Right Fix?' *Economist,* 1 Sept. 2003, http://www.economist.com/
    node/2020463.
Talaga, Tanya. 'AIDS Drugs Fiasco a Tale of Red Tape.' *Toronto Star,* 9 Aug. 2007.
Ubelacker, Sheryl. 'Canada's Untapped Access to Medicines Program to
    Export First AIDS Drug.' Canadian Press, 8 Aug. 2007.
Universal Declaration of Human Rights. GA Res. 217 (III), UNGAOR, 3d Sess.,
    Supp. No. 13, UN Doc. A/810 (1948).
United Nations Commission on Human Rights. *Access to Medication in the
    Context of Pandemics such as HIV/AIDS, Tuberculosis and Malaria.* CHR Res.
    2001/33, UN Doc. E/CN.4/RES/2001/33 (2001).
– *Access to Medication in the Context of Pandemics such as HIV/AIDS,
    Tuberculosis and Malaria.* CHR Res. 2002/32, UN Doc. E/CN.4/
    RES/2002/32 (2002).
– *Access to Medication in the Context of Pandemics such as HIV/AIDS, Tuberculosis
    and Malaria.* CHR Res. 2003/29, UN Doc. E/CN.4/RES/2003/29 (2003).
– *Access to Medication in the Context of Pandemics such as HIV/AIDS, Tuberculosis
    and Malaria.* CHR Res. 2004/26, UN Doc. E/CN.4/RES/2004/26 (2004).
– *Access to Medication in the Context of Pandemics such as HIV/AIDS,
    Tuberculosis and Malaria.* CHR Res. 2005/23, UN Doc. E/CN.4/
    RES/2005/23 (2005).
United Nations Committee on Economic, Social and Cultural Rights. *General
    Comment 14: The Right to the Highest Attainable Standard of Health (Art. 12).*
    UN Doc. E/C.12/2000/4 (2004).
United Nations Development Programme. *Making Global Trade Work for People.*
    London: Earthscan Publications, 2003.
United Nations General Assembly. *Access to Medication in the Context of
    Pandemics such as HIV/AIDS, Tuberculosis and Malaria.* GA Res. 58/179, UN
    Doc. A/RES/58/179 (2003).

- *Global Crisis – Global Action: Declaration of Commitment on HIV/AIDS*. GA Res. S-26/2, UNGAOR, 26th Spec. Session, Supp. No. 1, UN Doc. A/RES/S-26/2 (2001).
- *Political Declaration on HIV/AIDS*. GA Res. 60/262, UNGAOR, 60th Sess., Supp. No. 49, UN Doc. A/RES/60/262 (2006).
- *2005 World Summit Outcome*. GA Res. 60/1, UNGAOR, 60th Sess., Supp. No. 49, UN doc. A/RES/60/1 (2005).
WHO Commission on Intellectual Property Rights, Innovation and Public Health. *Public Health, Innovation and Intellectual Property Rights*. Geneva: WHO, 2006. http://www.who.int/intellectualproperty/en.
WHO Commission on Macroeconomics and Health. *Macroeconomics and Health: Investing in Health for Economic Development*. Geneva: WHO, 2001.
World Health Assembly. *WHO Medicines Strategy*. WHA Res. WHA 54.11, 54th World Health Assembly (2001).
World Health Organization. *Counterfeit Drugs: Guidelines for the Development of Measures to Combat Counterfeit Drugs*. WHO/EDM/QSM/99.1 (1999).
- *Globalization, TRIPS and Access to Pharmaceuticals*. WHO Policy Perspectives on Medicines no. 3, WHO/EDM/2001.2 (2001).
- *Medicines: Counterfeit Medicines*. Fact sheet no. 275 (2010).
- *WHO Medicines Strategy: Framework for Action in Essential Drugs and Medicines Policy 2000–2003*. WHO/EDM/2000.1 (2000).
- *The World Medicines Situation*. Geneva: WHO, 2004.
World Health Organization and Joint UN Programme on HIV/AIDS. *Progress on Global Access to HIV Antiretroviral Therapy: A Report on '3 by 5' and Beyond*. Geneva: WHO & UNAIDS, 2006.
- *Treating 3 Million by 2005: Making It Happen: The WHO Strategy*. Geneva: WHO & UNAIDS, 2003.
World Health Organization and UNAIDS. *Progress on Global Access to HIV Antiretroviral Therapy: A Report on '3 by 5' and Beyond*. Geneva: WHO and UNAIDS, 2006. http://www.who.int/hiv/fullreport_en_highres.pdf.
World Health Organization and World Trade Organization Secretariat. *WHO Agreements and Public Health: A Joint Study by the WHO and WTO Secretariat*. Geneva: WHO & WTO Secretariat, 2002.
World Trade Organization General Council. 'General Council Chairperson's Statement of 30 August 2003.' In WTO Doc. WT/GC/M82.
- *Implementation of Paragraph 6 of the Doha Declaration on the TRIPS Agreement and Public Health*. Decision of the General Council of 30 Aug. 2003. WTO Doc. IP/C/W/405 (2003).
World Trade Organization Ministerial Conference. *Declaration on the TRIPS Agreement and Public Health*. WTO Doc. WT/MIN(01)/DEC/2 (2001).

World Health Organization, UNAIDS, & UNICEF. *Towards Universal Access: Scaling Up Priority HIV/AIDS Interventions in the Health Sector*. 2009 http://www.who.int/hiv/pub/2009progressreport/en/index.html.

World Health Organization, UNAIDS & UNICEF. *Towards Universal Access: Scaling Up Priority HIV/AIDS Interventions in the Health Sector – Progress Report 2010*. Geneva: WHO, UNAIDS & UNICEF, 2010.

Yamin, Alicia Ely. 'Not Just a Tragedy: Access to Medications as a Right under International Law.' *Boston University International Law Journal* 21 (2003): 325.

8 Ubuntu, AIDS, and the *King II Report*: Reflections on Corporate Social Responsibility in South Africa

JUDITH KING AND STEPHANIE NIXON

Corporate governance is concerned with holding the balance between economic and social goals and between individual and communal goals ... the aim is to align as nearly as possible the interests of individuals, corporations and society.[1]

Introduction

This chapter outlines how the second *Report of the King Committee on Corporate Governance for South Africa of 2002* (*'King II'*) posits a means by which, as an ethical imperative, businesses might 'hold the balance' described above. *King II* focuses on the experience of South Africa, one of the most highly HIV-affected countries in the world, making it a useful case study on the interactions of corporate social responsibility (CSR) and access to antiretroviral drugs (ARVs). The chapter begins with an introduction to the *King II Report*, followed by an exploration of the notion of *ubuntu*, the African communitarian philosophy that serves as *King II*'s foundational principle for the private sector's response to social concerns. We then chart the links to HIV and implications for approaching the issue of access to ARVs.

Introduction to the *King II Report*

King II was an update of the *King Report on Corporate Governance for South Africa* (*'King I'*), published in 1994 as an initiative of the Institute of Directors in Southern Africa (IoD).[2] Led by Mervyn King, a retired Supreme Court judge and CEO, the King Committee on Corporate Governance had been constituted in 1992 coinciding with profound social and political transformation at the time, with the dawning of democracy and the readmission of South Africa into the community of nations and the world economy.[3] The year 1994 marked the end of the racist, oppressive, and exclusionary apartheid regime in South Africa. In its wake, the country faced a daunting legacy of economic and social inequity, widespread poverty, and an unchecked HIV epidemic.

In this context, the IoD and various other national institutions foresaw a need to determine a code of corporate practice and conduct suitable for the country's special circumstances in the post-apartheid era. To this end, the King Committee was mandated to define – and in 2002, to refine – principles relating to the highest standards of governance in response to evolving social and ethical developments, both in South Africa and globally. One of the crucial aspects setting the South African code apart from the leading standard developed in the United Kingdom[4] was the broadening of terms to include non-financial aspects of corporate governance, to address pressing social and environmental concerns.

The report was produced by an entity elected by IoD members (the King Committee on Corporate Governance), comprising high-level representation of social forces normally associated with orthodox seats of material power. The text, therefore, is informed by a depth of expertise and credibility, and addresses matters of organizational rectitude and integrated sustainability in a grounded and judicious manner.

The report is targeted primarily at local companies listed on the Johannesburg Stock Exchange (JSE), financial services, and public sector entities, although it has also come to be regarded as a 'bible of corporate governance'[5] in Africa and many European countries. It serves as an indispensable reference for organizations seeking, at the very least, to understand and comply with these standards of governance, and beyond this, to advance and exemplify the highest of these standards in innovative ways.

Ubuntu: An African Principle with Global Relevance

King II's definitive stance on the cultivation of a particularly African philosophical mindset for 'corporate ethos and conduct' is clearly stated in Item 38 of the report's 'Introduction' and is derived from the Committee's extensive research and consultation on South Africa's 'wide range of value systems and rich diversity.'[6] Briefly, this section lists several precepts as key characteristics of ubuntu: spiritual collectiveness, the communal nature of life (interdependence), consensus rather than dissension, humility and helpfulness, reconciliation and the eradication of prejudice, belief in fairness, the notion of the extended family, commitment to upholding moral values, an ideology of consultation, and a 'perpetual optimism.'

These are presented as constituting a world view within which relevant ethical values and aims can be promoted. Moreover, *King II* calls for the principle of ubuntu to be recognized as a founding tradition for business ethics in the new millennium. Archbishop Emeritus Desmond Tutu has expressed the essence of this African cultural paradigm with particular succinctness: 'Ubuntu … is part of the gift that Africa is going to give to the world. It embraces hospitality, caring about others, being willing to go that extra mile for the sake of another. We believe that a person is a person through other persons; that my humanity is caught up and bound up in yours. When I dehumanise you, I inexorably dehumanise myself. The solitary human being is a contradiction in terms, and therefore you seek to work for the common good because your humanity comes into its own in community, in belonging.'[7]

To dismiss, discard, and disregard others is, in the language of ubuntu (since 'I am because you are') nothing short of self-neglect. *King II* spells out this tenet in the context of corporate social responsibility: 'Co-existence with other people is highly valued. The essence of Ubuntu (humanity) that cuts across Africa is based on the premise that you can be respected only because of your cordial co-existence with others.'[8]

The authors then collate these traits as factors for the regeneration of human resources management, leadership attitudes, and social cohesion, within and beyond the company gates.

King II's ideas reflect the trend of an international shift in values in ethical business theory and practice, and, in addition, offer a succinctly African solution to the challenges facing the private sector and its engagement with social well-being and development. The report's section on integrated sustainability reporting is prefaced with an inscription that translates the isiZulu phrase *'Umuntu ngamuntu ngabantu'* into English as 'I am because you are; you are because we are,' concluding with the interpretation, 'Humanity is interdependent.'

One of the reasons for the King Committee's expansion of parts of its 1994 submission (*King I*) was so that concurrent global trends in corporate governance during the twenty-first century could inform and be integrated into its recommendations. This motivation arose not only from cognisance of the need for local companies to produce reliable information that would attract global investors, but also from the

emerging worldwide recognition of sound corporate governance acting as 'a lever to address the converging interests of competitiveness,
corporate citizenship, and social and environmental responsibility.'[9]

King II's unique contribution to the global effort in this regard is articulated in its exposition of the qualities of ubuntu as a management
model:

> The notion of sustainability and the triple-bottom-line in the corporate
> world is evolving to an approach that recognises the importance of inter-
> dependent relationships between an enterprise and the community in
> which it exists. Ubuntu has formed the basis of relationships in the past
> and there is no reason why it could not be extended to the corporate
> world. International experience, which reveals a growing ... emphasis
> on non-financial issues, is a wake-up call to Africans not to abandon their
> cultures ... but to import and infuse these practices into the corporate world.[10]
>
> ...
>
> The Ubuntu philosophy and the community concept of the corporation ...
> provide a cultural hot-bed for such important values as creative co-operation,
> empathetic communication and team-work. They provide a basis for what
> should be corporate culture on African soil. In implementing best prac-
> tices with regard to the triple-bottom-line, corporate South Africa would
> be well-advised to build on the foundation of African values. They can not
> only form the basis for effective practices in this regard, but also have the
> potential to set South Africans apart as world leaders in this area.

Enterprise with Integrity

Drawing from work already done by numerous international bodies on
accountability and reporting (such as the AA1000 AccountAbility
Standard, the SIGMA Sustainability Guidelines,[11] the UN Global
Compact,[12] and the Global Reporting Initiative[13]), *King II* encodes seven
basic precepts – discipline, transparency, independence, accountability,
responsibility, fairness, and social responsibility – within a framework
of guidelines that inform and enhance ethical business practice.

Three of these seven core facets of governance relate tangentially
(and one, specifically) to social responsibility – accountability, fairness,
and responsibility – and as such, the report provides a valuable guide to
the formation of a just and sustainable business response to crucial

human challenges such as HIV and AIDS, notably since they emphasize an inclusive approach in all commercial operations. This approach is a seminal attribute of both King reports, and one that sets them apart from their equivalents elsewhere in the world, in that their espousal of 'a participative corporate governance system of enterprise with integrity' originates in 'the King Committee in 1994 successfully formalis[ing] the need for companies to recognise that they no longer act independently from the societies and the environment in which they operate.'[14]

King II's proposals promote the idea of an equilibrium and interaction between structure and agency. Similarly, its conjugation of commercial enterprise with social concern represents the notion of the 'good corporate citizen,' which is in perfect alignment with the concept of a company as a communitarian self. Moreover, by clearly articulating ubuntu as its philosophical foundation, *King II* specifies a uniquely African derivation of business-in-community. By linking this to the growing global awareness of the role of the corporation in society, *King II* presents a pivotal construct for an applied form of the communitarian business model.

The report is replete with conceptual elements that have one common feature: an appreciation of the relational nature, as opposed to disconnection, of entities and concepts (such as government and the private sector, investment and return, society and the market, enterprise and integrity, profits and people, financial and non-financial information). Its special achievement lies in its rigorous formulation for the marriage of corporate social responsibility (CSR) – of which corporate social investment (CSI) is one activity – with other core strategic components of business operations such as production, marketing, and accounting, from which it has traditionally been divorced.

In its briefing document on *King II*, the South African Grantmakers' Association[15] refers to this merging: 'Just as a focus on sustainable business management is a key aspect of sound governance practice, so CSI is a key component of the "mosaic" that is sustainable business management ... South African business's assumption of CSI responsibilities presents it with an opportunity to leverage its role in shaping public policy in ways that benefit itself and the broader national community.'[16]

'Triple-Bottom-Line' Reporting

King II conjoins moral obligation with business intelligence information. For example, the report's authors urge that all companies should report at least once every year on the nature and extent of their social, transformation, ethical, safety, health, and environmental management policies and practices. This advances company reporting from the level of the 'single' to the 'triple-bottom-line,' that is, from an account of purely economic data to a more comprehensive narrative and figures describing expenditure on, commitment to, and strategic results of social and environmental activities.

By 2003, the effects of *King II* were visible. Its recommendations generated an awareness of full and transparent reporting as a normative procedural requirement for companies listed on the Johannesburg Stock Exchange, such that corporate social responsibility (CSR) programs began to be designed with in-built mechanisms for measuring impacts, acknowledging and describing deficiencies and limitations, and proposing solutions. Global accounting specialists Deloitte & Touche reported on surveys of top 100 companies that had devised management courses on CSR integration and showcased their achievements through the media and via the Internet.[17]

King II's authors also advise companies to identify HIV and AIDS as a matter for specific consideration, in managing its impact both within and around the company's ambit.[18] This philosophy is expressly defined as 'business decision-making linked to ethical values ... and respect for people, communities and the environment ... [evidenced by] a comprehensive set of policies, practices and programs that are integrated throughout business operations, and decision-making processes that are supported and rewarded by top management.'[19]

Non-Contractual Obligations within a Communitarian Ethic

In the practice and application of business ethics theory, there is a distinct difference between cursory compliance and sustained, solid contribution. The King Code of Corporate Practices and Conduct is not prescribed by law in all areas of business; currently, only JSE-listed companies, public sector enterprises and agencies, banks, and financial and insurance institutions are required to demonstrate adherence to the code. As noted by JSE Chief Executive Russel Loubser, the JSE is not a 'policing agent' and the greatest stick that he, as CEO, can wave against errant executives is 'bad publicity.'[20]

For this reason, it is the non-contractual relationship inherent in the South African private sector's response to HIV and AIDS that is espoused in *King II*. This approach is built, applied, and advanced on the

model of an Afro-European communitarian ethic as a product of fundamental virtuous concern. As such, it works through a process that pro-
liferates beyond the confines of contracts and statutory obligations.

In contrast to the idea that codes of conduct require blanket enforcement mechanisms or, at least, structured monitoring systems, Epstein
argues for a modern communitarian idea that, in the interests of genuinely responsible and responsive social organization, there should be
no formal obligation to comply with such codes. He contends that, because individuals enter voluntarily into 'multiple overlapping forms of
association,' they can generally be relied upon, at the very least, to 'find
some limited areas of compromise and co-operation.' If that critical element of trust can be established on some limited grounds, then the
seeds are planted for its expansion over time into other areas. But this
program will work only through voluntary interaction that takes place
with the prospect of mutual advantage, and it cannot work when moral
over-confidence breeds social intolerance. 'Forced associations will
only compound ... high levels of distrust and make matters worse ...
there is no way to force-feed a viable social community. It has to be the
outgrowth of voluntary interactions by free and responsible men and
women.'[21]

This echoes Etzioni's illustration of the modern communitarian setting being made up of intersecting relationships, within and through
which individuals are naturally inclined to caring and sharing, despite
cultural and ideological differences.[22] Similarly, the conviction in such
voluntary, adaptive, and innovative virtuous approaches taking root
and flourishing over time within a supportive wider world view is reflected in the principle of ubuntu – which is specified in *King II*.

This is not to ignore or deny that our contemporary society suffers
from a lack of these strongly supportive connections, and indeed, radical disconnection is precisely what the HIV and AIDS pandemic is ex-
posing.[23] Even a fleeting survey of contemporary life reveals ubiquitous
and pervasive threats to human well-being: violent crime, abuse of
women and children, armed conflicts, corrupt government, mass poverty, and unchecked spread of infectious disease. As Campbell indicates, it would also be unrealistic, if not unreasonable, to suggest that
such voluntary, virtuous approaches, because they constitute a moral
ideal rather than a universal reality, could be rapidly and readily adopted by key role-players in society with a longstanding tradition of
oppositional attitudes, and that the public in general would respond in
kind with the urgency that the pandemic demands.[24]

The report's pragmatic recommendations are based on a clear grasp of this reality, and on a persuasive vision of social reconnection, which would gradually invigorate and advance an ethos of mutual and collective responsibility, balanced with individual rights. Behaviour change occurs within a highly complex matrix of social and cultural influences, but also depends on individual inspiration and self-leadership. The economic, racial, and gender imbalances and divisions in South African society, which have patently reduced opportunities for individuals to exercise their natural rights, responsibilities, and choices, and which continue to drive the spread of HIV, have been constructed and bolstered over centuries. Narrowing these gaps and ensuring the nation's recovery from these wounds will accordingly be a process requiring protracted and ongoing attention and vigilance.

Impacts of *King II*

Despite the non-contractual nature of *King II*'s recommendations, the ideas embodied in the report have the potential to carry weight in the courts. Mervyn King, chair of the King Committee that compiled both reports, has explained that, in terms of corporate governance as it relates to the fiduciary duties of directors, the King guidelines have been used by a legal body as a benchmark against which to weigh degrees of negligence by company leadership: 'The interesting thing now about having acceptable corporate governance guidelines in South Africa [is that] courts can actually assess whether a director has exercised care and skill, having regard to guidelines ... the guidelines complement the law and the law complements the guidelines.'[25]

The mandate of the King Committee was only to recommend. However, if, as exemplified here, a reciprocal dynamic between the letter of the law and the communitarian interests embodied in ubuntu can be established, a normative state of responsible business practice might be a realistic vision.

An additional marker of *King II*'s potential to effect positive change occurred in May 2004 when the Johannesburg Stock Exchange announced its first Socially Responsible Investment Index (SRI Index) for listed companies. This was described as 'a triple-first' because it is also the first index of its kind in an emerging market, and a world-first as one launched by a stock exchange.[26] Nicky Newton-King, CEO of the JSE, described the SRI Index as a means of helping to focus the debate on embracing the triple-bottom-line reporting method, and of encouraging more companies to voluntarily benchmark their CSR activities in this way.[27] Newton-King's comment implies a commitment to motivating corporate citizens to adopt and embed – rather than adhere desultorily to – a moral framework for business practice. As such, it manifests the notion of the corporate citizen as a virtuous individual entity engaged in refining its stance as a communitarian self, and adding its voice to the call for committed and co-ordinated action on social issues like HIV/AIDS. By structuring the measurement of the actual impact of ethical responses from business to the pandemic, this refinement process can be supported and advanced throughout society as a method of unification.

This has been borne out to an extent by a study of fifty-five SRI companies conducted by the University of Pretoria's Centre for Business and Professional Ethics;[28] a qualitative content analysis of these companies' annual and sustainability reports was conducted to measure their compliance with the *King II Report* and its Code of Corporate Practices. The study concluded that the majority (82 per cent) of the companies surveyed referred to *King II* as their benchmark for ethical consciousness, commitment, and practice.

Interconnections with HIV and AIDS

Chapter 4 of the *King II Report* gives particular attention to HIV and AIDS in South Africa in the section on health. Citing statistical indicators prevailing in 2002 showing that 'over 20% of South Africa's economically active population [would] be directly affected within the [coming] five years,' the report lists six practical impacts of the pandemic on the country's economy generally: decreased productivity, increased overhead costs, reduction in the available skills and customer base, along with changes in consumer spending patterns, lowered profitability, and diminished investor confidence.[29]

The report's authors note that 'there [was] little evidence of measures taken to promote business sustainability in the face of the pandemic.' They urge boards of directors to adopt appropriate plans and policies based on an exhaustive understanding of the multiple and trans-sectoral effects of HIV and AIDS on business operations and objectives, and to regularly evaluate and report to stakeholders on performance in the implementation of such strategies.[30]

In Chapter 5 of the report, the committee turns to social and transformation issues, which – as a result of their nexus with HIV and AIDS prevention, treatment, and care programs – relate directly to 'the greater well-being of society generally.' Here again, the model of an ubuntu business ethic is motivated as having the potential to contribute to sustainability through addressing inequality, advocating that the process should be 'underpinned by supportiveness, co-operation and solidarity.' The committee calls for businesses to move beyond compliance with the existing laws that have already helped to effect change, and to commit to their 'underlying objectives.'[31] At this point, the report makes specific mention of the need to empower women in terms of access, contribution and benefit, through workplace policies that advance their opportunities and status at every level, consideration of their parental and care-giving roles, representation of women's issues and gender discrimination, and the obligation to ensure women's full participation in the economy.

This is closely followed by guidelines for the prioritization of diversity management and social investment programs designed to propagate growth and security in communities.[32] Bearing in mind that South Africa's youth are particularly vulnerable to HIV infection and its labyrinth of challenges, business funding for a range of community-based upliftment projects – in other words, responses that extend beyond the workplace and into focus areas such as education and income-generation – is crucial for the future of both society and the market. As such, the health of future generations and their economic prospects depend upon such commitments. Furthermore, given that all these measures are vital to the containment of HIV/AIDS and the provision of relief to those most susceptible to its effects, these recommendations demonstrate clearly the report's holistic approach to the responsibility of companies operating in a society wracked by the pandemic as a global health crisis of daunting proportions.

The message of *King II* thus resonates: if the AIDS pandemic is society's physical manifestation of its spiritual and philosophical dislocation, then it is urgent that companies, as corporate citizens and communitarian selves, perceive the healing of this fractured social reality not only as a commercial imperative, but also for the sake of the intrinsic worth of people as ends in themselves, and as everyone's responsibility to address. The significance of this message lies in the distinctive lesson of the pandemic itself, which resides in the fact that no single person, irrespective of race, age, gender, or creed, is immune to HIV infection and impact. In prescribing the internalization of communitarian thinking, *King II* urges boards of directors, CEOs, managers, and business owners to value their employees at every level, and their stakeholders from every quarter, as highly as they would themselves and those close to them.

In foregrounding ubuntu as an appropriate ethical model for use by companies in response to the pandemic, the report indicates how to perceive the systems, behaviours, and impacts (both internal and external) relating to HIV infection and AIDS mortality, as analogous to those relating to the body of society – the immune systems, behaviour, and impact of our human family, as it were. This understanding is consistent with traditional African approaches to health care, specifically in their concern for the whole person rather than isolated symptoms of illness, or only bodily predicaments. HIV infects and affects people at every level of existence, so that a multiplicity of caring processes is required to address the variety of afflictions the disease syndrome can cause. It is in this context that we turn our attention to the issue of access to antiretroviral treatment.

Implications for Access to Antiretroviral Treatment

The contest for accessibility to ARV treatment for HIV-positive South Africans has become a world-renowned saga of post-apartheid struggle and solidarity that will feature distinctively in this nation's economic, political, and cultural history for many decades to come. While analysis of the myriad aspects of this particular chronicle is important, it is not pertinent here. What are crucial to the overall argument for ubuntu as a communitarian business ethic in the context of ARV treatment in South Africa are two facts:

1. That ARVs offer a prognosis of extended, enabled life, and therefore hope; and
2. That the biomedical, psychological, and social complexities of administering ARVs are such that nothing less than a holistic approach to the individual patient, her sense of self, and her communal relationships, will ensure successful adherence to treatment and overall well-being.

On the first fact, the support given to the employee patient by a workplace ARV program addresses both the moral and the monetary costs of HIV and AIDS, as a simple correlative concept. From the material and commercial perspective, business faces the reality that 'HIV and AIDS raises costs, reduces the productivity of individual workers and alters the firm's operating environment.'[33] These authors project that the SA customer base will grow slowly until 2010, with the demographic impact of AIDS becoming starkly visible, and this base declining by 18 per cent. By 2015, consumption patterns are expected to change as consumers reallocate what income they have to coping with illness and death. Providing agency and structure for access to a life-saving treatment not only mitigates the impact of HIV and AIDS on individuals and their collective relationships, but it also fosters an ethos of belonging and regard. This constitutes a substantial affirmation of the humanity in each and every employee, and in communities beyond the company gates. *King II* presents ubuntu as the basis for an argument that there is a vital ethical role for businesses to play in restoring the balance between nurturing and self-interest, such that these two motivations are not mutually exclusive, but twinned and interdependent. Through this argument, we come to understand society's vulnerability to HIV and AIDS as also being business's vulnerability. However, such provision is not a simple process. Peter Doyle, CEO of the Metropolitan Group, noted survey findings from the South Africa Business Coalition on HIV/AIDS (SABCOHA): businesses spend over US$40 million per year on ARV treatment services alone, but that much more is needed to address stigma and psychosocial needs around HIV and AIDS generally.[34] It is within this context that the second communitarian premise – that the epidemic can be fought only on broad social fronts with open-hearted commitment from business leadership and policymakers – can be understood. An HIV-positive health promoter who works with youth in KwaZulu-Natal has observed that 'getting to antiretroviral treatment is not an instant event – it is a journey ... So much is involved and ... it is not an easy decision to make ... it all begins with knowing your HIV status.'[35] Cultivating a workplace ethos that lowers stigma around HIV and AIDS and encourages uptake of voluntary counselling and testing involves an understanding of the value of peer education in the workplace. Dickinson's seminal research has examined the informal activities of employee volunteers in this sector, noting their reliance on the company to provide training, campaign materials, and visibility for these programs.[36] Management faces competing demands in this regard, and he recommends that peer educators leverage their ability to creatively address challenges such as 'AIDS myths' and the ways in which HIV is transmitted through sexual networks, to secure the support and resources needed to conduct this work.

Forming a Serious Relationship: ARV Treatment and HIV Prevention

Messages from the research arena, campaign advocates, and the media, in commentary on ARV roll-out in South Africa programs, emphasize that treatment cannot be regarded as an alternative to prevention, but should be approached in tandem. While ARVs provide hope by prolonging life and enabling employees to remain active for longer, they do not diminish the pressures on all social players to reduce new infections, nor the enduring risks of unsafe sex and the contexts of susceptibility in which these are embedded. Furthermore, in a generalized epidemic such as that in South Africa, the goal of universal ARV treatment is impossible without a reduction in the growing number of people newly infected each day. Fourie presents the argument for treatment and prevention to be seen 'in complementary terms' within a framework of improved relations between government and other policy actors and agents, based on a 'bottom-up' impulsion towards policy design.[37]

Creative HIV and AIDS information and awareness campaigns are crucial girders in a framework that integrates – and so helps to normalize – the shared effects, impacts, and implications of the epidemic. Whiteside[38] argues that in attempting to mitigate these impacts, we need a massive social movement to take charge of how the epidemic is allowed to progress, deploying a three-pronged approach of prevention, effective, affordable and deliverable treatment, and care.

Setswe describes the new frontiers of HIV and AIDS research as spanning 'the spectrum of basic science, clinical research, prevention interventions, policy development, ethics, social science and operations research.'[39] He urges an informed and practical response, with researchers working in multidisciplinary teams on innovative, evidence-based studies focusing on gender relations, media messaging, effective policy formulation, and implementation, to 'address a pandemic that increasingly affects the poor, women and young people throughout the world.' The overall architecture of such fully evolved programs involves a spherical continuum of knowledge-sharing, counselling, testing, treatment for both HIV and opportunistic infections, nutritional advice, and familial and community engagement in household viability and sustainability. Services should be constructed to bridge the philosophical gulf between mechanistic Western medical models and the more holistic African cosmological approach to healing.

It is also a design that begins and ends with elements targeted at destigmatization of HIV and AIDS at every level of the company and its surrounding areas of influence, while simultaneously demonstrating a commitment to confidentiality for the protection of individual rights to privacy and non-discrimination. In ethical terms, the communitarian approach to advocacy and policy around management of HIV and AIDS allows and argues for both, with the disease being exceptional only in the urgency and magnitude of the vulnerabilities that cause and perpetuate infection.

Conclusion

The crisis wrought by HIV and AIDS can be the catalyst for radical and urgent reconstruction of society. The epidemic is fuelled by massive social lacunae, originating in and replicating through an inherited environment of abject poverty and age-old gender inequality. As such, it is a metaphorical tutor that assigns complex and demanding tasks with urgent deadlines and harsh penalties in the form of social dissolution. To break the intergenerational cycle of disease, degradation, and division, investment must be made in humanity itself, so that a new ecology of social conscience can evolve through a focused learning of the best aspects of human character – in heightened relief to the worst. Both the pandemic and ubuntu co-create a meta-ethical nexus for such institutional and individual learning and change, by demonstrating that division and exclusivity result in dysfunction, and ultimately, pathology of the social body, mind, and spirit.

For the business sector, an authentic ethical response to HIV and AIDS requires a profound effort that acknowledges more than the clinical impact on profits, productivity, and morale that fosters meaningful partnerships to maximize results and that offers resources towards structural and cultural transformation. Corporate citizenship calls for relational concern for the human suffering caused by the pandemic, arising from the sense that we are all infected and affected by it, and from the belief that the poorest and frailest among us are co-founders of a desirable future.

NOTES

1 Adrian Cadbury, *Developing Corporate Governance Codes of Best Practice*, http://www.ifc.org/ifcext/cgf.nsf/AttachmentsByTitle/Toolkit2-read .pdf/$FILE/Toolkit2-read.pdf, 1.

2   The Southern African Chapter of the Institute of Directors (IoD) was
    formed in Johannesburg in 1960 by Harry Oppenheimer and is the only
    organization of its kind in Southern Africa. The organization represents
    directors, professionals, and business leaders in their individual capacities.
    The membership is prestigious, providing a unique opportunity for
    networking and business development in all spheres of business. The
    organization aims to bring about continual development and lifelong
    learning by facilitating internationally recognized director development
    and educational programmes. See http://www.iodsa.co.za.
3   King Committee on Corporate Governance, Institute of Directors in
    Southern Africa, *King Report on Corporate Governance for South Africa*
    (*King II*), 2002, 5.
4   Adrian Cadbury, *Corporate Governance Overview* (Washington, DC: World
    Bank, 1999).
5   Alec Hogg, 'Interview with Mervyn King,' *MoneyWeb*, 4 Sept. 2002.
6   *King II*, 18.
7   L. Mbigi, 'Leadership: In Search of an African Spirit,' *Mail & Guardian
    Online – Business in Africa*, 8 Apr. 2004.
8   *King II*, Item 38.5, p. 18.
9   Ibid., 14.
10 Ibid., Items 7, 8, Section 4, p. 99.
11 SIGMA (Sustainability Integrated Guidelines for Management)
    Guidelines, http://www.proveandimprove.org/new/tools/sigma.php.
12 The Global Compact is a framework for businesses committed to aligning
    their operations and strategies with ten universally accepted principles
    in human rights, labour, the environment and anti-corruption. As the
    world's largest, global corporate citizenship initiative, the Global Compact is
    concerned with exhibiting and building the social legitimacy of business and
    markets. See http://www.unglobalcompact.org/AboutTheGC/index.html.
13 The Global Reporting Initiative (GRI) has pioneered the development of
    the world's most widely used sustainability reporting framework and is
    committed to its continuous improvement and application worldwide.
    This framework sets out the principles and indicators that organizations
    can use to measure and report their economic, environmental, and social
    performance. See http://www.globalreporting.org/Home.
14 *King II*, 5.
15 The Southern African Grantmakers' Association (SAGA) was a member-
    ship association providing professional support to the corporate social
    investment and donor community.
16 South African Grantmakers' Association. *The King Report 2002: Implications for
    Corporate Social Investment in South Africa*. SAGA Briefings, 1 Nov. 2002, 10.

17   Deloitte & Touche South Africa, 'Have Corporate Governance Guidelines Changed Our Business Environment?' 17 Feb. 2004. Accessed 23 Mar. 2005. http://www.deloitte.com/dtt/press_release/0,2309,sid%253D47395 %2526cid%253D51000,00.html#Top.

18   *King II*, 35–6.

19   Ibid., 96.

20   J. Cameron, 'Boardroom Detectives,' *Acumen* 7 (no date): 57.

21   R.A. Epstein, 'Toleration: The Lost Virtue,' *Communitarian Network* 14, nos. 2–3 (2004): 51, http://www.gwu.edu/~ccps/rcq/Epstein.pdf.

22   Amitai Etzioni, 'Communitarianism,' *Encyclopaedia of Community: From the Village to the Virtual World*, ed. Karen Christensen and David Levinson (Thousand Oaks, CA: Sage, 2003), 1:A308.

23   Catherine Campbell. *Letting Them Die: Why HIV/AIDS Prevention Programmes Often Fail* (Cape Town: Double Story Books, 2003).

24   Ibid.

25   Mervyn King, Hogg interview.

26   M. Brady. 'A Measure for Corporate Citizenship,' *Mail & Guardian*, 11 Aug. 2004.

27   Ibid.

28   Centre for Professional and Business Ethics, University of Pretoria, SA, 'Ethics Reporting Practices of JSE-listed Companies,' 2007, http://web.up.ac.za/UserFiles/EthicsReporting.pdf.

29   *King II*, 116.

30   Ibid., 117.

31   Ibid., 123.

32   Ibid., 124.

33   Tony Barnett and Alan Whiteside, *AIDS in the Twenty-First Century: Disease and Globalisation* (Basingstoke, UK: Palgrave Macmillan, 2002).

34   Mervyn King, Hogg interview.

35   Oziel Mdletshe, editorial in *Informer*, May 2007, 14.

36   David Dickinson, 'Talking About AIDS: A Study of Informal Activities Undertaken by Workplace HIV/AIDS Peer Educators in a South African company' (Johannesburg: Wits Business School, 2007).

37   Pieter Fourie, *The Political Management of HIV and AIDS in South Africa: One Burden Too Many?* (Basingstoke, UK: Palgrave Macmillan, 2006), 182–3.

38   Alan Whiteside, 'The Impact of the HIV/AIDS Epidemic,' presentation to MRC/HIVAN KZN AIDS Forum, 24 June 2003.

39   Geoffrey Setswe, 'Challenges 25 Years into the Pandemic,' *Leadership in HIV/AIDS* 15 (Mar. 2007): 14.

REFERENCES

Barnett, Tony, and Whiteside, Alan. *AIDS in the Twenty-First Century: Disease and Globalisation*. Basingstoke, UK: Palgrave Macmillan, 2002.

Brady, M. 'A Measure for Corporate Citizenship.' *Johannesburg Mail & Guardian*, 11 Aug. 2004.

Cadbury, Adrian. *Corporate Governance Overview*. Washington, DC: World Bank, 1999.

Cameron, J. 'Boardroom Detectives.' *Acumen* 7 (n.d.): 57.

Campbell, Catherine C. *Letting Them Die: Why HIV/AIDS Prevention Programmes Often Fail*. Cape Town: Double Storey Books, 2003.

Centre for Professional and Business Ethics, University of Pretoria. 'Ethics Reporting Practices of JSE Listed Companies.' 2007. http://web.up.ac.za/UserFiles/EthicsReporting.pdf.

Deloitte & Touche South Africa. 'Have Corporate Governance Guidelines Changed Our Business Environment?' 17 Feb. 2004. Accessed 23 Mar. 2005. http://www.deloitte.com/dtt/press_release/0,2309,sid%253D47395%2526cid%253D51000,00.html#Top.

Dickinson, David. 'Talking about AIDS: A Study of Informal Activities Undertaken by Workplace HIV/AIDS Peer Educators in a South African Company.' Johannesburg: Wits Business School, 2007.

Epstein, R.A. 'Toleration: The Lost Virtue.' *Communitarian Network* 14, nos. 2–3 (2004): 41–51. http://www.gwu.edu/~ccps/rcq/Epstein.pdf.

Etzioni, Amitai. 'Communitarianism.' In *Encyclopaedia of Community: From the Village to the Virtual World*, edited by Karen Christensen and David Levinson, vol. 1, A308. Thousand Oaks, CA: Sage Publications, 2003.

Fourie, Pieter. *The Political Management of HIV and AIDS in South Africa: One Burden Too Many?* (Basingstoke: Palgrave Macmillan, 2006).

Hogg, Alec, 'Interview with Mervyn King.' *MoneyWeb*, 4 Sept. 2002.

King Committee on Corporate Governance, Institute of Directors in Southern Africa. *King Report on Corporate Governance for South Africa (King II)*, 2002.

Mbigi, L. 'Leadership: In Search of an African Spirit.' *Mail & Guardian Online – Business in Africa*, 8 Apr. 2004.

Setswe, Geoffrey. 'Challenges 25 Years into the Pandemic.' *Leadership in HIV/AIDS* 15 (2007): 12–14.

SIGMA (Sustainability – Integrated Guidelines for Management) Guidelines. http://www.proveandimprove.org/new/tools/sigma.php.

Whiteside, Alan. 'The Impact of the HIV/AIDS Epidemic.' Presentation to MRC/HIVAN KZN AIDS Forum, 24 June 2003.

Annex: Human Rights Guidelines for Pharmaceutical Companies in Relation to Access to Medicines[1]

Preamble

a. Almost two billion people lack access to essential medicines; improving access to existing medicines could save ten million lives each year, four million of them in Africa and South-East Asia.

b. Millennium Development Goals, such as reducing child mortality, improving maternal health, and combating HIV/AIDS, malaria and other diseases, depend upon improving access to medicines.

c. One of the Millennium Development Goal targets is, 'in cooperation with pharmaceutical companies, (to) provide access to affordable essential drugs in developing countries.'

d. Medical care and access to medicines are vital features of the right to the highest attainable standard of health.

e. Access to medicines depends upon effective, integrated, responsive and accessible health systems. In many countries, health systems are failing and collapsing, constituting a grave obstacle to increasing access to medicines. While a range of actors can take immediate steps to increase access to medicines, health systems must be strengthened as a matter of priority and urgency.

f. States have the primary responsibility for realising the right to the highest attainable standard of health and increasing access to medicines.

g. In addition to States, numerous national and international actors share a responsibility to increase access to medicines.

h. As confirmed by the United Nations Global Compact, the Special Representative of the Secretary General on Human Rights and Transnational Corporations and Other Business Enterprises, the

Committee on Economic, Social and Cultural Rights, the Business Leaders Initiative on Human Rights, and many others, the private business sector has human rights responsibilities.

i. Pharmaceutical companies, including innovator, generic and biotechnology companies, have human rights responsibilities in relation to access to medicines.

j. Pharmaceutical companies also have other responsibilities, for example, a responsibility to enhance shareholder value.

k. Pharmaceutical companies are subject to several forms of internal and external monitoring and accountability; however, these mechanisms do not usually monitor, and hold a company to account, in relation to its human rights responsibilities to enhance access to medicines.

l. Pharmaceutical companies contribute in various ways to the realisation of the right to the highest attainable standard of health, such as providing individuals and communities with important information about public health issues. Enhancing access to medicines, however, has the central place in the societal mission of pharmaceutical companies. For this reason, these non-exhaustive, inter-related Guidelines focus on the human rights responsibilities of pharmaceutical companies in relation to access to medicines.

m. Pharmaceutical companies' human rights responsibilities are not confined to the right to the highest attainable standard of health. They have human rights responsibilities, for example, regarding freedom of association and conditions of work. These human rights responsibilities, however, are not addressed in these Guidelines.

n. While most of the Guidelines address issues that are highly relevant to all pharmaceutical companies, including innovator, generic and biotechnology companies, a few of the Guidelines address issues of particular relevance to some companies within the pharmaceutical sector.

o. These Guidelines apply to pharmaceutical companies and their subsidiaries.

p. These Guidelines are based on human rights principles enshrined in the Universal Declaration of Human Rights, including non-discrimination, equality, transparency, monitoring and accountability. The Constitution of the World Health Organisation affirms that the 'enjoyment of the highest attainable standard of health is one of the fundamental rights of every human being.' This fundamental human right is codified in numerous national constitutions, as well as international human rights treaties, including the Convention on the Rights of the Child and International Covenant on Economic, Social and Cultural Rights. Accordingly, these Guidelines are informed by some features of the right to the highest attainable standard of health, such as the requirement that medicines are of good quality, safe and efficacious. The Guidelines also draw from other widely accepted standards, such as instruments on medicines adopted by the World Health Organisation.

q. For the purposes of these Guidelines, medicines include active pharmaceutical ingredients, diagnostic tools, vaccines, biopharmaceuticals and other related healthcare technologies.

r. For the purposes of these Guidelines, neglected diseases are defined as those diseases primarily affecting those living in poverty, especially in rural areas, in low-income countries. Sometimes called tropical or poverty-related diseases, they include, for example, leishmaniasis (kala-azar), onchocerciasis (river blindness), Chagas disease, leprosy, schistosomiasis (bilharzias), lymphatic filariasis, African trypanosomiasis (sleeping sickness) and dengue. Although in recent years HIV/AIDS, tuberculosis and malaria have attracted increasing attention and resources, they may also be regarded as neglected diseases.

s. These Guidelines adopt the World Bank definition of low-income, middle-income and high-income countries.

General

1. The company should adopt a human rights policy statement which expressly recognises the importance of human rights generally, and the right to the highest attainable standard of health in particular, in relation to the strategies, policies, programs, projects and activities of the company.

2. The company should integrate human rights, including the right to the highest attainable standard of health, into the strategies, policies, programs, projects and activities of the company.

3. The company should always comply with the national law of the State where it operates, as well as any relevant legislation of the State where it is domiciled.

4. The company should refrain from any conduct that will or may encourage a State to act in a way that is inconsistent with its obligations arising from national and international human rights law, including the right to the highest attainable standard of health.

Commentary: Formal, express recognition of the importance of human rights, and the right to the highest attainable standard of health, helps to establish a firm foundation for the company's policies and activities on access to medicines (Guideline 1). Such recognition, however, is not enough: operationalisation is the challenge (Guideline 2). Many of the Guidelines signal ways in which right-to-health considerations can be operationalised and integrated into the company's activities. There are numerous national and international (including regional) legal provisions that safeguard aspects of the right to the highest attainable standard of health. It is axiomatic that they must be respected, at all times, by all pharmaceutical companies, in accordance with elementary principles of corporate good governance (Guidelines 3–4).

Disadvantaged Individuals, Communities, and Populations

5. Whenever formulating and implementing its strategies, policies, programs, projects and activities that bear upon access to medicines, the company should give particular attention to the needs of disadvantaged individuals, communities and populations, such as children, the elderly and those living in poverty. The company should also give particular attention to the very poorest in all markets, as well as gender-related issues.

Commentary: Equality and non-discrimination are among the most fundamental features of international human rights, including the right to the highest attainable standards of health. They are akin to the crucial health concept of equity. Equality, non-discrimination and equity have a social justice component. Accordingly, the right to the highest attainable standard of health has a particular pre-occupation with disadvantaged individuals, communities and populations, including children, the elderly and those living in poverty. Like equity, the right-to-health also requires that particular attention be given to gender. All the other Guidelines must be interpreted and applied in the light of Guideline 5, which has fundamental importance.

Transparency

6. In relation to access to medicines, the company should be as transparent as possible. There is a presumption in favour of the disclosure of information, held by the company, which relates to access to medicines. This presumption may be rebutted on limited

grounds, such as respect for the confidentiality of personal health data collected during clinical trials.

7. In conjunction with other pharmaceutical companies, the company should agree to standard formats for the systematic disclosure of company information and data bearing upon access to medicines, thereby making it easier to evaluate the performance of one company against another, as well as the performance of the same company over time.

8. Either alone or in conjunction with others, the company should establish an independent body to consider disputes that may arise regarding the disclosure or otherwise of information relating to access to medicines. This body may be the monitoring and accountability mechanism referred to in Guideline 14.

Commentary: Transparency is another cardinal principle of international human rights, including the right to the highest attainable standard of health. It is not possible to properly understand and meaningfully evaluate access to medicines policies and practices without the disclosure of key information. There is a presumption in favour of disclosure, which may be rebutted on limited grounds (Guideline 6). Commonsense confirms that the principle of transparency not only requires that information be made publicly available, it also requires the information be made publicly available in a form that is accessible, manageable and useful (Guideline 7). An independent, trusted and informal body should be established to consider any disputes that may arise about whether or not a particular piece of information relating to access to medicines should be disclosed (Guideline 8). This body should also provide guidance on the legitimate grounds of non-disclosure. While Guidelines 6–8 have general application to access to medicines, other Guidelines apply the cardinal principle of transparency in specific contexts, such as public policy influence, advocacy and lobbying (Guidelines 17–19).

Management, Monitoring, and Accountability

9. The company should encourage and facilitate multi-stakeholder engagement in the formulation of its policies, programs, projects and other activities that bear upon access to medicines. In keeping with Guideline 5, this engagement should include the active and informed participation of disadvantaged individuals, communities and populations.

10. The company should have a publicly available policy on access to medicines setting out general and specific objectives, time frames, reporting procedures, and lines of accountability.
11. The company should have a governance system that includes direct board-level responsibility and accountability for its access to medicines policy.
12. The company should have clear management systems, including quantitative targets, to implement and monitor its access to medicines policy.
13. The company should publish a comprehensive annual report, including qualitative and quantitative information, enabling an assessment of the company's policies, programs, projects and other activities that bear upon access to medicines.
14. In the context of access to medicines, internal monitoring and accountability mechanisms have a vital role to play, but they should also be supplemented by a mechanism that is independent of the company. Until such a mechanism is established by others, the company should establish an effective, transparent, accessible and independent monitoring and accountability mechanism that:
    i. assesses the impact of the company's strategies, policies, programs, projects and activities on access to medicines, especially for disadvantaged individuals, communities and populations;
    ii. monitors, and holds the company to account in relation to, these Guidelines.

Commentary: All human rights, including the right to the highest attainable standard of health, require effective, transparent and accessible monitoring and accountability mechanisms. The mechanisms have a variety of forms; usually a mix of mechanisms is required. While some mechanisms are internal, others are external and independent; both types are needed. Guidelines 9–13 address the issue of internal corporate monitoring and accountability regarding access to medicines. Guideline 14 addresses the issue of an external, independent monitoring and accountability mechanism regarding access to medicines.

Corruption

15. A company should publicly adopt effective anti-corruption policies and measures, and comply with relevant national law implementing the United Nations Convention against Corruption.

16. In collaboration with States, the company should take all reasonable measures to address counterfeiting.

Commentary: Corruption is a major obstacle to the enjoyment of the right to the highest attainable standard of health, including access to medicines. Those living in poverty, for example, are disproportionately harmed by corruption because they are less able to pay for private alternatives where corruption has depleted public health services. Numerous features of the right to the highest attainable standard of health, such as transparency, monitoring and accountability, help to establish an environment in which corruption can neither thrive nor survive. In short, a right-to-health policy is also an anti-corruption policy. As emphasised in the Preamble, improving access to medicines is a responsibility shared by numerous national and international actors; Guideline 16 provides one specific example of this shared responsibility in relation to counterfeiting.[2]

Public Policy Influence, Advocacy, and Lobbying

17. The company should disclose all current advocacy and lobbying positions, and related activities, at the regional, national and international levels, that impact or may impact upon access to medicines.
18. The company should annually disclose its financial and other support to key opinion leaders, patient associations, political parties and candidates, trade associations, academic departments, research centres and others, through which it seeks to influence public policy and national, regional and international law and practice. The disclosure should extend to amounts, beneficiaries and channels by which the support is provided.
19. When providing any financial or other support, the company should require all recipients to publicly disclose such support on all appropriate occasions.

Commentary: Like many other businesses, pharmaceutical companies devote considerable resources to advocacy, lobbying and related activities. While some of these activities may impact positively on access to medicines, for example, lobbying to lower taxes on medicines, other activities may impact negatively. Guidelines have already emphasised, in general terms, the central importance of transparency in relation to access to medicines (Guidelines 6–8). Guidelines 17–19 apply this general principle of transparency to the specific context of public policy influence, advocacy and lobbying.

Quality

20. The company should manufacture medicines that comply with current World Health Organisation Good Manufacturing Practice Guidelines, as well as other appropriate international regulatory requirements for quality, safety and efficacy.

Commentary: Guideline 20 reflects the elementary right-to-health requirement that all medicines must be of good quality, safe and efficacious.

Clinical Trials

21. A company's clinical trials should observe the highest ethical and human rights standards, including non-discrimination, equality and the requirements of informed consent. This is especially vital in those States with weak regulatory frameworks.
22. The company should conform to the Declaration of Helsinki on Ethical Principles for Medical Research Involving Human Subjects, as well as the World Health Organisation Guidelines for Good Clinical Practice.

Commentary: The right to the highest standard of health encompasses medical ethics. Guidelines 21–22 emphasise the right-to-health responsibility of pharmaceutical companies to observe the leading international standards on ethics and clinical trials. Guidelines 9–14 emphasise the importance of effective, transparent and accessible monitoring and accountability mechanisms; these mechanisms should monitor, and hold to account, pharmaceutical companies in relation to their policies and practices on clinical trials.

Neglected Diseases

23. The company should make a public commitment to contribute to research and development for neglected diseases. Also, it should either provide in-house research and development for neglected diseases, or support external research and development for neglected diseases, or both. In any event, it should publicly

disclose how much it contributes to and invests in research and development for neglected diseases.

24. The company should consult widely with the World Health Organisation, WHO/TDR[3] and other relevant organisations, including leading civil society groups, with a view to enhancing its contribution to research and development for neglected diseases.

25. The company should engage constructively with key international and other initiatives that are searching for new, sustainable and effective approaches to accelerate and enhance research and development for neglected diseases.

Commentary: By providing an incentive for pharmaceutical companies to invest in research and development, the intellectual property regime makes a major contribution to the discovery of new medicines that save lives and reduce suffering. Where there is no economically viable market, however, the incentive is inadequate and the regime fails to generate significant innovation. For this reason, a different approach is needed to address the vitally important right-to-health challenge of neglected or poverty-related diseases. Defined in the Preamble, neglected diseases mainly afflict the poorest people in the poorest countries. The record shows that research and development has not addressed key priority health needs of low-income and middle-income countries. More specifically, research and development has given insufficient attention to neglected diseases. There is evidence, however, that some pharmaceutical companies are taking active measures to reverse this trend.[4] The right to the highest attainable standard of health not only requires that existing medicines are accessible, but also that much-needed new medicines are developed as soon as possible. Neglected diseases demand special attention because they tend to afflict the most disadvantaged (Guideline 5). Guideline 23 does not make the unreasonable demand that all companies provide in-house research and development for neglected diseases. Rather, all companies should make some contribution towards research and development for neglected diseases. Guidelines 23–25 signal other steps that companies should take to address the historic neglect of poverty-related diseases.

Patents and Licensing

26. The company should respect the right of countries to use, to the full, the provisions in the Agreement on Trade-Related Aspects of

Intellectual Property Rights (TRIPS) (1994), which allow flexibility for the purpose of promoting access to medicines, including the provisions relating to compulsory licensing and parallel imports. The company should make and respect a public commitment not to lobby for more demanding protection of intellectual property interests than those required by TRIPS, such as additional limitations on compulsory licensing.

27. The company should respect the letter and spirit of the Doha Declaration on the TRIPS Agreement and Public Health (2001) that recognises a State's right to protect public health and promote access to medicines for all.

28. The company should not impede those States that wish to implement the World Trade Organisation Decision on Implementation of paragraph 6 of the Doha Declaration on the TRIPS Agreement and Public Health (2003) by issuing compulsory licences for exports to those countries, without manufacturing capacity, encompassed by the Decision.

29. Given that some least-developed countries are exempt from World Trade Organization rules requiring the granting and enforcing patents until 2016, the company should not lobby for such countries to grant or enforce patents.

30. As part of its access to medicines policy, the company should issue non-exclusive voluntary licences with a view to increasing access, in low-income and middle-income countries, to all medicines. The licences, which may be commercial or non-commercial, should include appropriate safeguards, for example, requiring that the medicines meet the standards on quality, safety and efficacy set out in Guideline 20. They should also include any necessary transfer of technology. The terms of the licences should be disclosed.

31. As a minimum, the company should consent to National Drug Regulatory Authorities using test data (i.e. the company should waive test data exclusivity) in least-developed countries and also when a compulsory licence is issued in a middle-income country.

32. In low-income and middle-income countries, the company should not apply for patents for insignificant or trivial modifications of existing medicines.

Commentary: The preceding Commentary recognises the major contribution made by the intellectual property regime to the discovery of life-saving medicines. Crucially, this regime contains various 'flexibilities' and other features that are designed to protect and promote access to existing medicines. Carefully constructed, they were agreed, after protracted negotiations, by the world community of States. Because they protect and promote access to existing medicines, which is a key component of the right to the highest attainable standard of health, these 'flexibilities' and other features should not be limited, diminished or compromised. Some of the key 'flexibilities' and other features are addressed in Guidelines 26–29. In brief, pharmaceutical companies should not seek to limit, diminish or compromise the 'flexibilities' and other features of the intellectual property regime that are designed to protect and promote access to existing medicines. Voluntary licences have a vital role to play in extending access to medicines (Guideline 30). Consistent with a company's responsibility to enhance shareholder value, commercial voluntary licences are designed to generate revenue for the patent holder. The terms of the licences should include appropriate safeguards, for example, relating to the quality, safety and efficacy of the product. Non-exclusive licences are more likely to extend access than exclusive licences. Voluntary licences respect, and depend upon, the intellectual property regime. Because data exclusivity has the potential to hinder access to medicines, companies should waive such exclusivity in all appropriate cases; while Guideline 31 identifies two occasions when the company should waive data exclusivity, there will be other occasions when a waiver is appropriate as a way of enhancing access to medicines for disadvantaged individuals, communities and populations. Access to medicines may be hindered when a company applies for a patent for improvements to an existing medicine; Guideline 32 is designed to mitigate this problem in low-income and middle-income countries.

Pricing, Discounting, and Donations

33. When formulating and implementing its access to medicines policy, the company should consider all the arrangements at its disposal with a view to ensuring that its medicines are affordable to as many people as possible. In keeping with Guideline 5, the company should give particular attention to ensuring its medicines are accessible to disadvantaged individuals, communities and populations, including those living in poverty and the very poorest in all markets. The arrangements should include, for example, differential pricing between countries, differential pricing within countries,

commercial voluntary licences, not-for-profit voluntary licences, donation programs, and Public Private Partnerships.

34. The arrangements should take into account a country's stage of economic development, as well as the differential purchasing power of populations within a country. The same medicine, for example, may be priced and packaged differently for the private and public sectors within the same country.

35. The arrangements should extend to all medicines manufactured by the company, including those for non-communicable conditions, such as heart disease and diabetes.

36. The company should have a board-approved policy that fully conforms to the current World Health Organisation Guidelines for Drug Donations.

37. The company should ensure that its discount and donation schemes and their delivery channels are:
    i. as simple as possible e.g. the schemes should place the minimum administrative burden on the beneficiary health system;
    ii. as inclusive as possible e.g. the schemes should not be confined to delivery channels that, in practice, exclude disadvantaged individuals and communities.

38. The company should disclose:
    i. as much information as possible about its pricing and discounting arrangements;
    ii. the absolute quantity and value of its drug donations;[5]
    iii. where possible, the number of beneficiary patients treated each year;
    iv. the amount of any tax benefit arising from its donations.

Commentary: While recognising they have a responsibility to enhance shareholder value, companies also have a human rights responsibility to extend access to medicines for all, including disadvantaged individuals, communities and populations (Guideline 5). In this context, pricing has a critical role to play. Lower prices do not necessarily mean lower profits. Sometimes the goal of enhancing access to medicines coincides with commercial interests. There are numerous arrangements that may reduce prices and increase sales, some of which are mentioned in Guidelines 33 and 34. Because the lives and health of millions are at stake, companies must approach such arrangements with urgency, creativity and boldness. They cannot act alone: here is another example of the shared responsibility emphasised in the Preamble. Inventive arrangements should neither be confined to a company's 'flagship' products nor a narrow range of communicable diseases (Guideline 35). Although unsustainable in the long-term, a carefully constructed donation program may extend access (Guidelines 36–37). Guidelines have already emphasised, in general terms, the central importance of transparency in relation to access to medicines (Guidelines 6–8); Guideline 38 applies this general principle of transparency to the specific context of pricing, discounting and donations.

Ethical Promotion and Marketing

39. The company should take effective measures to ensure that all information bearing upon the safety, efficacy, and possible side effects of a medicine are easily accessible to individuals so they can take informed decisions about its possible use.
40. The company should have a board-approved code of conduct and policy that fully conforms to the current World Health Organisation Criteria for Medicinal Drug Promotion. In the context of this code and policy, the board should receive regular reports on its promotion and marketing activities.
41. The company should publicly disclose its promotional and marketing policies and activities, including costs.

Commentary: Guidelines have already emphasised, in general terms, the central importance of transparency in relation to access to medicines (Guidelines 6–8); Guidelines 39–41 apply this general principle of transparency to the specific context of ethical promotion and marketing. Promotion and marketing give rise to a wide-range of access to medicines issues, such as advertising to health professionals and the general public, packaging and labelling, and information for patients. Based on ethical considerations, the World Health Organisation Criteria for Medicinal Drug Promotion provides authoritative guidance on these important matters (Guideline 40).

Public Private Partnerships

42. When participating in a Public Private Partnership, a company should continue to conform to these Guidelines.
43. If a company joins a Public Private Partnership, it should disclose any interest it has in the Partnership's decisions and activities.

44. So far as these Guidelines bear upon the strategies, policies, programs, projects and activities of Public Private Partnerships, they shall apply equally to such Partnerships.
45. A company that joins a Public Private Partnership should take all reasonable steps to ensure the Partnership fully conforms to these Guidelines.

Commentary: Public Private Partnerships can make an important contribution to enhancing access to medicines. They are subject to right-to-health considerations corresponding to those set out in these Guidelines. Where conflicts of interest may arise, disclosure is important, consistent with the human rights requirements of transparency.

Associations of Pharmaceutical Companies

46. So far as these Guidelines bear upon the strategies, policies, programs, projects and activities of associations of pharmaceutical companies, they shall apply equally to all such associations. The Guidelines on lobbying (Guidelines 17 and 26) and financial support (Guideline 18), for example, shall apply equally to all associations of pharmaceutical companies.
47. A company that is a member of an association of pharmaceutical companies should take all reasonable steps to ensure the association fully conforms to these Guidelines.

Commentary: A company has a responsibility to ensure that its professional associations are respectful of the right-to-health considerations set out in these Guidelines, otherwise a company could use an association as a way of avoiding its human rights responsibilities.

NOTES

1 Published in the report to the *Report of the Special Rapporteur on the Right of Everyone to the Enjoyment of the Highest Attainable Standard of Physical and Mental Health*, UN Doc. A/63/263 (2008).
2 Counterfeit drugs (medicines) are defined by the World Health Organisation in *FAQ's on Counterfeit Drugs*, 2008.
3 UNICEF, UNDP, World Bank, World Health Organisation Special Programme for Research and Training in Tropical Diseases.

4 M. Moran and others, *The New Landscape of Neglected Disease Drug Development*, The Wellcome Trust, 2005.
5 'Value' as defined in Guideline 11, World Health Organisation Guidelines for Drug Donations.

Contributors

Asher Alkoby, associate professor of law, Department of Law and Business, Ted Rogers School of Management, Ryerson University, Canada

Richard Elliott, executive director, Canadian HIV/AIDS Legal Network, Canada

Lisa Forman, Lupina Assistant Professor, Dalla Lana School of Public Health and Munk School of Global Affairs; director, Comparative Program on Health and Society, Munk School of Global Affairs, University of Toronto, Canada

Paul Hunt, professor, Department of Law, University of Essex, United Kingdom

Patricia Illingworth, associate professor of philosophy, Northeastern University, United States

Rajat Khosla, policy coordinator on health, Demand Dignity and ESCR Programme of Amnesty International. The work on this book was done by Rajat prior to joining Amnesty International, and the views expressed are entirely his own and do not necessarily reflect Amnesty International policy.

Judith King, communications and advocacy manager, Centre for Economic Governance and AIDS in Africa, Cape Town, South Africa

Jillian Clare Kohler, associate professor, Leslie Dan Faculty of Pharmacy, University of Toronto, Canada

Matthew Lee, pharmacist, Overwaitea Pharmacies, Canada

Joel Lexchin, professor, School of Health Policy and Management, York University, Canada

Stephanie Nixon, assistant professor, Department of Physical Therapy, University of Toronto, Canada; and research associate, Health Economics and HIV/AIDS Research Division, University of KwaZulu-Natal, South Africa